More Advance Praise for
13½ Reasons Why Not to Be a Liberal

"So glad I was able to cajole Judd into actually finishing *13½ Reasons Not to Be a Liberal—and How to Enlighten Others* during the taping of *Bulletpoints* (our web series on YouTube) for a *year*! Well worth the wait!"

> —**Michael Loftus**, Fox regular, *The Loftus Party, Freedom to Laugh Comedy Tour*, TV writer of *Anger Management* and *Kevin Can Wait*

"Judd Dunning not only empowers conservative readers with the critical thinking and forensic tools to survive a liberal rhetorical onslaught, but also enables them to emerge from the battle with a convert or two as well."

> —**Lowell Cauffiel**, *New York Times* Bestselling Author of *House of Secrets*

"My new lucky number is 13½, because of Judd Dunning's eye-opening, insightful new book. If you're a conservative or want to be, this is a *must* read!"

> —**Seth Swirsky**, no. 1 hit songwriter, four-time Bestselling Author, and Award-winning Documentarian

"The best teachers of enlightenment are those who've once lived in darkness. As a former liberal, Judd Dunning's book, *13½ Reasons Not to Be a Liberal—and How to Enlighten Others*, is an important tool that can potentially help you save family or friends duped by the (very) evil forces of the world. And after the onslaught of 2020, we all need as much help as we can get!"

> —**Ann-Marie Murrell**, Bestselling CoAuthor of *What Women Really Want* and *PolitiChicks: A Clarion Call to Political Activism* and editor/owner of PolitiChicks.com

13½ Reasons Why Not to Be a Liberal

And How to Enlighten Others

JUDD DUNNING

with Eric Golub

Humanix Books

www.humanixbooks.com

Contents

PART II
CULTURE AND SOCIAL ISSUES

PART III
SAFETY AND SECURITY

Introduction

The Belly of the Beast

The disturbing 11 p.m. phone call came from my good friend Larry during the second term of the Obama administration. Ironically, he called when I was watching an episode of the conflict-ridden political drama *House of Cards*.

He got right to the point. "Judd, I want to give you the dignity of calling before I delete you from my Facebook, my phone, and my entire life."

I laughed. I thought he was joking. I'd known Larry for a good 10 years. We met through a circle of friends and shared the highs and lows of working in the entertainment industry. Larry had an unconventional show-business angle. He was a performer in a popular female impersonator showcase where he and his fellow players impersonated female actresses and celebrities. The shows were full of raucously funny song and dance numbers. I valued Larry's friendship. Knowing him had helped me understand the difficulties of being a gay man, even in liberal Hollywood.

"Hey, Larry," I said. "Great to hear from you. It's been a while, buddy. I hope you're well."

He wasn't doing well. He was near tears and so upset that he was whispering. He'd been reading my Facebook posts. He said, "I need to know if the horrible things you write challenging our President Obama and our country are really you—or is this just some type of act?" He'd read that I believed in free markets, a strong military, gun rights, preservation of traditional family values, and religious freedom. He also knew that I opposed Obamacare and wanted more research on climate change.

I took a breath and tried to meet him on common ground. I acknowledged how inherently positive it was that Obama was the first black president, and how his election could potentially help heal the racial divide that had been ever present in our American history. However, I didn't ask Larry any questions about his own beliefs. Instead, I went on to tell him how I struggle with certain liberal policies and why I believed the way I do on the topics at hand. I did so awkwardly, offering a lot of broader opinions with few facts. To his credit, he listened.

Then he hung up. I haven't heard from him since.

The call was just the beginning of a seismic shift and an oncoming wave. I began hearing snide comments about me from liberals at parties. Others I knew stopped returning my calls. Other Facebook friends dropped me. Even then I wasn't aware that this was just the tide sucking back from shore. The rejection tsunami would soon come with the election of Donald Trump.

What followed threatened to be emotionally traumatic. I don't reject liberals for being progressives. All are welcome in my circle. It seemed outrageous that I could lose more than 2,000 people off of my Facebook page simply because I expressed my political views. People started calling me an idiot and a bigot. On some existential level I was faced with a sense of abandonment, that I was fatally flawed on some conscious or unconscious level. I could have believed this had I not heard similar stories from other conservatives, libertarians, and even moderate Republicans who were experiencing the same rejection.

I concluded that the rejection wasn't personal. It was universal.

It got me thinking about my own and my family's political journey. I come from some very old school Americans. The Dunnings landed in 1770 fleeing British oppression and moved to Tennessee and Virginia, fought the British in the American Revolution, and fought on both sides of the Civil War. The other side of my family was made up of the Whitners and Kresges. The Whitners arrived in South Carolina in 1764 after fighting on the American side of the Spanish-American War. After the war, part of the family moved to Cuba in 1898 as cattle ranchers. When Fidel Castro overthrew Fulgencio Batista and seized my family's ranch, they fled communism and came back to America. The Kresges arrived in 1906 via Ellis Island from the Polish-Ukraine border. They escaped the violent pogroms to seek a new way of life in Massachusetts and later New York. Although I came from a historically Republican household, my parents rarely discussed politics. As I grew up in the 1970s and 1980s, politics still had considerable ongoing conflicts. Yet life seemed much more private than today. One's personal politics were not yet used as a key litmus test of who to have in your life, work, or social circle.

Full of youthful idealistic sentiments and low on facts, by default, I became a big-hearted superliberal (back then, I was just called a Democrat). The Ivory Tower only fueled the fire. Not one of my Colorado State University professors spoke positively of our country. I earned my bachelor's degree in social science and economics, declared myself prelaw, and took the LSAT. My plan was to work for the American Civil Liberties Union (ACLU) to fight injustice and racism.

Right before law school and increasingly disgusted with our country, I opted not to stay in school. I was full of anger fueled by socialist ideals and utopianism. Ironically, those same years saw

President Ronald Reagan empower our country. Reagan had engineered a new era of greater national security and booming prosperity, but I wanted none of it.

After school, I sold all the capitalistic material goods I owned, including a new car my father had given me for completing college. I decided to move to the more caring, socialized Europe, vowing never to return. One rainy, low-wage, bus-riding, depressive year later—and after three weeks in a British hospital experiencing socialized medicine firsthand—I quickly discovered that the land of milk and honey didn't exist in Europe. I humbly returned home.

I was still a liberal. Al Gore, Michael Moore, Hollywood, academia, National Public Radio, the liberal media, Planned Parenthood, democratic socialism, Gore Vidal, Oliver Stone, Howard Zinn, Spike Lee, and the Clintons happily consumed my next 20 years. I marched on ready as ever to convert everyone to my passions. My moral outrage dictated my vote. My highly charged emotional yet well-meaning liberal heart ruled all my reasoning.

It was the perfect mind-set for where I eventually landed—liberal ground zero. I started in San Francisco at the American Conservatory Theater. I built a successful local acting career. I later relocated to Hollywood to raise the stakes and go for the greater gold. I performed in everything from *The Young and the Restless* to *Poetic Justice* and numerous commercials and independent films.

It was a great journey, but Los Angeles is an expensive city. I wanted a family. Economic reality required that I support my show-business efforts with other income. Always athletic, I became a successful personal trainer with several employees. I was also on the lookout for other entrepreneurial pursuits.

The struggle to survive in Los Angeles, with its gauntlet of taxes, licenses, and regulations, soon began to nudge me into a different political mind-set. Life was harder here. The liberal rhetoric of California politicians and their concern for the working man was as thick as the fog that came off the Pacific. However, I found that their policies had not advanced my success. They hindered it through

$73 parking tickets, ever-increasing sales taxes, and larger taxes as a small corporation—even when it lost money.

By the time of the 9/11 terrorist attacks, I was challenging all my old liberal beliefs. I slowly transformed into a seasoned conservative man. I'm not some red-bellied repressive traditionalist who clings to the past. I'm a 20-year ex-liberal turned conscious conservative who struggled deeply to emerge from left-wing Hollywood, the belly of the beast, to challenge all my opinions.

I still do this, even today.

Along the way, I also transitioned to a more lucrative profession to further support my family. Years of auditions, countless stand-up gigs, and pitching film projects taught me the art of sales. This helped me launch a very successful career in institutional commercial real estate. However, I never gave up on my creative pursuits. Near the end of the Obama administration, I hatched the idea to marry humor, entertainment value, and my political passions. I created a TV project and webcast that sought to add a refreshingly light touch to the rancor that dominates American political discourse today. *Conservatively Unplugged* featured me as a self-effacing Republican, a humor-based conservative host in a format similar to *The Daily Show*. I have hosted numerous leading political commentators, including Ben Shapiro, Ann Coulter, and James Carville. Comedic guests ranged from Fox regular Michael Loftus to Paul Rodriguez, Adam Yenzer, and even *Dancing With the Stars* dancer Sharna Burgess. We've been showcased for three years at Politicon. We have a steadily growing audience on YouTube and other streaming venues. A year ago, writer and comedian Michael Loftus and I also launched a new weekly streaming and YouTube show called *BulletPoints! With Michael Loftus and Judd Dunning*.

BulletPoints! became the impetus of the idea that generated this book. After experiencing all those angry rejections from contentious liberals in my personal life, I didn't want to become just another one of those angry pundits railing about the left. On the new show, I wanted to fearlessly present myself as a conservative yet also reduce the number of people I lost because of my political views. I'd already decided that the future of the country was more important than hiding my beliefs so as not to lose friends. There had to be a way to completely come out politically while accommodating them and their views. Perhaps that would create opportunities to promote understanding of conservatism. Perhaps it could even change some hearts and minds. More important, I needed to serve my fellow conservative travelers. How could I design an easily accessible format that could help others on the right experiencing the wave of rejection and disdain?

The answer came from the front lines of my own commercial real estate sales experience. In a sales negotiation, there's something called the *takeaway*. This is when a party at the table makes a demand and threatens to kill the deal and walk away if it's not met. It's the most negative and aggressive of all sales techniques. The opposite of the takeaway is the *win–win solution*. The win-win seeks to understand the other party's needs and meet them without damaging your own position. The win-win, whenever possible, is the most effective way to open any negotiation.

I came to realize that an interaction with a liberal—whether face-to-face or on social media—is essentially a negotiation. The liberal wants something from you: the rejection of your political beliefs and the support of theirs. You want something from them: understanding, some basic respect, and ideally, their support of the policies you endorse.

In my experience, angrier liberals often open with the takeaway. You state that you're on the right or that you support a conservative policy, and the equivalent of the takeaway is unleashed. You're labeled a compassionless bigot supporting a misogynist orange Oval Office clown. All discussion is over. We on the right sometimes resort to the takeaway as well. We approach our opponents with a hard line. When offended by their inaccurate accusations, we react and walk.

The obvious solution to these situations is to employ the win-win approach. This requires an even-keeled rational temperament and the ability to understand the other party's position. This also requires having done some research on any position they might take. During the negotiation itself, it requires asking a lot of questions. Being inquisitive is a proven way to lower the temperature and disarm the other party. It cultivates goodwill and shows respect and, dare I say, some basic humanity.

Once that is accomplished—and perhaps most important—the win-win approach requires the ability to effectively answer the questions or assertions that come from the other party. You can't give away what you don't have. What is the factual basis of your beliefs? What critical thinking supports them? Do you simply parrot the talking points you've heard from the talking heads on the liberal-loathed Fox News? Do you resort to generalizations or even the same kind of shaming or name-calling prevalent on the left? No, of course not. Yet you also might not have the core conservative arguments clear enough in your head to defend and explain your beliefs after being attacked from your first opening lines.

To meet that need, I'm offering *13½ Reasons Why Not to Be a Liberal*. Ideally, my timeless ideological treatise is also a practical and easily accessible political handbook for today's times. You will find that my tone ranges from philosophical, intellectual, and historical analysis to bare-knuckled and humorous commonsense responses. Given the minefield that is politics today, this range is how political discourse must be conducted.

This book has been compiled into an indexed, easily understandable guide that covers the most important issues under discussion in the age of progressivism versus conservatism. Its segregated sections cover the hot-button categories of economics, cultural and social issues, safety and security, the presidency of Donald J. Trump, and a bonus section on abortion. Within those categories are the liberal arguments you have heard or will hear anytime you are confronted in a potentially divisive discussion. They are followed by the reasoned, factual responses that you can employ toward the goal of a win-win.

If you can't achieve a win-win civil discussion, at least you can use this book to land some clear, intelligent blows. You will no longer serve as a liberal's doormat. You will not be consumed by the belly of the beast. You can maintain your dignity and then move on to someone who really wants to both talk and listen.

My hope in offering this guide is to help us all preserve relationships with our fellow citizens. We have to preserve the country I've loved in my five decades as an American citizen. I'm concerned that we have embarked on a cold civil war where rash decisions could permanently harm our country. Despite the rabid resistance we face, we all must foster civil discussions with our fellow Americans. The country and even our humanity are at stake.

I wish that I could have made that point to my old friend Larry. I wish that I knew then what I know now. Maybe I would have gotten the chance.

Part I

ECONOMICS

CHAPTER 1

Big Government Fails at (Almost) Everything

The Republican Party Small Government Pro-Growth Platform

Dennis Prager wisely stated, "The bigger the government, the smaller the citizen."[1]

With everything at your fingertips thanks to Amazon, Uber, Facebook, and others, it is easy for Americans to get complacent. As the private sector has created new technologies that vastly improve our lives, the public sector has regressed. Big government expansion remains a dangerous problem to our American individual liberty and the health of our nation's future. The government destroys wealth faster than the private sector can create it. This is unsustainable. Even worse, a large segment of our society has been conditioned to see an overarching government leviathan as a positive. Nothing could be further from the truth.

The more people come to rely on the state to take care of them, the more they begin to develop a sense of entitlement. Feeling entitled creates two other negative character traits: ingratitude and resentment. The more people expect to be given, the less grateful they will be for what they receive. They become resentful when any entitlements are taken away.

Most people who go into government are good people with noble intentions and a commitment to public service. Yet, as economist Milton Friedman brilliantly stated, "One of the great mistakes is to judge policies and programs by their intentions rather than their results."[2] After all, the road to hell is paved with good intentions. Intentions are emotional. Results and facts are rational. The facts are that far too many government programs have resulted in unintended consequences that deliver crushing blows to the very people most in need of help.

Small government was the clear original vision of the people who founded the United States of America. It is the major reason that America fought the Revolutionary War—to escape the British. It has given more people more freedom and more opportunity to live a better life than any other country ever has.

Avoid the liberal straw man that creates a false dichotomy between big government and anarchy. Government is absolutely needed, but in limited form.

Liberal argument: Government economic intervention is best for our country to level the playing field and protect all Americans.

The facts: Most government programs fail. There have been countless catastrophic interventionist government mistakes that have destroyed lives and spread misery.

President Franklin Delano Roosevelt's New Deal failed to lift America out of the Great Depression. The Supreme Court struck down a significant chunk of his programs as unconstitutional. He then tried to retaliate by packing the court and was thwarted there as well. World War II ended the depression and created the jobs that FDR failed to create in his first nine years.

Later, President Lyndon Baines Johnson declared a war on poverty, and then poverty won out as well. LBJ's social programs of the 1960s destroyed lives, primarily minority lives. Seventy-two percent illegitimacy rates among blacks have decimated black neighborhoods.[3] When House Speaker Newt Gingrich and the Republican Congress dragged President Bill Clinton kicking and screaming into a strong welfare reform law, welfare rolls plummeted. When President Barack Obama gutted the work requirements, welfare rolls and the number of people on food stamps ballooned. When President Donald Trump reinstituted the work requirements, welfare rolls dropped again.[4]

The 2008 housing crisis was largely created by prior government policies. Liberal politicians led by Massachusetts Congressman Barney Frank and Connecticut Senator Christopher Dodd played racial politics with the banks. The banks, under threat of closure, were bullied into giving mortgages to poor minorities who could not afford them. When large numbers of those borrowers stopped making their payments, the market crashed. The nation got hurt by unnecessary government meddling. Blacks were hurt the most.[5]

Unlike FDR, Obama only failed to create jobs for eight years. His initial stimulus package failed. Attending a business panel, he joked, "Shovel-ready was not as shovel-ready as we expected."[6]

Obama's attempt at a government takeover of the American healthcare system was a spectacular failure. The Affordable Care Act was a giant ideological redistribution scheme. Premiums were raised on people more likely to vote Republican so that Obama's base of poor Democrats could have free healthcare. Cynical politics led to an even worse policy. Millions of people had their policies canceled and saw their premiums skyrocket. Those hurt by the law dwarfed the comparably few people who benefited. "If you like your doctor, you can keep your doctor. If you like your healthcare plan, you can keep your healthcare plan."[7] Those words by Obama became Politifact's 2013 "Lie of the Year."[8]

Obama tried to create a green energy revolution through brute government coercion. He forced Americans to buy newfangled light bulbs because the standard light bulbs Americans had been using for more than 100 years were no longer good enough. Obama's light bulbs were worse. Yet the light bulb in his head never turned on. He tried to bribe Americans into buying solar panels. The people rejected them. He wasted billions of taxpayer dollars on Solyndra[9] and other failures. With no budget constraints, he piled up more debt than the first 43 presidents combined out of a desperate zeal for "fundamentally transforming"[10] a nation that got plenty right before he was born.

Government should not be in the business of picking winners and losers. President George W. Bush got some pretty big things right, but even he was pushed into playing favorites on Wall Street. Throughout his presidency, Bush had refused to bail out failing companies. Democrats tried to tie him to Enron (not surprisingly a green energy and climate alarmism company), but when Enron begged for a bailout, he told them no. Six months before the financial crisis, he refused to bail out Bear Stearns. Then came the reckoning on Wall Street. In September of 2008, Lehman Brothers burned. Bush let them. Then Goldman Sachs was teetering. Bush was persuaded under extreme pressure to abandon his free-market principles.

Goldman was deemed too big to fail. Could it be that Goldman had powerful government friends and Lehman did not? Former Goldman CEO Robert Rubin was Clinton's treasury secretary. Former Goldman CEO Hank Paulson held the same position under George W. Bush. Paulson and Federal Reserve Chairman Ben Bernanke made a compelling argument. Credit had seized up. Without government liquidity in the form of bailouts, the global financial system could break down. The argument is powerful but still begs an important question. Why save Goldman but not Lehman? Where was the ethics in that? That was crony capitalism at its worst.

It opened the floodgates for the Obama administration to follow Bush and spend into the stratosphere under the mantra of "Never let a serious crisis go to waste."[11]

In America, people have the freedom to fail. Businesses also have that freedom. Every generation sees a few entrepreneurs create the next big thing that everybody must have. Turning from rags to riches is far more common than elites would have the rest of us believe. Michael Lindell was a drug addict whose addiction cost him his marriage and his savings. Today he is a multimillionaire.[12] The My Pillow CEO built a better mousetrap. It seems silly that something as simple as a pillow needed to be redone, but Lindell did it. People loved his pillows, told their friends, and gave him millions of dollars in sales.

This is America. We have bankruptcy laws that protect debtors from going to jail or worse. Entrepreneurs who fail in business move in with their family or friends and start again. Big business owners have friends and families with couches to sleep on as well. This is how it should be.

Creative destruction works. Trying to prevent it inevitably leads to stagnation (little or no economic growth). Japan and most of Europe have battled stagnation for decades.

When businesses fail, they do so with their own money (unless they are crony capitalists relying on government subsidies and bailouts). When government programs fail, they are wasting taxpayer dollars. In business, CEOs who fail frequently get fired. In government, it is often difficult to fire people. When there is no reward for success or punishment for failure, the result is usually indifference followed by more failure.

There are not enough pages to discuss the thousands of government programs that fail in every big-government presidency. A better challenge is to flip the question on its head. Ask every liberal to name one significant big-government program that has ever succeeded. They will cite Social Security and Medicare, but this is not true. These programs are constantly flirting with insolvency and eating up the largest portion of our federal budget. At their current pace, they may not exist in 30 years.

Name one big-government social program government has ever gotten right. Take your time.

> **Liberal argument:** We must raise taxes and make the rich pay their fair share to best take care of the middle class and poor.
>
> **The facts:** "The power to tax is the power to destroy."[13] Of all the ways government can damage an economy, raising taxes is the easiest and most destructive. Liberals would happily raise taxes on everyone because their vision of government requires it. However, massive tax increases on everybody is not politically feasible. Liberals insist that they are only raising taxes on the rich. They never specify what qualifies a person or family as rich. Most people do not see themselves as rich. They are fine sticking it to the wealthy until they figure out that the government is talking about them.

Slogans are useless. What matters is evidence in the form of results. The two conflicting schools of economic thought are between demand-side Keynesian economics and supply-side economics. Keynesians support active government intervention, including tax hikes to stimulate economic growth. Supply-siders support tax cuts to stimulate economic growth. The results are crystal clear.

In his significantly effective book, *The New Conservative Paradigm*, supply-sider Tom Del Beccaro provides a simple recap of tax policy attempts and their results. Supply-side tax cuts were enacted by President John Fitzgerald Kennedy in 1961. He considered them essential to stimulating economic growth. Republican President

Richard Nixon was against them, dismissing them as a gimmick. President Ronald Reagan enacted supply-side tax cuts again in 1981 with a significant push from Delaware Senator William Roth and Buffalo Congressman Jack Kemp. President George W. Bush enacted supply-side tax cuts in 2001, 2002, and 2003.[14]

Under the tutelage of economists Arthur Laffer, Larry Kudlow, and Steve Moore, Trump became America's newest supply-side president. His December 2017 tax cuts ended a decade of stagnation. Growth in 2019 was up by a respectable 3 percent from the fourth quarter of 2017.[15] During the more Keynesian President Obama's 31 quarters—from the start of the expansion in the third quarter of 2009 through the first quarter of 2017—growth was just 2.2 percent. History has shown that supply-side benefits take time and often show up predominantly in a supply-side president's second term. The 2019 trend already appeared to align with prior proven historical patterns.[16]

In 2020, the American economy cratered, but this was due to a global pandemic. The COVID-19 coronavirus escaped from a lab in Wuhan, China, and killed more than 2 million people worldwide, including more than 100,000 Americans. Medical experts convinced Trump to shut down much of the entire American economy to slow the spread of this new disease. The resulting severe economic contraction of 2020 was directly caused by economic closure. There was zero correlation between the Trump tax cuts and the unprecedented 2020 COVID-19 crash. The strong correlation came between the tax cuts and the prepandemic 2019 economic boom.

Four presidents tried this supply-side approach, one Democrat and three Republicans. All four times the result was exactly as intended. Supply-side tax cuts spurred spectacular economic growth and unleashed prosperity.

In contrast, demand-side tax hikes were tried five times. In the 1930s, FDR attempted the Keynesian approach to combat the Great Depression. In the 1970s, President Jimmy Carter attempted to combat "malaise." In the 1990s, Presidents George H. W. Bush and Bill Clinton both raised marginal rates. Four attempts under

four different presidents, three Democrats and one Republican, produced the same result: failure. FDR worsened the Great Depression,
Carter worsened the stagflation, and Bush worsened the recession.
Clinton got lucky. He inherited an economy that was growing at
nearly 5 percent in the fourth quarter of 1992.[17] His tax hikes slowed
growth, but he was bailed out by the stunning internet revolution
that began in 1995. Unparalleled wealth creation that most people
had never seen before made up for the tax hikes.

Obama apparently never read Del Beccaro's book, because
the fifth president to try demand-side economics failed just like
the first four. Growth was stagnant for Obama's entire eight years,
nearly tipping America back into recession. Obama made it easy for
Trump, who just had to do the opposite of Obama. By reversing the
Obama-Keynes policies, economic growth exploded under Trump.[18]
Trump is no dummy, but it helps to have Laffer, Kudlow, Moore,
Del Beccaro, and the *Wall Street Journal* editorial pages shouting on
a daily basis that supply-side tax cuts work.

In addition to supply-side income tax cuts in marginal rates,
another key rate is the capital gains rate on sales of stocks. Clinton
and his successor, Bush, one Democrat and one Republican, both
cut capital gains taxes. Clinton lowered the rate from 28 to 20 percent. Bush lowered it further to 15 percent. In both cases, millions
of dollars poured into the financial markets.[19] The rate ideally should
be 0 percent because the capital gains tax is inherently unethical
as double taxation. Unfortunately, try making this case to a politically cowardly Congress unable to articulate why good policy should
supersede optics. Liberals deride trickle-down economics without
having any idea how or why supply-side tax cuts work and have
already worked repeatedly.

One more tax that needs to be entirely repealed, even if only
temporarily, is the tax on repatriated assets. Approximately $2 to
$4 trillion are being held overseas to avoid confiscatory U.S. taxes.[20]
If that rate were lowered, overseas capital would flood the financial
markets and probably double the U.S. stock market.

Ardent tax-cutting New York Mayor Rudy Giuliani summed it up best: "Money is fungible. When you tax rich people, they leave."[21] Rich people have tax shelters and expensive tax attorneys and accountants. The rich can always find ways to legally evade confiscatory taxes and transfer the burdens onto those less fortunate. When business owners receive tax breaks, they do not stuff the money under their mattresses or in Swiss bank accounts. They invest it. When liberals push investment, they really mean spending. Far too often this spending is wasteful and creates nothing. Business owners engage in real investment. They purchase machinery and raw materials. They hire more employees to handle increased customer needs. Lower business taxes benefit everyone in the business from the owner to the receptionist. While the owner may receive a much larger raise, the secretary has far less risk. The secretary can find a new secretarial job. For many business owners, their business is their life. If their business fails, they have nothing. Lower taxes and regulatory burdens allow businesses to thrive. Raising taxes and increasing regulations are the best way to crush businesses and wreck an economy (outside of mandating businesses close altogether, as was done during the 2020 pandemic).

Raising taxes harms growth. Cutting taxes helps growth. It really is that cut and dry.

Liberal argument: Europe has democratic socialism and, as a result, is more caring. Big government in Europe provides the social safety net.

The facts: For some bizarre reason, many liberals worship Europe. They particularly idolize France. France is perfection, and perfection is France. Maybe they find sophistication in awful accents and a common bond in contempt for everyday Americans.

Liberal argument: Our country was created to spread equality. Big government is the only way to do this.

The facts: Nature is nature. People are different. We as human beings in the Modern Age intrinsically know that we are fully equal in regard to our natural rights. Nevertheless, each of us is inherently different from one another in our potential, talents, and merit. We cultivate these distinguishing traits in our society around us. Our Constitution states that "all men are created equal,"[22] but it does not anywhere say that the government's job is to force equality. The people are entitled to "Life, Liberty and the pursuit of Happiness."[23] The key word is *liberty*. Equality and liberty are incompatible. The Constitution chose to emphasize liberty. Equality is a noble aspirational goal, but not at the expense of liberty. Those who prefer equality at all costs have to shred the Constitution to enforce such equality. That is liberalism in a nutshell. Control government and use the levers of government to reward those who have less and punish those who have more. External factors such as work ethic and lifestyle choices are ignored. Communist nations emphasize equality over liberty and use brute force to carry out their goal of equality. These nations have failed wherever this approach has been tried, with great cost and far too much human suffering.

Enough speculation. The evidence is clear. While Europe may not be completely finished, it is in very deep trouble. The American economy is much larger than the entire European Union combined. Several European nations have gone bankrupt. Even in holy, sacred France, unemployment has been mired in double digits for decades.[24] Bureaucratic rules make it almost impossible to fire workers. This, in turn, makes it impossible to hire them. Stagnation is the norm. Despite shared stagnation, there is rampant political instability. Governments are frequently toppled. Britain voted for Brexit[25] because the people realized that Brussels was taking away their democracy. British voters concluded that they could do better on their own rather than be a part of failing Europe. Europe has no military, relying on the United States to defend it. France in particular has proven totally incapable and helpless to prevent its people from rampant crime and radical Islamic terrorism. Some Islamist parts of France are no-go zones where police fear to tread. The social safety net has not completely collapsed, but it is far from the romanticized dream of young college backpackers. I know. I was one. After one year in failed Old Europe, I returned home and found real paradise in the form of the American dream.

> **Liberal argument:** Rent control, wage control, affirmative action, national healthcare, progressive taxation, and large unions are necessary. The Environmental Protection Agency and a myriad of other agencies, policies, and governmental intervention are also vital. Otherwise, the rich would run over the country, the environment, and the middle class and poor.
>
> **The facts:** Combining a ton of nonsense into one argument sometimes saves time by allowing the debunking of everything all at once.

Nixon experimented briefly with wage and price controls. The result was a complete economic failure, and he quickly reversed course.[26]

Nixon created the EPA as well. The environment was being legislatively protected before the EPA existed. Try pointing to one significant positive EPA accomplishment that required the EPA's existence. If something truly is important enough, the legislature will act. This is what legislators are supposed to do.

Other nations have national healthcare. Their care is vastly inferior in quality to American healthcare. Europe has rationing. Old people barely rank higher than dogs because the government can declare them too old to have expensive lifesaving procedures. Waiting lines are long. It can take months to get approval for a procedure that would take mere days in the United States.

Plenty of people work in industries without a union presence. These people can be fired at any moment, but they can also voluntarily quit for a better job at their own convenience. For conservatives, unions can also be a political nightmare. Liberals love unions because unions collect involuntary dues and then spend that money on liberal political activities. Unions then spend more dues money on expensive marketing campaigns denying their political expenditures.

Union membership plummets when membership is voluntary. There was a time when unions were vitally necessary to prevent business abuses. Now there are labor laws in place. Despite the best union scare tactics, children are not being sent back to work in the coal mines and sweatshops. The most extreme Gilded Age labor abuses are in our past. Free markets and solely voluntary unionization remain most ideal in the present day. Conservatives fully respect the right of workers to voluntarily unionize, but great problems continue to arise with compulsory union membership. Mandatory union membership is still required by law in most states. As a result, large amounts of union dues are often spent on one-sided political agenda projects that run counter to the free individual political views of many mandated unions members and remain subject to abuses of power and graft.

Rent control makes it far more difficult for landlords to make upgrades to their units. The free market allows renters and seekers to find each other. Potential tenants and landlords both end up with many more options. Nobody is entitled to live in any particular neighborhood, city, or county. Americans are free to reject rent increases by voting with their feet and moving to more affordable areas. Living on the Upper Westside of Manhattan or the beach in Santa Monica is not a constitutional right.

Forget progressive taxation. Until the 16th Amendment to the Constitution was ratified in 1913, the United States had no federal income tax.[27] America also had zero debt. Although taxes are now an inherent part of our functional modern government (especially military defense of the nation and our borders), overall higher progressive taxation and penalizing our wealthier job creators have not strengthened America.

Affirmative action was supposed to help those who have been marginalized in society. Unfortunately, it frequently fails to get to the recipients who need it most.[28] Affirmative action should be based on income, not race. Surely most reasonable people would agree that poor whites have a greater need for financial help than wealthy blacks.

Affirmative action is one of the few government programs that can claim some success. At least it has not been a complete failure. However, the unintended consequences are now rapidly outweighing the benefits. The stigma of being perceived as a token hire can last a lifetime. More important, careers that rely on merit tend to provide real diversity. Professional sports owners focus on trying to hire the best players. Sales jobs boil down to which people are the best salespeople. The U.S. Armed Forces want people who can kill bad guys and protect America. These professions are as race neutral as any, and they function quite well. Industries with quota hires (despite the denials, the next step is inevitably token quota hires) such as public education and government are messes.

The notion that rich people are the problem is just nuts. There are always rich people who inherit money and sit around leading lazy lives. Most people have no idea what the many living members of the Kennedy family actually do. Inherited wealth often leads to an unfulfilling, unproductive life. However, most people become rich the old Smith Barney way. To quote the late John Houseman, "They earn it."[29]

Rich people provide jobs to other people. These new hires are not envious. They are grateful to be employed and willing to work hard in the hopes of one day becoming rich themselves. The government did not hire them. Private individuals did. In this country, busboys can own restaurants. Paperboys can own newsstands. Construction workers can start their own construction companies. The main thing that could mess this up is government getting in the way. When government forces companies with 50 employees working 30 hours per week to provide free healthcare, employers cut back to 49 employees working 29 hours per week.[30]

The best example of trying to soak the rich came in 1990. Congressional Democrats convinced Bush Senior to violate his "Read my lips: no new taxes" pledge.[31] Not only did he raise income tax rates, but he also enacted a luxury tax on yachts and expensive watches. The unintended consequences were catastrophic. The rich tightened their belts and delayed buying yachts and watches. The yacht builders and watchmakers saw their industries get devastated. Many of them went out of business. In 1993, the same Bill Clinton who would raise income tax rates quietly repealed the luxury tax.[32]

Liberals blame the rich. Conservatives want to become rich. Ask yourself which approach leads to a happier, better life.

Liberals want more government. Conservatives want less government. The evidence is overwhelming that with government, bigger is not better.

What *should* government do? Government should provide for the national defense through a strong military (under control of a civilian president) and ensure that Social Security checks and other similar administrative functions are handled. Everything else can be privatized, from the post office to the department of motor vehicles. The Constitution is a charter of negative liberties. Unless the federal government is specifically empowered to do something, it is prohibited from doing it. Government needs to be returned to its constitutional role, which the Founding Fathers deliberately and severely restricted.

CHAPTER 2

Life Is Not Fair and People Are Inherently Unequal

Free-Market Capitalism and Individual Liberty

The concerns about economic inequality are many: limited opportunities that leave the less fortunate behind; potential resentment and social unrest; excessive political power among the rich; the unfairness of huge financial gains among a tiny class of successful entrepreneurs and investors, those seemingly fortunate to benefit from, perhaps, good genes, a privileged upbringing, elite education, unique career options, even blind luck.

—CURT BIREN[33]

Life is not fair. Most of us cannot dunk a basketball as well as Michael Jordan. During his final years with the Chicago Bulls, Jordan was earning more than $30 million in annual salary. He was also earning millions more in product endorsements. Meanwhile,

schoolteachers were struggling to make ends meet. This is supposedly unfair.

Actually, it is totally fair. In professional sports, only the very
best get to play. Excellence is demanded, and players who fall short
get cut. In education, standards have been lowered to make it easier
for teachers to pass the requisite exams. They also receive job stability and security elusive to professional athletes. Teachers can last for
30 or 40 years. The average professional American football player
plays barely more than three years.[34]

Of larger significance, the best professional athletes pump billions into their local, state, and even the national economy. Jordan
added more than $10 billion dollars into Chicago.[35] When the
1990s Bulls were winning championships, more people attended
the games. This led to a need for more hot dog vendors, sellers of
team apparel, and even makers of a bizarre design called a *bobble-
head*. Beyond this commerce, Jordan has made numerous charitable
donations with his own earned money.

Contrast this with the education system. Lower standards
have created a glut of teachers. If enough people refused to become
schoolteachers, there would be a teacher shortage, and salaries would
rise. You will not see schoolteachers reach Jordan's salary, but again,
his contribution to the overall economy is far greater. He merits
his take-home pay because the free market says he does. This is the
fairness of recognizing talent. Government cannot accomplish this
recognition.

Governments can provide equality in opportunity but must not
try to force equality of outcomes. God gave each individual different
skills and aptitudes. Capitalism offers the best environment for success. Every other system (communism, socialism, fascism, etc.) has
failed to replicate the successful capitalist experiment. Capitalism
encourages failure in the pursuit of individual happiness and success.

The liberal dream of universal fairness is awesome in theory. For
25 years, I pursued proving it true; then I became a conservative.
My liberal friends and I both care for America in our own way. They

have their vision, and I have mine. Our healthy, peaceful conflict is what keeps us all free. Unfortunately, the liberal vision that life must be fair is wrong. Fairness is an ideal worthy of being strived for, but a free life is not always realistic.

Milton Friedman pointed out in his book *Free to Choose* that there are three categories for human equality: equality before God, equality of opportunity, and equality of outcome. He thinks the first is the Founders' use, the second is compatible with liberty, and the third is socialism.[36]

The liberal vision also has three main cornerstones to its failed mission: (1) life should be fair, (2) love the planet, and (3) we should all just get along within a more loving, homogeneous globalized community of world peace. Sadly, the first cornerstone that life should be fair is not reality (neither are the other two, addressed in other chapters).

We know well the heartstrings plucked on the liberal emotional violin. Give peace a chance, hope and change, and save Mother Earth are all based on living a heart-centered life. What kind of unconscientious marauding beast could object to this? To the left, the answer is greedy, uncaring Republicans. Disagree and you have no heart. With no heart, your personhood must be flawed and broken, and you once again must be a bigot.

Unfortunately for the liberal left, the exact converse is true. History has repeatedly proven life's unfairness. Supply-side economics works in an environment of inherent natural unfairness. Huge entitlements and overregulation only weaken those coddled.

Natural unfairness also has its time-tested roots in natural law and Neoplatonism. Our Judeo-Christian ethics are the essence of Republicanism and conservative individualism enshrined in our Constitution. This all flows from the biblical Torah.

Conservatives call for less government, knowing that a myriad of highly effective laws already exists in service of this very issue to the benefit of Americans. Our free-market incentive-based principles work well. Almost all prior institutional injustices regarding fairness have already been addressed in our laws and justice system. We already have over 100,000 pages of laws in our federal registry. We already have 27 constitutional amendments to address possible oversights of our Framers.

After 20 children died in the tragic 2012 Sandy Hook shootings, Los Angeles liberal-centrist Rabbi Mordecai Finley from Los Angeles Ohr Hatorah offered wisdom: "First . . . slow down and grieve. Then, get all the information from the many sides of the debate on how to reduce gun violence. Then, make a rational decision on your position and take proper action aligned with your carefully considered beliefs."[37] He was in essence counseling us not to jump to conclusions or reactively politicize the tragedy to try to change the Constitution.

Life hurts. Slow down, grieve the nature of reality first, and then take action. Maybe when you do, you'll see that the nature of life itself is the issue. It is important to grieve that life is not fair in a similar fashion. This is particularly important in America. Our special experiment here survived 244 years because of a lot of suffering to get this right.

Life is rough. Man (or woman) up. Anyone can complain. Work on the productive solution that already exists. If you truly want a fairer, more just, more equal society (with prosperity rather than shared misery), then the only economic solution is capitalism.

Liberal argument: Free markets don't work. Greed leaves behind the little guy.

The facts: Free-market capitalism has been the most powerful nonreligious force for good in the history of the world. Free-market capitalism has lifted billions of people worldwide out of poverty in the past two generations alone. It has brought consumers an embarrassment of riches in product variety. It rewards talented people for talents that dictators or central planners would never have even thought to exploit. Jeffrey Dorfman of *Forbes* perfectly encapsulates the wonders of free-market thinking in his brilliant article, "Ten Free Market Economic Reasons to Be Thankful." Here are his largely unredacted words:

1. **Median income is really rising.** Claims of stagnant middle-class wages rely on flawed data rather than official government statistics. Another problem is the misuse of government statistics. As the Manhattan Institute's Scott Winship has repeatedly shown, properly measured, incomes have risen rather steadily with labor productivity, as would be expected. Using data from the *Current Population Survey* and the Congressional Budget Office, Winship shows that from 1967 to 2009, median household income rose by more than $20,000. Median income growth was slowly positive during the Obama years and grew rapidly in Trump's first term (prepandemic). When more updated data are released, the cumulative gain since 1967 will be closer to $22,000 for the median household. These rising wages are thanks to a free labor market where employers have to compete for workers by offering competitive wages.

2. **Free trade saves us trillions.** From 2015 to the present, free trade has generally been a losing issue politically. The economic reality is that allowing the free market to extend past national boundaries allows people in both trading partners to increase the benefits of free markets. By exploiting more

differences in comparative advantage and the differences in tastes, preferences, resources, and talents
worldwide, American consumers save hundreds of
billions of dollars per year on the goods we purchase. In addition, we Americans gain variety in
our purchases, such as the ability to buy fresh fruit
in the winter. Some workers may temporarily lose
jobs and see wages rise more slowly thanks to the
increased competition trade brings, but on average,
we save much more in lower prices than we lose in
lower wages.

3. **Free markets know what we want.** Free markets
miraculously supply almost all our wants without
an obvious mechanism that lets them know what
to make and where to deliver it. Through the wonder of the infamous "invisible hand," we vote with
our dollars every day by how we spend our money.
The market continually adjusts to meet those needs
as efficiently and inexpensively as possible. The
average supermarket, for example, contains 50,000
different items for sale. It also has an inventory
control system and supply chain that are respon-
sive to consumer demand. On any given day, 99.8
percent or more of those items are waiting (on the
shelves) for you to buy them.

4. **Innovators are rewarded and consumers
benefit.** Economic rewards to innovators encourage businesses to invent things consumers don't
even know they need. Nobody needed an iPhone,
Velcro, Post-It notes, blind-spot warning systems,
or fitness trackers until somebody invented them.
The rewards to those who correctly guess the mood
of enough consumers are sufficient to make many

of them rich. This encourages innovation and enriches consumers by much more than any financial rewards to the innovators themselves.

5. **Failed businesses are punished and economic growth accelerates.** Economic judgments also put out of business those making things consumers don't want. When a business disappears, it frees up resources to be redeployed to the production of things society values more highly. This is exactly what the government frequently gets wrong when it bails out failing businesses under the mistaken pretext of protecting jobs. Bailing out failing companies traps resources and capital in a low-growth sector that could have been more profitably used in higher-growth areas of the economy. Stopping business failures slows down economic growth; let them die, and watch new businesses rise from the ashes.

6. **Free markets match buyers and sellers.** Free markets automatically pair up sellers and buyers. In a free-market system, producers rarely have to know, find, or ever meet the sellers of their products. Retailers stand between producers and consumers. Banks stand between savers and borrowers. Stockbrokers and real estate agents serve to match up those who want to sell and buy shares of stock or pieces of property. Because some money can be made through performing these matchmaking services, a free market allows customers to find the products they want without finding the people making those products. This greatly lowers the transaction costs for both buyers and sellers, making markets more efficient. The internet has

only accelerated the benefits gained in this regard, shrinking transaction costs ever further.

7. **Competition keeps prices low.** Competition among businesses keeps prices low. Inflation is mostly a problem in the industries with the most government involvement (e.g., healthcare, education). Industries that have more free-market competition find businesses reluctant to raise prices. These businesses are always looking for cost efficiencies to gain an advantage over their competitors. Think about prices for computers, food, and clothes to realize the gains consumers capture from robust competition in a free market.

8. **Price signals work.** Price signals tell people and businesses where to allocate their skills and efforts. A nursing shortage is signaled to the labor market through employers advertising higher wages for nurses, hopefully leading more people to go into that profession. High demand for a popular product will lead businesses to bid higher to get a share of the limited supply, encouraging producers to make more. Similarly, falling prices and wages tell producers and workers what products and fields some of them should abandon. When you think about how rarely a store is out of the item you want or has a huge overstock lingering on the shelves for months on end, you realize how well price signals work in a free market.

9. **Freedom.** Free markets let you choose what work you want to do, who to work for, where to shop, and what to buy. Without free markets, some government agency or (hopefully benevolent) dictator would have to match workers with jobs,

producers with retailers, and retailers with customers. Without free markets, you have no free choice. When we restrict free markets with government regulations, people lose freedom over what work to do, where and when to shop, and what to buy. Free markets, in contrast to government-controlled ones, let more than 100 million workers choose from thousands of professions and 300 million consumers choose from millions of goods and services for sale every day.

10. **Free markets make things work.** Think about sectors of our society where things are not working well: many government agencies (such as the department of motor vehicles), healthcare, transportation systems, and K–12 education, for example. These are areas where we have the fewest markets and the most government intervention. If you want low prices and high quality, keep government out of the way, and let free markets work. America's K–12 public education system, which has virtually no freedom of choice, consistently scores in the middle of the pack internationally. Yet our higher education system, where consumers can choose the college they want to attend, is universally rated as the best in the world.[38]

It remains undeniably clear that without free-market capitalism, much of what we are thankful for would be missing.

> **Liberal argument:** The coronavirus pandemic exposed the failure of free-market capitalism and free trade. Corporations do business all over the globe. When the pandemic hit, the supply chain was disrupted. There were shortages of basic items. Many Americans could not even purchase toilet paper because the stores had none in stock.
>
> **The facts:** Truly free trade requires that all trading partners abide by basic legal and ethical business principles. Trade agreements are only valid if there are enforcement mechanisms for compliance. America at a bare minimum should not trade with nations that have openly declared war on America.

Iranian leaders have been chanting "Death to America" for decades. Because Iran is a hostile actor on the world stage, it has sacrificed its right to engage in trade. The American government has placed tight sanctions on Iran. Doing business with Iran is prohibited in most cases.

Americans were prohibited from doing business with the Russians during the Cold War. A pair of blue jeans or a cassette tape of The Beatles could be purchased in the United States for under $10. Russians were willing to pay hundreds of dollars for these items. Americans who were willing to risk jail time illegally smuggled these items into Russia. The black market for these items was a multibillion-dollar industry. As the Cold War was ending, Ronald Reagan took Soviet President Mikhail Gorbachev to Bloomingdales.

America and Japan were enemies in World War II. Commerce with the enemy would have been unthinkable. After the war ended, these two warring nations made peace and over time developed a very friendly rapport. Today, Japan is one of America's strongest international allies. Japanese Prime Minister Shinzo Abe is a big fan of the late Elvis Presley. When Abe visited the United States in 2006, Bush took him to Graceland.

The late Iraqi dictator Saddam Hussein loved Frank Sinatra's music. Unfortunately for Hussein, he loved attacking his neighboring nations more. Had he minded his own business, he could have had access to all the records of Ol' Blue Eyes. Instead, he threatened America with the "mother of all battles." America responded with economic sanctions, war, and more sanctions. When he still did not get the message, he received a second war that led to his being captured, tried, and hung.

The examples are endless, but China is a far more complex situation. The government is communist politically but hypercapitalist economically. China's leaders do not overtly threaten to kill us. They bribe us. They smile at us publicly while trying to defeat us through cyberwarfare and buying up massive amounts of American products and political power. Many American corporations are so desperate to access the Chinese market that they ignore China's history of human rights abuses and deceptive business practices. In simple terms, the Chinese government murders its own citizens and steals America's intellectual property.

This brings us to the coronavirus in terms of trade.

COVID-19 began in the city of Wuhan, China. Initial reports claimed that it stemmed from Chinese "wet markets" where people eat bats.[39] Those initial reports were discredited. What is beyond dispute is that the virus began in a laboratory in Wuhan, China. The only unresolved question is whether the virus was released accidentally or deliberately as a bioweapon.[40]

Either way, this virus from China killed Americans and did threaten our supply chain. The panic and the toilet paper shortages were real. The solution is not to abandon free trade altogether. It is to abandon or drastically reduce trade with hostile actors.

America is not going to bomb China and start a new hot war. There will not even be a cold war. There may be severe economic sanctions. The Trump administration has a variety of tools at its disposal. Canceling American debt owed to China would be the least likely option because it could affect America's international credit standing. A more likely scenario would be a drastic increase in tariffs on Chinese goods. China could try to start a trade war, but its leaders know they would lose. Trump began pressuring American businesses to move operations out of China. Ideally, these companies would return jobs to the United States. At the very least, companies can exit China and move their overseas operations to democratic allies such as India. Trump has a very warm relationship with Indian Prime Minister Narendra Modi.[41] Another option Trump mulled was stripping China of its sovereign immunity status so that American COVID-19 victims could sue the Chinese government.[42] Whatever avenues the Trump government pursues, America must remain a nation that produces as much as possible at home but trades with friendly partners whenever it is beneficial to us.

America must continue to engage in trade, but not with nations that are hostile to American interests. The greater the level of anti-American hostility, the greater is the reduction in trade and increase in tariffs. If China becomes a most hostile nation like Iran, then outright total sanctions are the correct course of action. If the Chinese government ever completely ceases its hostility, America can and should trade with it as we do with Japan, Britain, Israel, and the rest of our many allies. Only time will tell.

> **Liberal argument:** Democratic socialism is a much better alternative. More government means more success for all.

The facts: Democratic socialism became hip and cool to millennials during the 2016 election. Vermont Senator Bernie Sanders became a cult favorite on campuses. Sanders, in his earlier years, identified with the full-blown communism of the former Soviet Union and was a Trotskyite.[43] Before addressing the ludicrous notion that this is what is best for America now to ensure fairness, what is democratic socialism anyway? Though often blended together in misunderstanding, there is a difference between socialism and social democracy.

John Haltiwanger of *Business Insider* offers a charitable distinction between democratic socialism and outright socialism: "Democratic socialism differs from outright socialism in the level of state control of the economy. Socialists want government to own almost all property and all means of economic production. Democratic socialists would allow for some private production, but still heavily regulated by government."[44]

A less charitable differentiation is that in outright socialism, government seizes the means of private production. In democratic socialism, the people freely vote to give the government the right to seize the means of private production.

Straight socialism generally ends with chaos, collapse, and massive deaths. Social democracy suggests redistribution of capitalistic gains. Several Scandinavian nations practice this latter form. The American left romanticizes Scandinavian nations, but the truth (as is often the case) paints a far darker picture.

Denmark and Sweden are small, homogeneous nations. Nordic lifestyles mean that Nordic life expectancy outclassed life expectancy in the United States. This was before the Nordic states tried radical redistributionist policies. Both Norway and Sweden are now moving in a politically right-wing direction. Contrast them with Switzerland, which is just as successful and far less socialistic. Generous welfare policies can only operate in small, homogeneous countries. If you open your borders, immigrants flood in and then sink the boat. This is why voters in Europe have been consistently moving toward a more restrictive view of immigration. This includes (wrongly perceived) leftist darling Sweden. The *Wall Street Journal* reported on January 9, 2019, that Sweden abandoned democratic socialism in 1991.[45] In 2018, the conservative Heritage Foundation rated Sweden as the fifteenth freest country in the world. It rated the United States as the eighteenth freest![46]

When the rubber meets the road, socialism and democratic socialism are still distinctions without real differences. They differ only about the means. They agree on reaching the same ends: total state control of the lives of everyone in a society. This leads to economic ruin, as experienced by the once-prosperous Cuba and Venezuela. In the worst cases, it leads to government murdering millions of its own citizens. Stalin, Mao, and Pol Pot were not capitalist conservatives.

Liberal argument: Even the richest of Americans in their 2019 letter, "An Open Letter to the 2020 Presidential Candidates: It's Time to Tax Us More Now,"[47] understand that we must redistribute wealth. It is immoral and even unjust in modern-day America to not do so.

The facts: Let us not wade into the great complexities of how the wealthy manage a large amount of their megawealth in offshore accounts in countries that protect them from ever being properly taxed. That's an entire chapter itself.

Political writer Curt Biren answered this argument with erudition. I humbly proffer his words in a recent article from the journal *The American Mind*: "As Harvard professor Eric Nelson stated, 'Moral egalitarianism (the idea that all individuals ought to be able to identify and pursue their own idea of the good life without coercion) and economic egalitarianism (the idea that coercion should be used to ensure a more equal distribution of wealth) cannot easily coexist in the same theory.'" Biren goes further to state with great clarity: "The concept of economic justice did not exist at the time of the Founding, nor was there any movement calling for a certain level of economic equality or some other preferred economic state of affairs. The Founders did not introduce the idea because they understood that justice is a political question. They focused on getting government right, and, for them, securing justice was the purpose of government."[48]

This meant first finding ways to limit the potential reach and abuse of government power. As James Madison explained in *Federalist Paper*, No. 51, "In framing a government which is to be administered by men over men, the great difficulty lies in this: you must first enable the government to control the governed; and in the next place oblige it to control itself."

Government is to be limited to its just purposes, namely securing justice. "Justice," Madison wrote in *Federalist Paper*, No. 51, "is the end of government. It is the end of civil society. It ever has been and ever will be pursued until it be obtained, or until liberty be lost in the pursuit."[49]

Madison recognized that everyone is different with different faculties. This did not mean that government should aim to equalize outcomes in order to adjust for such differences. "The protection of these faculties is the first object of government," Madison observed in *Federalist Paper*, No. 10. "From the protection of different and unequal faculties of acquiring property, the possession of different degrees and kinds of property immediately results."[50] Government exists to protect liberty and to protect property—in their inevitably diverse and unequal portions.

The evidence has been clear for a long time. Our government was never created to take away the realities of life but more so to continually allow us to pursue success. Our own merits are a realm of justice itself.[51]

> **Liberal argument:** Republicans are pro-business and therefore anti-American. Our society is run by big business. More government is required to ensure the safety and prosperity of the average American.
>
> **The facts:** If Republicans are pro-business, does this mean that Democrats are anti-business? They may actually be, but all except the most radicalized of Democrats vehemently deny this. Whether the denial is based on honest convictions or cynical calculated political considerations is a political question. What is not in dispute is that Democrats by and large vociferously reject the charge.

Whether Democrats are sincere or lying about what they believe, the conclusion is the same. The American electorate is overwhelmingly pro-business. Voters are certainly not anti-business. They understand that for the most part, businesses help their lives, while government detracts from them.

According to the Small Business Administration (SBA), nearly 95 percent of small businesses fail.[52] Respectable portions of the rest of them go on to become the institutions often referred to as big business. Although it is trendy on the left to attack big business, every single big business started out as a small business. The owners and CEOs often risked everything including their own financial livelihood. Government employees (outside of our beloved military) risk nothing.

Businesses produce jobs. Those jobs give people a paycheck they can use to spend on whatever they choose. Most of their paycheck is spent on necessities, but sometimes luxury items find their way into the checkout basket.

Government produces nothing. Government takes money out of your paycheck and spends it on God knows what. Government is never required to provide an accounting of how many dollars are seized or where those dollars go. Businesses have to be efficient to avoid going bankrupt. Governments can just print more money. This leads to currency devaluation and causes nations that do this to inevitably collapse. When business leaders lose value, they are often fired. Try firing government workers.

Businesses have a powerful motive to succeed. That motive is the profit incentive. The more a business succeeds, the more money that business makes. The free market gloriously rewards success and ruthlessly punishes failure.

Government has no motive to succeed. Most government workers are entrenched no matter who is in the White House. Many government workers may be good people who take pride in their jobs, but most of them are "clockers." They punch their timecard and go home. Do not expect them to be working at three o'clock in the morning trying to solve a customer problem or resolve a complaint. Anyone who has ever owned a business knows that there is no such thing as a true sick day or vacation day.

Most important, businesses have to innovate to stay competitive. Innovation is the key to everything. If Coca-Cola comes up with a water beverage, Pepsi must do likewise or lose that critical market. If McDonald's comes up with a new menu item, expect Burger King to be right on its heels, and vice versa. Taco Bell struck gold with its Doritos Locos Tacos, a taco shell flavored like a Dorito.[53] After decades of ordinary taco shells, somebody came up with the idea that taco shells must be as flavorful as the meat, cheese, and salsa inside the taco. This is innovation. This is the heart of business.

Governments cannot and do not innovate. Government is the bureaucracy, and bureaucracy is the exact opposite of innovation. Bureaucracy, also known as *red tape*, stifles innovation. Government is qualified to administer Social Security checks. It has proven zero ability to identify consumer trends. If it could, it would not keep subsidizing companies that go bankrupt once those subsidies end.

Business leader Steve Jobs invented the iPhone, turning around Apple from a company on the brink to a world leader. This forced competitors to come up with their own smartphones. Government did not lead the world-changing 1990s technology revolution. Microsoft, Intel, Dell, Cisco, and others had visionary CEOs in Bill Gates, Andy Grove, Michael Dell, and John Chambers. Private businesspeople with dreams created the social media revolution through Facebook, Twitter, and Instagram.

Mark Cuban became a multibillionaire in 1999 by selling his company Broadcast.com to Yahoo. He then purchased the NBA's Dallas Mavericks. He freely concedes that there is nothing as exhilarating as owning a professional sports team.[54] Cuban also did something important that only happens in the private sector. He used his success to help other entrepreneurs make it rich themselves. For the uninitiated, the television show *Shark Tank* is not about aquatic life. Cuban and several wealthy entrepreneurs (the sharks) hear sales presentations from eager individuals seeking investor capital. Many of the companies Cuban and his fellow sharks invest in go on to become successful companies in their own right.[55]

This is America. This is business. This is capitalism. This does not, cannot, and will not ever happen in government.

This does not make government evil. On the contrary, both business and government have vital roles to play in society. Neither is qualified to do the job of the other. Trump's former Secretary of Defense James "Mad Dog" Mattis was far more qualified to lead wars and preserve peace than any private-sector CEO. His job was to lead his soldiers in killing bad guys when necessary and protecting good guys whenever possible.

The job of a business is to make money. Period. Exclamation point. End of sentence. Businesses create wealth. Governments destroy wealth. For this reason, no sentient person should ever want to depend on government for financial survival. Those who disagree are free to turn in their smartphones and wait for the government to create a better one. It will be a long wait.

CHAPTER 3

Big Green Elephant

Climate Change, Responsible Progress, and Real versus Junk Science

We are at the beginning of a mass extinction, and all you can talk about is money and fairy tales of eternal economic growth. How dare you!
—Greta Thunberg, a 16-year-old Swedish student at her impassioned UN speech[56]

Climate researchers and activists suffer from depression and PTSD-like symptoms. For just such feelings, a Salt Lake City support group provides "a safe space for confronting" what it now calls "climate grief."
—2015 *Esquire* feature, "When the End of Human Civilization is Your Day Job"[57]

It remains very ironic that today's highly flawed new legislative proposal the "Green New Deal" was named in homage to FDR's original New Deal, referencing it as a model of

past legislative success when it was ultimately a well-known
big governmental failure.
—Dr. Marvin Treiger, Ph.D., Millennial Policy Center[58]

It's been three decades since climate change became a core political issue. Now we are buried in junk science and fake news. Even
prepubescent children are begging the United Nations to address
climate change to avoid imminent planetary extinction. As our fates
literally (or perhaps not) hang by a thread, where to start on this
hot topic is the elemental question. This chapter is dedicated to our
environment, but that is far from what is at stake. Left unchecked,
our entire American way of life is what now hangs in the balance.

National Geographic and NASA define global warming and
climate change.

> Global warming is the unusually rapid increase in Earth's
> average surface temperature over the past century primarily
> due to greenhouse gases released by people burning fossil
> fuels. This term was coined by geochemist Wallace Smith
> Broecker in 1975.[59]

> Climate change is the long-term alteration of tempera-
> ture and typical weather patterns in a place. Climate
> change could refer to a location or the planet.
> Climate change may cause weather patterns to be less
> predictable.

The competing views on climate change are the *anthropological*
and the *skeptical*. The anthropological view of climate change claims
that humans have ruined the climate. "Climate change is a present
reality that alters our physical environment and impacts human cultures around the globe. Climate change intensifies underlying problems—poverty and economic disparities, food and water security,

and armed conflict—heightening these issues to the point of wide-spread crisis."[60]

The anthropological view stems mostly from an Intergovern-mental Panel on Climate Change (IPCC) report stating that "[m]ost of the observed increase in global average temperatures since the mid-20th century is very likely due to the observed increase in anthropogenic GHG [greenhouse gas] concentrations."[61] The anthropological view believers insist that climate change exists and that ideally the climate is supposed to be stable.

The climate skeptical view states that there are other influences at play. Other factors include the sun, cosmic waves, water vapor, cloud cover, poles shifting, and other natural events. Climate change skepticism is a scholarly discourse that generally refers to a family of arguments and individuals that rejects, disputes, or questions the orthodox and often politicized anthropological view. Attribution skepticism may accept the trend claims but reject the view that humans are primarily responsible. Impact skepticism ideally accepts that humans are altering the climate but challenges the scale of potential negative effects from climate change. Process skepti-cism states that the massive funding of climate research became a biasing factor that corrupted the process of climate research.[62] Contradictory research is habitually ignored in mainstream climate research.

Climate change deniers believe in climate change but also believe that it has been around forever in inherently natural cycles. Deniers also specifically challenge the validity that carbon diox-ide levels are the key elemental factor of climate change. The term *deniers* is seen as pejorative, meant to link climate change skeptics to Holocaust deniers. A more neutral term is *hoaxers* because they believe the movement itself is a hoax.[63]

A 2016 Pew poll stated that 48 percent of people believe that climate change is caused by human activity, 31 percent believe that it is naturally caused, and 20 percent cite no evidence to prove accuracy either way.[64]

The anthropological viewers believe that we must all come together and take action against climate change now, even if individual rights or economic realities are sacrificed. Alternative views to demanding immediate action are buried deep in search engines globally. Media and politics are the central factors shaping beliefs about the effects of climate change.

To those in this massive unified anthropological chorus, global warming and climate change remain the greatest global existential threat. They view dissenters as obviously blind skeptics, backward, ignorant troglodytes and marauding capitalist dogs thinking only of profit and self-serving ends.

Skeptics (and many other apolitical Americans) consistently rank climate change as one of the least important issues of our lifetimes. Matters of global terrorism, immigration, and the economy consistently rank higher. Those demanding immediate action are viewed as zealots motivated by money, power, and communism disguised as environmentalism.

Despite being marginalized, many well-noted intellectuals and scientists with no plausible unified agenda are willing to commit societal and professional suicide to state their healthy rational convictions and doubts. At his 2018 Cambridge Union address, known hard-line rationalist and intellectual Jordan Peterson stated, after reading hundreds of recent books, scientific journals, and reports on the climate, that "I'm very skeptical of the models that are used to predict climate change" and that "[y]ou can't trust the data because too much ideology is involved."[65]

In 2019, a 16-year-old European girl with Asperger's syndrome named Greta Thunberg gave an angry speech to the UN about her fears of a climate emergency. On that same day, a group of 500 prominent scientists and professionals sent a registered letter to the UN Secretary-General contradicting Thunberg. Their letter stated that there is no climate emergency and that climate policies should be designed to benefit the lives of people. They were led by Guus Berkhout of the Friends of Science, a Canada-based "non-profit organization run by dedicated volunteers comprised mainly of active and retired Earth and atmospheric scientists, engineers, and other professionals."[66] They declared that

1. Natural as well as anthropogenic factors cause warming.
2. Warming is far slower than predicted.
3. Climate policy relies on inadequate models.
4. Carbon dioxide (CO_2) is not a pollutant. It is a plant food that is essential to all life on Earth. Photosynthesis is a blessing. More CO_2 is beneficial for nature, greening the Earth. Additional CO_2 in the air has promoted growth in global plant biomass. It is also good for agriculture, increasing the yields of crops worldwide.
5. Global warming has not increased natural disasters.
6. Climate policy must respect scientific and economic realities.
7. There is no climate emergency. Therefore, there is no cause for panic.

While polls of scientists actively working in the field of climate science indicate strong general agreement that the Earth is warming and human activity is a significant factor, 31,000 scientists say that there is "no convincing evidence" that humans can or will cause "catastrophic" heating of the atmosphere.

The Oregon Institute of Science and Medicine has an online petition that states:

We urge the United States government to reject the global warming agreement that was written in Kyoto, Japan, in December 1997, and any other similar proposals. The proposed limits on greenhouse gases would harm the environment, hinder the advance of science and technology, and damage the health and welfare of mankind. There is no convincing scientific evidence that human release of carbon dioxide, methane, or other greenhouse gases is causing or

will, in the foreseeable future, cause catastrophic heating
of the earth's atmosphere and disruption of the earth's
climate. Moreover, there is substantial scientific evidence
that increases in atmospheric carbon dioxide produce many
beneficial effects upon the natural plant and animal environ-
ments of the earth.[67]

Some opinions even reach the point of negation, stating that
we are being hustled. The Earth's temperature is currently cooling
slightly. Ocean heat is declining. Global sea-level rise has not accelerated. Tropical storm energy is at a 30-year low.

Few political causes bring as much liberal demagoguery as the
environmental movement. While some would declare environmental issues to be social issues, they are in the economics section for a
reason. The environmental movement involves money and power.
Big money funds it, and the goal is to assume power. It is a generally
corrupt movement that frequently perverts science. For each liberal
attack, there is a rational conservative response.

Liberal argument: 97 percent of scientists believe in
man-made climate change.

The facts: This oft-repeated falsehood is based on a
deliberate misrepresentation of one study. In honest science and statistics, outliers are thrown out.
Cherry-picking the outliers is the height of dishonest
science. The key to any credible study is the sample
size. If a poll claims that 100 percent of people vote
Republican, but the poll asks only one Republican,
the study is invalid. A sample size of one person is too
small to be statistically significant.

With the famous 97 percent poll, around 10,000 scientists involved with one single conference were sent a questionnaire. Ninety-nine percent of the scientists never answered the questionnaire for various reasons. Of the approximately 100 scientists who answered the survey, 97 percent sided with the extreme leftist position on human-made climate change. The sample size was just under 1 percent.[68]

Liberals then point to scientific academic journals that show overwhelming scientific support for the human-made causality argument. This falls apart on learning that the journals cited are owned by political ideologues, not scientists. Publishers blacklist many scientists who advocate against the human-made causality argument. These scientists are dismissed as crackpots, with the disagreement itself cited as evidence of mental illness. Real science involves debate. The left declares the issue settled by broad agreement. When those who disagree stand up, they are attacked for not understanding that the issue is agreed upon and settled. This is circular logic. The issue is anything but settled. Vehement disagreements are healthy in the scientific community. Absolutism is the enemy of honest science.

Most important, the track record of these liberal scientists is miserable. People who have been repeatedly proven wrong are demanding to have their declarations taken at face value. Their say-so is their evidence, and it is evidence because they say so. Again, the logical tires spin and go nowhere. In the 1970s, the fear was global cooling. The world was headed for an ice age. We were all going to freeze to death. Then in the 1980s, the scientists bemoaned global warming. We were all going to burn to death. Now they use the term *climate change*. That way they can never be wrong. True science must be based on the possibility of its falsification. The *falsification hypothesis* is a concept first introduced by philosopher of science Karl Popper.[69] If no data can possibly refute you, you can't call it science. If the temperature goes up or down, either way it has changed. This allows the human-made causal arguers to never be wrong.

Somehow they still find ways to be wrong anyway. People making outlandish apocalyptic claims tend to do that. The oceans have
not flooded us all. We have not burned or frozen to death. Polar ice
caps are doing fine. Polar bears are still enjoying them.

Liberal argument: Liberals care about the environment, and conservatives care about big business.

The facts: Again, Republican Nixon created
the Environmental Protection Agency (EPA).[70]
Republican Bush Senior signed into law major
amendments to the Clean Air Act.[71] Democrat
Clinton as Arkansas governor ignored home-state
business Tyson Chicken polluting local waters.[72]
The Republican Party remains what Reagan Legacy
Foundation Director Larry Greenfield calls the
"Big Green Elephant."[73] Both parties want a clean
environment. The trick is how to secure that clean
environment without strangling economic growth or
bankrupting the country. Conservatives tend to seek
a middle ground while understanding that businesses
power the American economic engine. Liberal solutions tend to be cost prohibitive and require massive
new regulations that have been proven to stifle growth.

Liberal argument: Republicans want dirty air and dirty water.

The facts: This is the least serious liberal environmental argument. Have you ever met anyone who woke up and took delight in destroying Earth? Bugs Bunny character Marvin the Martian wanted to blow up Earth because it was blocking his view of Venus.[74] Cartoon Martians do not represent everyday earthlings. Conservatives and liberals drink the same water. We breathe the same air. Poisoning either would be poisoning all of us. Most people want to live.

Liberal argument: If NASA says climate change must be true, it is.

The facts: The facts: NASA data show that the global temperatures dropped sharply in 2016 and 2017. Writing on RealClearMarkets, Aaron Brown looked at the official NASA global temperature data and noticed something surprising. From February 2016 through February 2018, "global average temperatures dropped by 0.56 degrees Celsius." That, he noted, is the biggest two-year drop in the past century. "The 2016–2018 Big Chill," he wrote, "was composed of two little chills, the biggest five-month drop ever (February through June 2016) and the fourth biggest (February through June 2017). A similar event from February through June 2018 brought global average temperatures below the 1980s average."[75]

On page one of NASA's website, the opening statement reads: "NASA: Climate Change and Global Warming." NASA first acknowledges the existence of Milankovich cycles, which describe three periodic variations in the way the Earth rotates around the sun and its effect on temperature:

> The earth's climate has changed throughout history. Just in the last 650,000 years there have been seven cycles of glacial advance and retreat, with the abrupt end of the last ice age about 7,000 years ago marking the beginning of the modern climate era—and of human civilization. Most of these climate changes are attributed to very small variations in earth's orbit that change the amount of solar energy our planet receives.

After this disclaimer, NASA then lists all our major climate issues proving climate change and global warming exist. These include warming oceans, shrinking ice sheets, glacial retreat, decreased snow cover, sea-level rise, declining arctic sea ice, extreme weather events, and ocean acidification.[76]

Yet, during the same short period, NASA and certain publications citing NASA released many contrary reports or data points:

1. "Cold Water Currently Slowing Fastest Greenland Glacier"[77]
2. "Study: Mass Gains of Antarctic Ice Sheet Greater Than Losses"[78]
3. "New NASA Data Blow Gaping Hole in Global Warming Alarmism"[79]
4. "Trump's NASA Chief Changed His Mind on Climate Change. He Is a Scientific Hero."[80]
5. "NASA Says That CO_2 Is a Coolant Not a Warming Gas"[81]

Our news media do not help. There is an obvious reason that even climate scientists are skeptical of the media. In a recent George

Mason University poll with a 4 percent margin of error, just 1 percent of climate scientists rated either broadcast or cable television news about climate change as "very reliable."[82]

With even scientists having reasonable doubt, some hesitancy by us common Americans is merited.

Liberal argument: Deregulation of the oil industry caused the *Exxon Valdez* debacle and the BP oil spill.

The facts: The 1989 *Exxon Valdez* tanker crash was one of the worst environmental disasters in American history. However, the problem was not caused by oil or government policies. Captain Joseph Hazelwood was drunk.[83] There are already laws on the books dealing with drinking and driving. Most of these cases involve automobiles. Comedian Bill Murray in 2007 was briefly detained in Europe after getting drunk and operating a golf cart on a golf course. He did not know it was illegal, but golf carts are motor vehicles. He paid the $10 or so fine and posed for pictures with the officers.[84]

Not all situations are this amusing. Airline pilots have been caught flying their passenger airplanes while intoxicated. The solution to flying a plane while drunk is not to ban airplanes or gasoline. It is to arrest the pilots, which is exactly what happened.

The *Exxon Valdez* lesson is a simple one: do not get drunk and operate an oil tanker. Hazelwood was sentenced to four years in prison.

As for the 2010 Deepwater Horizon oil spill, no American law could have prevented that incident. BP stands for British Petroleum. BP is not an American company.

While the original spill was BP's fault, the American government exacerbated the problem. For 86 days, the Obama administration abused and threatened BP rather than working with the company to solve the problem. Obama was a former faculty lounge adjunct professor, not an oil industry expert.

He threatened to put the "boot on the throat" of BP to get the company to comply with cleaning up the mess.[85] BP was losing billions of dollars in lost oil and bad publicity. The company had every reason to want to clean up the spill as quickly as possible. Obama demanded that the company "plug the damn hole."[86] BP executives responded with the equivalent of, "Gee, Yogi, why didn't we think of that?"[87]

The Obama administration should have delayed all additional regulations and sanctions until after the spill was cleaned up. Our government spent more time on public relations and meaningless tough talk than on solving the problem. BP had to fight a two-front war of closing the leak itself and fending off counterproductive government meddling. The government even threatened to shut down BP permanently. Had it succeeded, BP could have retaliated by quitting and demanding that the government fix the problem itself. For nearly three months, the government pencil-necks sabotaged the oil roughnecks.

The Mineral Management Service (MMS), at the time a subdivision of the Department of the Interior, had its limits. "The Mineral Management Service cannot check every oil rig every day. It only takes one series of mistakes to cause an explosion such as the Deepwater Horizon. Accidents cannot be prevented in all cases."[88] As much as it bothers government experts to hear, the Deepwater Horizon explosion that caused the oil spill was a tragic accident. Some accidents are just that. They happen.

> **Liberal argument:** Trump pulled out of the Paris Climate Agreement and repealed environmental regulations.
>
> **The facts:** The Paris Climate Agreement is flawed at its core. It exempted China and India, two of the world's biggest polluters. Each of those nations has more than 1 billion people, more than triple the population of the United States. Without their compliance, the agreement is meaningless. Whereas the process of reporting and reviewing climate goals was mandatory, the climate targets themselves were only aspirational.[89]

China wouldn't have to voluntarily abide until 2030. As per the UN's own model, the EPA-backed agreement could not be quantified. Obama's Clean Power Plan, if fully implemented for 14 years, would do nothing. If it worked and somehow all other countries complied, it would reduce the temperature 0.0023 degrees in the year 2100. If the plan worked, it would put off global warming (if it existed) by eight months. The cost would be $2 trillion a year according to Stanford and Asian forecast models. The total cost would be $100 trillion to change the temperature by 0.003 degrees by 2100 per the UN's own model. By then, technology will have evolved regardless.[90]

The Paris Agreement was a massive redistribution scheme. The purpose was to transfer wealth from rich nations to poor nations in order to right supposed past wrongs. This is socialism, not environmentalism. Many declared communists, including former Obama Green Jobs Advisor Van Jones, support the environmental movement specifically because of its commitment to wealth redistribution.[91] Green is the new red.

On the regulatory front, Trump did not do anything unprecedented or even unusual. Obama engaged in massive overregulation.
Obama's actions in size and scope were unprecedented. Obama's
new regulations crippled businesses, contributing to a flat economy. All Trump did was repeal the Obama regulations.[92] Businesses
immediately responded, and the economy grew. Trump did not take
us back to the Stone Age out of Bedrock. Far from the *Flintstones*,
Trump took America back only a few years to 2008. Many of the
Obama regulations were passed in his final year in office. Trump
took America back in one year. This is barely more than daylight
savings time. It's the time equivalent of a rounding error.

Liberal argument: Fracking poisons the water.

The facts: Hydraulic fracturing, or fracking, for short,
is a private-sector drilling technology that is safer,
more efficient, and more effective than traditional
drilling. Far too many Hollywood celebrities are
against fracking without actually knowing what it is.
It is somehow connected to oil, so it just sounds like
something that must be bad. With fracking, water is
injected into rocks to split the rocks open. This has led
to some of the largest natural gas and shale oil finds in
American history. The price of natural gas plummeted
when oil companies began fracking. In September
2019, America for the first time became a net exporter
of petroleum.[93] By the end of 2020, America is pro-
jected to be a net exporter of all energy, including
crude oil, rather than a net importer.[94]

Phelim McAleer and Ann McElhinney produced the outstanding 2013 documentary *Fracknation* that discredits the anti-fracking

lobby. Phelim and Ann, as they are known, are from Ireland. They have no emotional stake in the American political system. One important and hysterically funny scene in their movie shows a water inspector delivering what should be good news to a homeowner. The water around her home was repeatedly tested and deemed safe to drink. Rather than be relieved, the homeowner angrily demands that the water be retested. After the inspector insists that the tests were done multiple times and corroborated, the woman explodes in rage. She wanted the drinking water to be poisoned so she could sue the oil companies who fracked the land. The safety of her family took a back seat to her love of money. How dare oil companies refuse to poison her water by using safe drilling technology![95]

Liberal argument: Investing in green energy and technology is sound business.

The facts: Ask a liberal to name one alternative energy source that is as functional, fungible, and cost-effective as oil. The late T. Boone Pickens was an oil man to his core. The only thing oil magnates love more than oil is making money from oil. Pickens invested $1 billion of his own money in wind power. He lost every penny of it and kept his remaining billions in oil.[96] Windmills also kill birds. Columnist Mark Steyn hilariously referred to these windmills as the "Condor Cuisinart."[97]

Dr. Gal Luft is passionate about finding alternative energy sources. He deeply believes in flexible-fuel cars, now well-known as *hybrids*. Dr. Luft concedes that many forms of alternative energy are cost prohibitive. Hydrogen would be better than oil, but splitting and re-forming hydrogen cells is still far too costly.[98]

The Obama administration provided subsidies for people to put solar panels on their homes. His government spent millions retraining unemployed individuals in how to install these solar panels. Once this subsidy (in reality, a straight-line income redistribution of your tax dollars to pay someone else's energy bills) ended, people stopped buying the solar panels, and the newly created jobs disappeared.[99] Solar energy may one day be affordable, but as of now, nobody has figured out how to make this happen. Elon Musk wasted billions of tax dollars on failed solar experiments.[100] At least Pickens wasted his own money.

Attempts to find alternative energy profits in the financial markets have been illusory. The concept of carbon credits was begun by the most selfish of liberal Hollywood celebrities. They wanted others to cut down on energy consumption while they flitted around the globe in private jets. They paid others to be more environmentally conscious to offset their own rapaciousness. In the real world, this is called *bribery*. Offsetting is feel-good nonsense. Yet enough liberals believed that there was a financial market for carbon offsets. This led to the creation of the Chicago Climate Exchange (CCE). Liberals were not willing to put their money where their mouths were. The scam soon folded and the CCE shut down.[101] Meanwhile, many rich liberal celebrities, including Michael Moore, continue to invest heavily in oil stocks.[102] They love money and know deep down that big oil works best.

Liberal argument: Extreme weather is caused by climate change.

The facts: Any extreme weather incident can be blamed on climate change because it is impossible to disprove a negative. Fires, floods, earthquakes, hurricanes, and blizzards are now all blamed on climate change. The facts tell a contradictory story. The Earth existed long before human beings. Every single extreme weather event cited in the modern era can be compared with a more devastating event ages ago. Long before the industrial revolution created factories, extreme weather existed. Additionally, extreme weather conditions are actually not trending upward.[103]

Liberal argument: Drive a Prius, not a big gas-guzzler.

The facts: The Prius is made by Toyota. Buying Japanese cars is not the best way to help the American economy. Much more important, the Prius is not an environmentally friendly car. Prius batteries are bad for the environment. Liberals insist that these lead-acid batteries can be properly recycled. When they are not recycled properly, they release high levels of toxins into the surrounding atmosphere.[104]

Liberal argument: Campus studies prove climate change.

The facts: The most honest and credible scientific trials involve double-blind studies, where neither the tester nor the subjects know the results in advance. Drug companies rely on double-blind studies to truly determine whether their drugs are more effective than placebos. These companies get in trouble when they break the double-blind seal and look at the results in advance. This often corrupts future trials. Honest science involves following the data and letting the data dictate the conclusion. Dishonest science starts with a predetermined conclusion and then forces the data to fit that conclusion. College campuses are over-whelmingly liberal. An unhealthy majority of wealthy individuals who fund these studies demand that the results match their desires. Results that contradict the human-made causality theory are often followed by threats to pull research grant money. When grant money is pulled, research departments close down. This inherent conflict of interest can corrupt the process from the inception. Most young researchers, desperate to survive financially, are not going to bite the hand that feeds them. If the human-made causal-ity argument keeps their facilities open, so be it.

Liberal argument: Climate change is based on truth, honesty, and morality.

The facts: The climate change movement is rid-dled with lies, fraud, and immorality. In addition to the corrupt campus problems, email scandals have plagued the movement. The "Climategate scandal" of November 2009 revealed that several scientists did not believe their own public words. Kevin Trenberth of the National Center for Atmospheric Research (NCAR) said, "The fact is that we can't account for the lack of warming at the moment and it is a travesty that we can't."[105] While these scientists were the victims of an illegal email hack, it does not mitigate the emails themselves. Supporters of their agenda claimed that the emails were deliberately taken out of context. This is the common phrase used by people who get caught being quoted verbatim.

A new study in November of 2018 by Australian researchers says that data on how sea levels are rising, relied on by the UN, were adjusted upward in "arbitrary" ways. This is a polite way of accusing the movement of cooking the books. At least something got warm. The ocean rise prediction was based on one Yemeni study of the Indian Ocean where 40 years of data from 1970 to 2010 were completely missing.[106]

Information itself is easy to corrupt. Any small input change in the initial data of a computer simulation tends to magnify greatly over lengthy future projections. Climate projections are 80 or more years into the future. Garbage in leads to much more garbage out. We already see this problem because the IPCC revises its estimates in each report. The IPCC also failed to predict a 15-year pause in warming.[107]

Corruption and fraud have extended far beyond the campuses, scientific organizations themselves, and the private sector. It bled into the highest levels of government. Obama's EPA Director Lisa Jackson was the zealot who declared that the carbon dioxide humans breathe out was a public health threat. She then assumed power herself to have the EPA regulate it. Obama's EPA inspector general launched an audit of Jackson's record-keeping practices. Jackson was caught using a private email server under the assumed name Richard Windsor (her dog) for government business. She also ignored environmental concerns involving the Clinton Global Foundation for obvious reasons. As she left her government job in 2013, she joined the foundation's board of directors.[108]

The bottom line is that there is serious disagreement on a myriad number of proposed environmental solutions. Far too many liberals trot out the typical insults toward climate change skeptics. These skeptics are labeled evil, stupid, anti-science, and climate deniers. Again, the last slur is meant to link climate skeptics to Holocaust deniers. This trivializes the Holocaust, which actually happened. The human-made causality movement insists that shouting down opponents, refusing to publish them, rigging data, and declaring the issue settled actually accomplish that. Its effect is just the opposite. The issue is fiercely disputed and as unsettled as an issue can be. The left claiming that there is nothing to debate makes it seem as if they are terrified of having an honest debate. Given how consistently the green movement has been wrong, its fear of an honest debate where opposing views are allowed makes sense.

As for Hollywood celebrities obsessing over climate change, conservative comedian Evan Sayet has it totally right.[109] Hollywood celebrities are experts at playing make-believe for a living. They get paid to create fantasy. Their expertise is in pretending, not real science. Demagogic politicians are no better. Al Gore is not a scientist. He flunked out of law school and divinity school and entered politics because of his famous powerful father with the same name.[110] His predictions have been vastly discredited, which is why he refuses to debate real scientists.

Liberal argument: The Green New Deal is the answer.

The facts: Our political system is well crafted. Just like the weather, change is always inherent. Yet one major storm arrived in 2019 regarding environmental legislation that was so radical and significant that it cannot be ignored—the Green New Deal.

After the 2016 election, the left was in shambles and willing to do anything to delegitimize President Donald J. Trump. Claims of an Electoral College crisis elicited yawns. The Russia hoax collapsed. The attempt to impeach Trump over a Ukrainian phone call failed. Attempts to blame Trump for the coronavirus pandemic fizzled as Americans rallied around the president (as they typically do after acts of war against America). Former Vice President Joe Biden won the 2020 Democrat nomination by being anti-Trump and without advocating anything resembling a belief system, political philosophy, or governing agenda.

Desperate Democrats still to this day have been unable to offer a tangible alternative or more attractive vision for America's future. Then first-term New York Congresswoman Alexandria Ocasio-Cortez (AOC) and Massachusetts Senator Ed Markey led the relatively unknown Green New Deal into a blinding spotlight.

The Green New Deal (GND) is a left-wing congressional Democrat legislative proposal that aims to address climate change and economic inequality. Its name refers to the New Deal, a set of social and economic reforms and public works projects undertaken by FDR in response to the Great Depression. The GND combines FDR's economic approach with modern ideas such as renewable energy and resource efficiency.

Soon enough, the GND strayed from its purported environmentalism and became a rallying cry of socialist policy goals. Among its more radical provisions: Phase out conventional fuels (oil, natural gas, and coal) by 2030, only a decade from now; implement a federal jobs guarantee; retrofit all U.S. buildings; overhaul transportation with high-speed rail; and provide universal healthcare.[111]

AOC declared:

> The Green New Deal we are proposing will be similar in
> scale to the mobilization efforts seen in World War II or
> the Marshall Plan. It will require the investment of trillions
> of dollars and the creation of millions of high-wage jobs.

We must again invest in the development, manufacturing, deployment and distribution of energy, but this time green energy. Half measures will not work. The time for slow and incremental efforts has long passed.[112]

AOC even insisted that if action was not taken in 12 years (later revised down to 10), the world in April 2031 would cease to exist.[113] Her misguided doomsday followers believe this sham. The IPCC encouraged the hysteria.[114]

With a price tag approaching $100 trillion, presidential candidates who initially rushed to embrace the GND soon ran from it. When Senate Majority Leader Mitch McConnell of Kentucky put the GND to a vote, the Senate soundly rejected it.[115]

It would be easy to dismiss the GND as an impossible progressive dream, but that would be a mistake. No one has bothered to teach millennials the first law of socialism—abolish private property. The GND is a direct threat to the American spirit, which would be transformed irretrievably if it became law.

The conservative solution is to keep an open mind, ask questions, and demand uncorrupted evidence. This is real science, which has traditionally been supported by the Big Green Elephant Republican Party.

Part II

CULTURE AND SOCIAL ISSUES

CHAPTER 4

You Are Not a Bigot

Colorblind Conservatism
and the Myth of the GOP as Racist

Issues of racism and bigotry are far different from standard political issues. With most issues, logical arguments can successfully persuade reasonable uninformed people. Issues of bigotry, including racism, are far different. Those involve deep-seated emotions.

Convincing somebody to support supply-side tax cuts is a cold, bloodless exercise. Present some facts and figures, and people can be taught why tax cuts stimulate economic growth.

Taxes involve stuff. Race and bigotry are about people. People have human emotions, and appealing to emotional people with logic is at best a waste of time and at worst dangerous. The standard, cool logical approach found in almost every other part of this book must be largely discarded in this chapter. Emotion must be dealt with emotionally. Keeping a cool head is not necessary.

This advice will not lead to harmony and understanding in the short run. In many cases, it will exacerbate the conflict. Before enjoying a steak, cows have to get slaughtered. In this case, it is the sacred cows that must meet the butcher's knife. Either everybody is allowed to discuss everything or nobody gets to discuss anything.

There is no reason to provide a lengthy explanation to a false charge that does not deserve to be dignified to people who have no interest in hearing the truth.

With race and bigotry, conservatives and Republicans are always on the defensive. Liberal Democrats accuse us of being racist bigots, and we give them a laundry list of why we are not. Then they ask why we are being so defensive.

As arrogant as they are, the question is one I would ask. Why are you being so defensive?

To those many good conservatives and Republicans who start a sentence by saying, "I'm not a racist, but," stop immediately. Of course they are not racist. Why would they bring it up? Why start on defense? Why are they so desperate to get approval from people? Good people don't need to offer disclaimers. Getting the benefit of the doubt unless proven otherwise must be nonnegotiable.

I could give you a lengthy history of the Republican Party and the many conservatives who have been champions on race. I could give you an even lengthier history of the evil deeds done toward minorities by Democrats. Guess what? It will not matter. If someone with predetermined opinions is hell-bent on judging you, all the facts in the world will not matter. For those wanting an excellent source on race and ideology, read, *What's Race Got to Do with It?* by Larry Elder.[116]

Again, tax policy is complex and requires lengthy explanations. You don't need a blackboard to write down racial discussions. Keep it short, simple, and anything but sweet. Venom does not require sweetness in return. It also does not require facts in its response. Opinions are just fine in this one chapter.

Liberal argument: Republicans are racist.

Conservative response: Unless you want to discuss policy issues and only policy issues, I have no use for this conversation (stronger language is fine, but for exceedingly polite conservatives, "Go to hell" will suffice).

Liberal argument: Republicans have always been the racist party.

Conservative response: Conservative response: You have no idea what you're talking about. Go read a history book.

Liberal argument: The system is embroiled in white privilege and not fair to this modern day.

Conservative response: I'll tell white Holocaust survivors to check their privilege at the door before getting shot at or gassed again.

Liberal argument: There is no endemic difference in various ethnicities across America. If there are, white people caused them.

Conservative response: This conversation is boring. Continuing it serves no purpose.

Liberal argument: We need to redistribute white wealth to make this fair and okay. White people should pay for weakness they have caused in others.

Conservative response: Good. Break into a trailer park, steal whitey's last can of Spam, and give it to Oprah Winfrey. Don't blame whitey if you get shot to death trying to rob his trailer park. If you survive, go to the poorest white neighborhood in West Virginia and demand equal access to the meth that's killing them. How dare poor whites not share their narcotics and hallucinogens with you!

Liberal argument: Trump is racist. You voted for Trump, which makes you a racist. White Republicans care only about their own and should be ashamed of their own class and stature.

Conservative response: I can see why you voted for Hillary Clinton. She is angry, boring, and shrill, and so are all of her voters. See how easy that was?

Liberal argument: You're using dog whistle language.

Conservative response: Are you a canine? Dog whistles are for dogs. We're people, not dogs. Trivial accusations of racism must be ignored. Real racism does exist, and those accusations must be taken seriously. So now let's get serious.

The facts: Providing the entire history of race and bigotry in America would make this book longer than Tolstoy's *War and Peace*.[117] Offering no history at all would give the false impression that this issue itself doesn't matter. It matters greatly. It matters very deeply. Besides, under the slimmest of chances that a liberal has any intention of listening to you, be prepared.

The Grand Old Party (GOP), the party responsible for the vast majority of civil rights legislation, began in a little schoolhouse in Ripon, Wisconsin, in 1854. A small assembly of abolitionists came together to bring an end to slavery. That led to a political party dedicated to freedom, equal opportunity, and civil rights, the Republican Party.

Formal organization of the GOP took place in July of 1854 at a convention in Jackson, Michigan. Thousands of anti-slavery activists were present. Two years later, in 1856, in Philadelphia, the GOP constitution was written at the first Republican National Convention.[118]

On January 1, 1863, President Abraham Lincoln's Emancipation Proclamation called for abolishing slavery.[119] The 1864 Republican National Convention followed suit.

The KKK was founded in Tennessee in 1866 as a social club. It then spread into just about every state in the South and eventually into the North in various locations. According to Columbia University history professor Dr. Eric Foner:

In effect, the Klan was a military force serving the interests of the Democratic Party, the planter class, and all those who desired the restoration of white supremacy. It aimed to destroy the Republican Party's infrastructure, undermine the Reconstruction state, reestablish control of the black labor force, and restore racial subordination in every aspect of Southern life.[120]

From 1870 to 1930, Democrats used fraud, lynching, whippings, mutilation, murder, and intimidation to suppress the black population. Democrats also enforced Black Codes and Jim Crow laws that legalized racial discrimination and denied blacks equal rights. Gun control measures were enacted to "disarm the Negroes and leave them defenseless."[121]

It was radical Republican Senator Charles Sumner of Massachusetts who introduced the landmark 1875 Civil Rights Act.[122]

In the years following 1900, the solidly Republican women's rights movement began to gain steam. Most suffragists, including Susan B. Anthony, favored the GOP. The Nineteenth Amendment guaranteeing women the right to vote was written by a Republican senator and received greater support from Republicans than from Democrats. It was passed by Congress on June 4, 1919, and ratified on August 18, 1920.[123]

Prior to the passage and ratification of the Nineteenth Amendment, Republican Jeannette Rankin of Montana in 1916 became the first woman elected to Congress.[124]

On June 2, 1924, the Republican-controlled 68th Congress and President Calvin Coolidge granted citizenship to Native Americans with the Indian Citizenship Act.[125]

Republican Octaviano Larrazolo of New Mexico in 1928 was sworn in as the first Hispanic U.S. senator.[126]

On May 17, 1954, the legendary *Brown v. Board of Education* ruling struck down racial segregation in public schools. The majority decision was written by Chief Justice Earl Warren, the former California Republican governor and vice presidential nominee.[127]

President Dwight D. Eisenhower, who appointed Judge Warren, sent Congress a proposal for civil rights legislation. The end result was the Civil Rights Act of 1957, which established the Civil Rights Section of the Justice Department.[128]

On August 21, 1959, Republican Hiram Fong of Hawaii became the first Asian-American elected to the U.S Senate.[129]

On June 10, 1964, Republican Senate Minority Leader Everett Dirksen of Illinois broke a Democratic filibuster and passed the 1964 Civil Rights Act. The House version of the Civil Rights Act of 1964 was embraced by 80 percent of Republicans but supported by only 61 percent of that chamber's Democrats. In the final Senate vote on the act, it received 82 percent support from Republicans and was opposed by 69 percent of Democrats.[130]

Ninety-four percent of Senate Republicans voted in favor of the Voting Rights Act of 1965 versus 73 percent of Democrats. The final vote on the House's version was even starker because only one Senate Republican voted against it, while 17 Democrats opposed it. In the House, 82 percent of Republicans supported the bill versus 78 percent of Democrats.[131]

On September 25, 1981, Ronald Reagan appointed Sandra Day O'Connor to become the first woman on the U.S. Supreme Court.[132]

Now that we honestly covered history, let's very briefly discuss policy.

- **Welfare reform.** GOP efforts were meant to give people their dignity back. Liberals want to keep as many people as possible dependent on government so that they have no choice but to support the party of government. It's a vicious never-ending cycle on the new liberal plantation.
- **Gun control.** Again, Democrats passed laws to disarm blacks so that they could kill them. Republicans want all citizens to be able to defend themselves.
- **Illegal immigration.** Illegal workers steal jobs from black and Hispanic laborers who are in this country legally. Democrats want endless illegal immigration and open borders to gain more Democratic votes.

- **Abortion.** Planned Parenthood founder Margaret Sanger was a known racist. Abortion was her way of reducing the black population.[133]

It is long past time for a lesson in personal responsibility. Melanin content does not make anyone competent at their job. It also does not make them terrible at their job. If someone calls you incompetent, it is not because they are racist. It is because you (like most people) don't like being told that you suck at your job. If you hear this criticism frequently enough, maybe you *do* just suck at your job. Be better or get out and do something else. This was the message that former Republican Florida Governor and now Senator Rick Scott essentially delivered to Democrat Brenda Snipes. She tried to play the race card when he fired her from her post as Broward County supervisor of elections. Scott refused to back down, and her firing was upheld.[134]

Losing an election or a job is not always because of racism. Maybe the defeated individual is just a basket case out of step with mainstream voters or values. There are plenty of normal mainstream minorities in America. Former Obama Attorney General Eric Holder, 2018 Florida gubernatorial candidate Andrew Gillum (who would be found passed out naked in a hotel room with a male escort and drug paraphernalia),[135] 2018 Georgia gubernatorial candidate Stacey Abrams, and California Senator Kamala Harris are not among them. Neither is Alexandria Ocasio-Cortez (AOC). The rule for minorities is the same as for whites: Be normal. Don't be a basket case.

Also, people who have to pretend to have deep roots in a minority community are not authentic anything. Robert O'Rourke called himself "Beto" so that voters in his heavily Hispanic district would think he was also Hispanic. O'Rourke is Irish.[136]

Massachusetts Senator Elizabeth Warren spent her life insisting she was part American Indian because her ancestors had "high cheekbones." This is as valid as insisting that a big nose is proof of being Jewish or that a large posterior makes someone a black woman. These stereotypes are real racism. Warren is 100 percent white, give or take 1/1024th.[137]

Senator Kamala Harris portrayed herself as a woman who lived the American black experience. During the 2020 Democratic presidential primary, she played the race card on front-runner Joe Biden. There is plenty to criticize Biden for, but intentional animus toward black people is not on the list. The criticism from Harris fell apart when it was revealed that she held the exact same position as Biden on the school busing issue at the heart of her attack.

Harris also invented an entire fictional racial narrative for herself. The truth was that her father is Jamaican and her mother is Indian. Harris was raised in Canada in a middle-class home. Both her parents were white-collar workers. Her mother was a medical professional in a hospital, and her father was an economics professor at Stanford University. Harris keeps her husband away from the cameras. Most Americans would not care that she married a white man, but it does go against her carefully crafted image as a champion of the black community.[138]

O'Rourke, Warren, and Harris are hard leftists who spent more time pushing their own fake racial narratives to gain political power than helping real downtrodden minorities.

Last, and most important, if you actually *are* a racist or bigot, please come closer so that I can slap the daylights and bigotry out of you. It is tough to push away fake claims of racism when real ones are cherry-picked and used to paint with a broad brush. Everybody should just shut up and love each other. Done.

Now that the emotion is out of the way, we can return to more nuts-and-bolts policy issues and a kinder, gentler tone that the late Barbara Bush (rest in peace) would approve.

CHAPTER 5

Justice Does Not Need an Adjective

Constitutionalism, Social Justice, and Special Rights

Our great American experiment is only 244 years old, yet the present-day war on the very concept of American justice has never been more emotional and ridiculous than today. Reading and history are systematically being replaced by the liberal *causes célèbres* or adjectives of the day. A huge swath of emotionally charged misguided Americans now overreact daily to various cries of injustice. Our 24-hour emotionally manipulating mainstream media news cycle drops social-justice-driven buzzwords with reckless abandon. Channels showcase pained liberals weeping in the streets. Television news anchors fanning the flames remain unaware that almost all historical institutionalized injustices have already been solved in America.

Justice is not 100 percent perfect. We fallible humans must ultimately be the ones to interpret it. To expect otherwise is pure folly, but America, with her undeniably good conscience, is quick to solve problems through checks and balances. American justice remains globally superior to that of all other countries worldwide. Our justice remains mostly blind but certainly not as blind as the social, environmental, LGBTQ, and other leftist warriors desire. They are desperate to convince you that our system is broken and that we should hate our flawed country.

Let's start with the deep roots of American justice. After that, we can address the inane adjectives added by anyone with a feeling who seeks to hijack American justice for his or her own agenda.

Our successful American system of justice comes from two foundational wellsprings, one here and the other greater and less tangible than here. On this earthly plane, American justice is the direct product of our Constitution. The Constitution includes our establishment of federal and state court systems to further protect our constitutional principles as well as the freedom and rights of our people.

The opening lines of the Constitution are crystal clear:

We the People of the United States, in order to form a more perfect Union, establish justice, insure domestic tranquility, provide for the common defense, promote the general welfare, and secure the blessings of liberty to ourselves and our posterity, do ordain and establish this Constitution for the United States of America.[139]

Article III states:

The judicial Power of the United States shall be vested in one Supreme Court, and in such inferior courts as the Congress may from time to time ordain and establish. The judges, both of the Supreme and inferior courts, shall hold their offices during good behavior, and shall, at stated times, receive for their services a compensation which shall not be diminished during their continuance in office.[140]

The Eleventh Amendment explained in detail what the courts are to do. All these recent liberal adjectives are covered already. The Thirteenth, Fourteenth, and Fifteenth Amendments gave blacks full equality under the law.[141] On June 26, 2015, the U.S. Supreme Court ruled that the Constitution grants same-sex couples the right to marry.[142] Our greater systemic injustices in our democracy have overwhelmingly adjusted.

On a higher plane, our justice comes from several core sources. The Bible and its Judeo-Christian ethics provide the Ten Commandments and the Golden Rule. Then came the ancient Greeks and later Neoplatonism, a third-century Greek Platonic doctrine-based philosophical system founded chiefly in Eastern mysticism (with later influences from Christianity).

Neoplatonism holds that all existence consists of emanations from the One whom the soul may be reunited with. Neoplatonism was a core influence on our well-studied Framers' use of natural rights later in our legal history.[143] The English played another key role. Although we broke from England, the English common-law system effectively remained in place after the Revolution and continues to this day. The English court system particularly uses the Magna Carta[144] as its core legal basis. Legal scholars state the lasting impact of the Magna Carta on the American legal system.

The Magna Carta is more present in American constitutional law than in the United Kingdom to this day. The right to a trial by jury, the right to travel, and the right to due process (habeas corpus) all come from the Magna Carta. Ideas of natural law and natural rights shaped the founding of the United States and in its 1860s refounding. Natural law involves the use of reason to analyze human nature to deduce binding rules of moral behavior from nature's or God's creation of reality and humankind.

With so much careful ethical evolution, maybe your man-bun-adorned neighbor tinkering with justice is more serious business that you thought. The stakes of changing justice or the Constitution from which it emanates have long-lasting implications for individual liberty.

Our eternally and rationally well-grounded, world-leading justice system is already in place. Social justice warriors want to make what is already "right and just" fit their own feelings. This has greater consequences than one can imagine. New rights desired by leftists range from tree rights to human-dolphin relational rights. Far from strengthening our society, these new rights tear it down.

Liberal argument: Our U.S. Constitution is a Living Constitution. The Constitution has a dynamic meaning. It changes as the needs of Americans progress and evolve. Loose construction reflects that dynamic.

The facts: This entire argument is an opinion lacking a single fact to back it up anywhere. It cannot be backed up. The Founding Fathers never explicitly stated that their document was evolving. To the contrary, the Tenth Amendment in the Bill of Rights explicitly puts the federal government in a strict constructionist straitjacket: "The powers not delegated to the United States by the Constitution, nor prohibited by it to the States, are reserved to the States respectively, or to the people."[145] If the federal government cannot unilaterally alter the Constitution, how can the courts?

The judicial branch was set up to be the weakest of the three branches of government. In the 1803 case *Marbury v. Madison*, the Supreme Court assumed to itself the power of judicial review (whether a law was constitutional). The decision angered Thomas Jefferson, who wanted the legislature to have that power. The

Supreme Court had assumed the right to reduce the Constitution to a "mere thing of wax in the hands of the judiciary."[146]

The Founding Fathers were very specific. They left open a process to amend the Constitution. They made it difficult to amend the Constitution in keeping with the view that doing nothing beats acting in haste (a rebuke to those obsessed with change).

A *textualist*, or *strict constructionist*, looks at the words of the Founding Fathers as written. The Constitution is exactly what it says it is. Everything is literal.

A loose constructionist wants us to look beyond what the Founding Fathers said and instead focus on what they meant but did not say. If this sounds like Deepak Chopra mystical gobbledygook, it's because it is. It requires ignoring the *Federalist Papers* and reading the minds of a bunch of dead men. Unless you own a Ouija board made before December 14, 1799, you have no idea what George Washington was thinking. To think that you could possibly know is the height of arrogance.

One of the great originalist judges was also one of the finest legal minds the world has ever known. Appointed by Reagan in 1986, Justice Antonin Scalia summed up best why a living Constitution makes a mockery of jurisprudence: "If the Constitution does not speak to a matter, it's for the democratic process to provide an answer. If you want something, you persuade your fellow citizens that it's a good idea and pass a law."[147]

Liberals love the evolving Constitution argument because it is a lazy argument. Getting legislation passed is difficult. Getting bad legislation repealed is even tougher. The legislature is the closest representation of the people. Scalia understood that nine justices in black robes should not be making new laws. They were only there to interpret existing ones. In recent years, liberals have stymied conservative legislation by getting one liberal Ninth Circuit Judge in Seattle, San Francisco, or Hawaii to invent law out of thin air.

What if the Constitution is wrong? Amend it.

What if enough people are against amending it? Too damn bad. The people spoke. Respect their will, and try to find consensus. Laws passed by consensus stand the test of time. Laws created by the courts only exacerbate conflicts.

Nowhere has this been truer than with the 1973 *Roe v. Wade* decision legalizing abortion. The issue is not whether life begins at conception or if a woman has a right to choose what to do with her body. That is the abortion question itself, which will be debated forever without resolution. The constitutional question is what the original document says about abortion.

Documents are specific. Catholic doctrine clearly forbids abortion. Jewish doctrine forbids eating bacon. Islam forbids drinking alcohol. These are all examples of explicit codified religious law.

Abortion is not even mentioned in the Constitution. Abortion was declared legal in 1973 by a 5–4 margin under some invented right to privacy that is found nowhere in the Constitution.[148] The end result is that 45 years later, advocates on both sides are still locked in a death struggle on the issue. *Stare decisis* (respect the precedent) is an advisory tradition but not binding. In 2020, an abortion vote could go 5–4 the other way. We have no idea. This is why both sides fight to the death over court nominations.

What the Supreme Court should have done in 1973 is what Justice John Roberts did regarding the Affordable Care Act in 2012. Conservatives were angry that Roberts (through some very tortured legal reasoning) voted to uphold the law.[149] Grounds for repeal were strong. What Roberts did was give a polite but stern message to the legislature. They created this mess, and they needed to fix it.

Using the courts to invent new laws allows the legislature to duck responsibility for doing the hard work they were elected to do. Legislative work is hard because forging consensus in a divided nation is hard. Try passing a nonbinding resolution declaring apple pie to be delicious. Some anti-apple-pie lobby will convince one gutless congressperson to kill the resolution because apple pie is somehow racist. This may be frustrating to the rest of us, but such stalemates are not a failure of the system. They are the system working perfectly.

Loose constructionism is a sneaky way of allowing politicians to avoid responsibility for serious life and death matters. Strict constructionism forces lawmakers to take personal responsibility. What a novel concept. In a world where politicians generally want more power, judges are in theory supposed to be above politics. Strict constructionists want to give themselves less power. It takes moral courage for a judge to say, "I hate that law. I would love to strike it down. However, I can't. The Constitution won't let me."

Good judges do this on a regular basis. They put America and our Constitution above their own ambitions and desires. That was Scalia. That is strict constructionism.

Liberal argument: White Republican males created originalism to keep society trapped in the past.

The facts: This argument is so senseless that a short rejection of it should confine it, Lord willing, to the dustbin of history forever. While the term itself is a twentieth-century term, the concept of originalism has existed since the original justices and the Founders. Imagine going up to Washington or Jefferson and saying, "I know what you said, but what did you mean?" You would be considered an uneducated dolt and laughed out of the room, deservedly so. You would also justifiably be told to stop talking so much and spend more time paying attention and listening. So how do we know that the Republican Party had nothing to do with the original way the Constitution was viewed by the Founders and the original justices?

Until 1854, the Republican Party did not exist! This argument needs to be turned upside down. Judicial activism (living
Constitution advocates) was created by emasculated white leftist
legislators too gutless to take tough stands that might anger voters. Why show bravery when you can hide under your desk and let
judges with lifetime appointments take the heat?

If an issue is important enough, the legislators will get off
their duffs and get the job done. Slavery was evil. After the Civil
War ended, the legislature passed the Thirteenth, Fourteenth, and
Fifteenth Amendments in the political equivalent of warp speed.
Most issues are just not as serious as slavery. Naming a post office
after your Aunt Edna may seem noncontroversial, but maybe it is
controversial to another legislator who disliked her for cheating at
bridge (allegedly). If the process bogs down, then your precious issue
is just not that important to enough people. Voters are very diligent
about letting their elected representatives know when they are upset.
As the late Senator Everett Dirksen used to say, "When I feel the
heat, I see the light."[150] This is the system working as intended.

The argument is actually dangerous for liberals as well. They may
be incapable of picturing a world where they are voted out of power.
It still shocks many of them that a large segment of the population, dare it be said, disagrees with them. Let's say that one man
wants to marry another man. Gay marriage is legal, so this on the
surface seems noncontroversial. Now let's say that one of the men
self-identifies as a walrus and the other one self-identifies as a platypus. Should they have the right to demand that the person or animal
performing the ceremony concludes by saying, "I now pronounce
you walrus and platypus. You may kiss the walplat (platwal?)." The
law sees plenty of silliness. If a liberal judge decides that this should
be legal because of biases (he may have a thick mustache and is often
mistaken for a walrus), he can declare it law.

What if a conservative judge decides not to act like Scalia or
another originalist, Justice Clarence Thomas? What if Judge Thomas
decides to ignore text in favor of his personal biases? He may one

day wake up and decide, "I know the Constitution says it's wrong to kill based on race, but I hate the Smurfs. Anyone wearing blue can be shot to death without consequences." Should this be allowed? Anyone who says that this is impossible needs to spend much more time in a courtroom. Frivolous lawsuits are filed every day.

> **Liberal argument:** Justice by itself is biased. To be in tune with the people, we need social justice, environmental justice, LGBTQ justice, and Sharia justice.
>
> **The facts:** This argument is downright dangerous. While all human beings possess inherent biases, the goal for a justice is to truly be a nonpartisan referee. Judge Roberts compared it with being a baseball umpire. Just call balls and strikes, nothing else.[151] The liberal argument says that judges are incapable of upholding this honorable requirement. To be fair, far too many liberal judges are failures in this area. Rather than admit their own shortcomings, they attempt to justify a character flaw as necessary for the common good. Judges are supposed to be better than this. This is why they go through a rigorous confirmation process. More is expected of them.

It takes only one judge to upend the law for political reasons. This is why liberals keep running to their West Coast Ninth Circuit friends. What will they do when the other side turns the tables? The electoral college showed us in 2016 that much of the nation thinks differently from California. Do liberals really want to be subjected to the whims of Mississippi and Alabama judges?

The responsible course of action is for all Americans to encourage their judges to seek impartiality whenever possible. Innate imperfection is no excuse to give up striving for perfection. It is fine for Congress to have 535 members as biased as the voters who elected them. Judges with lifetime appointments must be those aforementioned umpires.

Many of America's institutions are in tatters. The presidency has been degraded, the media have been discredited, and Congress is held in low esteem. The only institution outside of our military that still garners respect is the Supreme Court. The only way for this respect to be maintained is for judges to be seen as fair, impartial, and rendering decisions based on clearly codified laws and statutes.

> **Liberal argument:** Social justice warriors are the most evolved, woke[152] people in our time. Those who aren't in alignment are morally flawed.
>
> **The facts:** *Social Justice* was an anti-Semitic American Roman Catholic periodical published by Father Charles Coughlin during the late 1930s and early 1940s. *Social Justice* was controversial for printing anti-Semitic polemics such as, "The Protocols of the Elders of Zion." Coughlin claimed that Marxist atheism in Europe was a Jewish plot against America.[153]

It is no surprise that the current iteration of social justice has maintained its hostility toward capitalism and especially toward Jews.

Nobel Prize–winning economist Friedrich Hayek wrote in 1976, "I have come to feel strongly that the greatest service I can still render to my fellow men would be that I could make the speakers and writers among them thoroughly ashamed ever again to employ the term 'social justice.'"[154]

Most liberals can't even articulate what social justice is. Social justice means anything its emotionally charged advocates want it to mean to get what they want. It's socialism rebranded as well as an emotional tool to try to alter the highly functional system of American justice already in place.

The term has been hijacked from its original meaning. A Jesuit priest named Luigi Taparelli first coined the term *social justice*. He never intended it to mean that government would swoop in and take over every aspect of your life. Taparelli's mission was to further the thoughts of Thomas Aquinas: that truth is to be accepted no matter where it is found.[155] This definitely does not mean getting what you want with a buzzword by altering the eternal concept of justice. It means the precise opposite.

Social justice was subsequently equated politically with economic justice. Like socialism, the basis was rooted in the concept of redistribution of wealth for the common good of all. This remains the fundamental basis of Marxism still championed by progressives.

As columnist Jonah Goldberg points out:

The Mission Statement of the AFL-CIO (which could be the mission statement for a thousand such organizations) states: 'The mission of the AFL-CIO is to improve the lives of working families—to bring economic justice to the workplace, and social justice to our nation.' In short, social justice is code for good things no one needs to argue for and no one dare be against. Ultimately, social justice is about the state amassing ever-increasing power in order to do 'good things.' What are good things? They are whatever social justice champions decide this week. But first, last and always it is the cause of economic redistribution. Compassion, or social justice, is when government takes your money and gives it to someone else. Greed is when you want to keep it.[156]

The term *warrior* is a totally inaccurate label for these overly sensitive, politically correct crybabies. They retreat to safe spaces to avoid healthy conflict when they don't get what they want. These easily triggered overgrown toddlers can't handle hearing anything other than what they think fits their own internal constitution and bills of self-generated rights.

Hating capitalism is not being woke. Hatred of Jews is not woke. It's bigoted. Being woke is not being enlightened. It's being either an angry America-hating, capitalist-hating, Jew-hating female with bad grammar or an emasculated beta male who desperately wants to date them (well-adjusted women date alpha males, not sissies).

CHAPTER 6

Life Is Not a Safe Space

Free Speech versus
Leftist Political Correctness

Warning: If you are a liberal crybaby, this chapter may hurt your feelings. When it comes to free speech, our Declaration of Independence and First Amendment are more important than your precious feelings.

A 2018 Cato Institute poll showed that 71 percent of Americans say that political correctness has silenced dialogue that society must have. Fifty-eight percent have political views they're afraid to share.[157] This is what political correctness has done to free speech and personal expression in America. Unlike climate change, this is a real crisis, and we must act now.

Political correctness, safe spaces, trigger warnings, and their supporting language corrections have turned its proponents into clerics of linguistic hysterics. Insults are not emotional rape.

This is not to imply that insults are good. People should be nicer to each other. The Golden Rule is golden indeed. When libertarian Milo Yiannopoulos walks into a room of students and yells, "F*ck your feelings," he is being a provocateur.[158] Of course we should care about another person's feelings. We should also act within reason.

Most people would not approach a grieving widow at a funeral and say, "Hey, sorry your husband is dead, but I'm raising money for a Hawaiian vacation. How much would you like to donate?" Most people would not go up to a black person and ask, "Hey, we're having a local KKK meeting this Thursday. Do you want to come? They're serving lemonade!" Reasonable people had better be able to agree that these are examples of hurting a person's feelings where the outrage would be justified.

Now let's go to the other extreme. Try telling a woman that she is wearing a very pretty dress and that you like the pattern. Then try asking her where she bought it.

She could respond with gracious appreciation. She could tell you the name of the store. Maybe the dress was a gift from her favorite grandmother who recently passed away. You made her day by complimenting the taste of someone she deeply cared about.

Alternatively, she could scream, "Stop judging me by my looks, you sexist pig! Respect me for my intelligence!"

You may have hurt her feelings, but is it really your problem that she is a hysterical basket case? More important, is it sexist for you to point out that she is a hysterical basket case? No, and no. A reality check is necessary to keep this hysterical basket case from inflicting herself on another innocent human being.

Political correctness, like most political issues, can be dealt with using our favorite political document. A quick consultation with the Constitution again settles the issue.

The First Amendment states: "Congress shall make no law respecting an establishment of religion or prohibiting the free exercise thereof; or abridging the freedom of speech, or of the press; or the right of the people peaceably to assemble, and to petition the government for a redress of grievances."[159] Nowhere in the Constitution is there a First Amendment exemption for feelings. It says nothing about protective restrictions due to being triggered or offended. Your right to obnoxiously push your grievances on others ends with their right to choose to ignore you.

Contrary to what many liberals believe, the Constitution does not grant a right to happiness. It grants "life, liberty, and the pursuit of happiness." Pursuit is not a guarantee of anything. High school science geniuses are free to pursue the prom queen. She is free to say no and most likely will.

This differs sharply from our current politically correct environment. Political correctness stems from an entitled imposition that your right to happiness supersedes someone else's. My refusal to call your self-identified pan-gender[160] (or whatever) friend pan-gender doesn't mean that I demean his/her/its value. He/she/it still has the same legal rights under the law. None of their civil rights are violated because I choose to use the same pronouns that have been around since ancient times. Conversely, my insistence on traditional pronouns does not take away your own right to enjoy your "they-ness" in all its glory.

You can even call yourself "His Majesty," as one college man did.[161] His self-appointed title came with zero special powers. He still had to complete his homework assignments on time like everybody else. Civil discourse allows you your idiosyncrasies. It does not require my embracing them.

Equality under the law and free speech leave no room for victims or tyrants. Welcome to America. This is the real safe space that free speech itself creates. Unless it's specifically covered under the laws of the land (truly violating your rights or unjust to our American standards of natural law) and not just a personal politically correct demand, it is simply not law. Unlawful acts are society's problem. Your pet peeves are your personal problem.

Political correctness often morphs into condemning those who disagree. It leads to trying to damage or impinge the freedom of speech of people who hurt your feelings. This terribly wrong behavior has its roots in the darker forces of socialism and communism.

Jonah Goldberg covers this well in his book, *Liberal Fascism*. Tyrannical empires quickly move to take control by confiscating three rights: freedom of speech (including the press), freedom of religion (to later make the groupthink of the state the new religion), and guns.[162] This is so that they may later take away liberty and private property, usually by force.

As an ex-liberal, I concede that the emotional heart passionately calls for change and action to protect others who are less fortunate. The right has heated emotions as well. Emotions themselves are not the abuse of political correctness. Emotions are God given and often beautiful. People have a right to feel things, but emotional outrage and tears must not become a cover to propagate political correctness and impinge on my speech.

Cry all you want. Anger at losing an election is not a justification for repeatedly trying to impeach a president. Being upset is not a legal defense against slander or libel. As the Rolling Stones sang, "You can't always get what you want, but if you try sometimes, you just might find, you get what you need."[163] Not getting what you want often leads to creativity and better opportunities. Slipping into a soul-damaging victim mentality can hinder your ability to generate internal happiness regardless of external outcomes. Pull yourself up by your bootstraps. Toughen up, chin up, march on, and take the next right action. That is America.

The challenge now is that politically correct groupthink is gaining momentum. The self-generated rights of the few are becoming the new meta-laws, with consequences being doled out to those who don't obey. Its power now calls for protests and rallies of thousands. These mobs move beyond peaceful protest into emotionally charged violence. This is how individual intentions become societal problems. If you're an American and love your country with any kind of gratitude and selflessness, you cannot in good conscience rally people to repress others.

JFK, Dr. Martin Luther King, Jr., Mahatma Gandhi, and Ronald Reagan all successfully connected to millions of people through rational, peaceful actions within our already existing system. Their approach resulted in much better outcomes than that of the many more intrusive and oppressive leaders in history we all know so well. Whether it's the planet, the #MeToo movement (which did achieve some positive measure of justice for deserving women),[164] Trump, or the cause of the day, peaceful solutions are available. These solutions can be achieved without running away, hiding behind a safe space, bullying, slandering, or pressuring others to conform.

Liberals and leftists have mind meltdowns and become dominated by their feelings because their ideology is about conditioning you to behave this way. The left wants you to think, not feel. Feelings are in direct accordance with the power of the liberal dream of ultimate fairness in all things.

Be it sexual, societal, racial, or environmental, everything must be fair. Someone somewhere experiences an inequality. All the tears and rage are then justified and easily recruited for whatever agenda the left wants. It's a very effective form of political brainwashing. Don't think in this age of marketing that it just happens organically on the other side of the political spectrum.

Wikipedia defines this phenomenon well: "Mind control (also known as brainwashing, coercive persuasion, mind abuse, thought control, or thought reform) refers to a process in which a group or individual systematically uses unethically manipulative methods to persuade others to conform to the wishes of the manipulator(s), often to the detriment of the person being manipulated."[165] The technique is also clear:

The manipulator offers you a number of choices, but the choices all lead to the same conclusion. The same idea or phrase is frequently repeated to make sure it sticks in your brain. Intense intelligence-dampening is performed by providing you with constant short snippets of information on various subjects. This trains you to have a short memory, makes the amount of information feel overwhelming, and the answers provided by the manipulator to be highly desired due to how overwhelmed you feel.[166]

The most powerful technique is emotional manipulation. "Emotional manipulation is used to put you in a heightened state, as this makes it harder for you to employ logic. Inducing fear and anger are among the most popular manipulated emotions."[167]

It is no leap of logic that our academic, political, and media systems are predominantly liberal. Those needing power over others often suffer from low self-esteem, egotism, narcissism, and in extremes cases, sociopathic tendencies. It takes a clear view and calm mind to be more accepting of others who differ. Many wounded people in life are just doing the best they can.

It's not universally easy to be a human being and constantly choose internal happiness during life's ups and downs. The Buddha taught that life is suffering.[168] Christ suffered. Most of the people in the Bible and Torah suffered in their journeys. To hurt, be offended, or not get what you want is an unavoidable part of the natural process of life.

Self-control is an important attribute of maturity and a vital component of relatedness. Control is an essential element of responsibility. Loss of control under pressure (or of a feeling of a loss of power) leads to anxiety, unhappiness, anger, resentment, stress, helplessness, and even depression. Abdicating control, acting powerless, and playing the victim are irresponsible. Our freedom ends where it begins for others. We must balance control with the rights and needs of others and respect for others.

The last thing for social justice warriors to consider is that every army runs the risk of encountering a superior army. Rome is a small shell of what it was during its Roman Empire glory days. The Spanish Armada was the envy of the world until the British shredded it. The sun never set on the British Empire until it did. Even France had a brief period of relevance. Social justice warriors win battles because they attack peaceful people unaccustomed to fighting.

It takes little courage for a football team captain to beat up a girl in a wheelchair suffering from cerebral palsy. It takes little effort for a schoolchild to burn ants with a magnifying glass. Hard-core leftist comedian Sarah Silverman in her book and movie ironically makes the case against her own views without a hint of self-awareness. She mercilessly ridicules Christians but will not dare mock Muslims because she doesn't want to get blown up or have her head cut off.[169] She refuses to make fun of blacks. Why does she make fun of Chinese people? Because, in her words, "We're not afraid of you."[170]

Liberal argument: If you offend someone, you violate that person's rights.

The facts: This is false. Rights are not self-declared. Moral rights come from God. Having a God complex does not make a person God. Our legal rights come from the Constitution. There are no legal protections against being insulted. A woman once said to British Prime Minister Winston Churchill, "You sir are a drunk." He responded, "You madam, are ugly, but I'll be sober in the morning."[171] A common refrain of protest is, "Well, I never (have been insulted in all of my life)!" The proper rebuttal, courtesy of Benny Hill, is, "Well, you should have been!"[172] Having your sensibilities offended is not the same as having your rights violated.

When college campus social justice warriors yell, "Shut it down," at invited conservative speakers, they do so knowing the school chancellor is a liberal. They know it is easy to win a rigged fight. What if the other side shows up and enters the ring? Wait until these pseudo-warriors encounter a conservative chancellor or, better yet, a conservative governor. That authority figure could turn the tables, expel them all, and permanently close down the entire institution until further notice. Imagine the irony if the police or government locked up the buildings as conservatives in the area yelled, "Shut it down."

Rights violations cause injury to your person. Insults injure your pride. Children learn in school at an early age that "sticks and stones may break my bones, but names will never hurt me."[173] If names do hurt you, then you have regressed beyond childhood. Your immaturity is your problem alone.

> **Liberal argument:** Trigger warnings and safe spaces are a right.
>
> **The facts:** The Constitution says nothing of the sort. Leaving home places people at the mercy of life and all its cruelties. Home is the ultimate safe space. Nobody has the legal right to enter your home without your permission. Assuming that you paid your bills, you own everything in your home.

Once you leave your driveway, you own nothing. If this is too much to handle, do the world a favor and stay home. You may not improve your life, but you will certainly improve everyone else's by reducing one of our aggravation sources. If you choose to venture into the world and make demands of others, be prepared for consequences when you mouth off to somebody bigger and stronger than you.

Liberal argument: Hate speech is not free speech.

The facts: Hate speech is the very speech deserving of the most protection. It is at the heart of free speech. Nobody is allowed under the Constitution to instigate violence or riots. The common examples of yelling fire in a crowded theater and threatening to assassinate the president have stood the test of time. They are prohibited. The U.S. Supreme Court case of *New York v. Irving Feiner* settled this matter.[174] Hate speech is terrible. In an ideal world, nobody would be a racist, anti-Semite, or other kind of bigot. The real world is what it is.

British writer Evelyn Beatrice Hall said it best when paraphrasing Voltaire, "I disagree with what you say, but I will defend to the death your right to say it."[175] Social justice warriors, including their violent Antifa (anti-fascist) contingent, may wish to ponder a potential concern. What happens to them when somebody decides that they are the offenders?

The revolution always eats its own. It is the same reason that all empires fall. When everyone has been conquered, there is nothing left to do but turn inward. Until that inevitable conclusion, accept living in an imperfect world with bad people saying bad things. The far worse alternative is a world where even one innocent person is wrongly shunned, jailed, or killed over misunderstood innocent speech.

You say undocumented workers. I say illegal aliens. You label it workplace violence. I label it radical Islam. You say handicapable. I say handicapped. You call them African-Americans. I call them blacks. You call them LGBTQIASANDEVERYOTHER ACRONYMINTHEBOOK. I call them Dave or Bill or Janice or whatever first name they claim.

Liberal argument: If you don't believe in safe spaces and trigger warnings as valid, you are bigoted, racist, regressive, sexist, and morally unconscious.

The facts: Keep boring me to death, and I *will* be unconscious. You are fully entitled to live by your rules. You have zero right to force anyone else to live under those rules (with an exception for parents raising their own children). Even if you have executive power as the head of a corporation, city, state, or nation, living in a first-world nation means you will have people who disagree with you.

You believe meat is murder. I enjoy a good steak. You insist animals have rights. I insist we can love animals, but they have no rights. "Go ahead and lick that frog!"[176]

You believe my complimenting your beauty is offensive. I believe that you do not speak for all women. I will cease complimenting you and save myself a headache by not speaking with you again. I will not stop sincerely flattering other women who appreciate that sincere flattery just because you are offended.

You believe I should justify why I disagree with you. I know that I am not required to justify anything to you. God created us both. Your existence may bother me, but I am legally required to accept it. That goes both ways.

We are all on this Earth together, and the world is becoming a smaller place. We are stuck with each other. Safe spaces are becoming fewer and even more far between. We might as well just get along. This means listening more than we talk and being tolerant of others. The people who speak words we disagree with often deserve even more tolerance. Otherwise, tolerance is as meaningless as a degree in community organizing.

CHAPTER 7

American Exceptionalism
Is Not a Hate Crime

Patriotism, Excellence, and Gratitude

The concept of American exceptionalism runs much deeper than buzzwords from the left and right. Americans have always thought their country was exceptional. They thought it since hearing of Jesus' Sermon on the Mount. "A City upon a Hill" is covered in Matthew 5:14.[177] John Winthrop delivered a famous sermon calling his Puritan community a "city on a hill" around 1630, long before the United States of America existed.[178]

Frenchman Alexis de Tocqueville has been credited (apparently erroneously) in the 1830s for labeling American society exceptional. De Tocqueville has been repeatedly credited (again seemingly erroneously) for saying, "America is great because America is good; and if America ever ceases to be good, she will no longer be great."[179]

Take a few weeks traveling across our country, and you'll find that Americans are mostly happy, good, warmhearted, kind, down-to-earth, hardworking people.

Let's dumb it down. It's okay to win and be grateful for winning the first-place "best nation in the world" trophy and not have that be an offense or a hate crime to lesser nations. Life is inherently competitive, and it's okay to win and lose.

This is the essence of democracy based on individual freedom and liberty. The opportunity to be good and say "I'm good" does not mean "you're bad" and thus a lesser human being.

Many people often fantasize about a world where everybody just gets along. Take one look at the news and see that this idealized world is a long way off. This global homogenized one world community is a fantasy.

In America, gratitude and confidence are choices. The United States has remained imperfect yet predominantly good ever since our tough, religious, hardworking immigrants fled European religious, financial, and government oppression.

Stalin's resentment of America in 1929 led him to declare us as the "heresy of American exceptionalism."[180] Stalin's communism was a doomed progressive experiment that could only be held in place by brute force. Marx said so himself.[181]

JFK also used the "city upon a hill" phrase.[182] Later, Reagan and his followers gratefully lauded America as a "shining city upon a hill."[183] After 9/11, George W. Bush and his supporters asserted America's exceptional distinctiveness with a renewed vigor. Islamic terrorists hated our freedoms. They wished to kill Americans because they envied this exceptional inheritance.

Obama in 2009 made a mockery of the term when asked if he believed in American exceptionalism: "I believe in American exceptionalism, just as I suspect that the Brits believe in British exceptionalism and the Greeks believe in Greek exceptionalism."[184] As Dr. Charles Krauthammer succinctly pointed out: "Interesting response. Because if everyone is exceptional, no one is."[185]

Trump's desire to "Make America Great Again" mirrors Reagan's entreaties after Carter. It's a call to move past the Obama era and recognize our exceptionalism again.[186]

The left still derides American exceptionalism as an outdated philosophy of manifest destiny. Academia and Hollywood label conservatives racist, neocolonialist, and xenophobic for claiming themselves as exceptional, blessed, and holding a vision of freedom for those in the world under despotic tyranny.

American history was hijacked regarding our claims to our own greatness. Leftism with its direct roots in socialism, communism, fascism, and the like cannot have a country too great or too proud of itself. Otherwise, there would be nothing left for government leftists to fundamentally transform in order to seize and maintain their own power and agenda.

Hollywood was very pro-American during World War II. Now it sells "Ameri-shame" the most. Remember that Hollywood is not real. It's a fantasy playland.

From baby boomers to millennials and beyond, the brainwashing continues. Declaring America great may be racist, xenophobic, and hurt other nations and their people's feelings. Patriotism evokes moral outrage. This is a far cry from the traditional American value system once imbued in our society. Simply staying together in marriage was a patriotic commitment to our country.

Many of Obama's speeches contained classic socialist economic themes. Demonizing the rich, claiming businessmen "didn't build" their businesses, wealth redistribution, and his belief that government spending creates jobs were peppered with his disdain for American exceptionalism.[187] During Obama's presidency, Republican leaders even expressed concern that, in Newt Gingrich's words, there was "a determined group of radicals in the United States who outright oppose American exceptionalism."[188]

It is vital to understand why America truly is exceptional.

It was only America's Revolutionary War victory over the British that stopped the Europeans from taking over America and displacing the Indians (in time as well). After much prolonged strife, our constitutional values and the better angels of our nature prevailed. Freedom from oppression often involves migration. We see this from the biblical age through modern times, including a big and often messy sorting-out process.

> **Liberal argument:** The Pilgrims confiscated America from Native Americans, Mexicans, Hawaiians, and Alaskans. The United States should be ashamed of its colonialism and imperialism.
>
> **The facts:** North American culture is far from alone. Persian, Indian, and European nations have all invaded and been invaded. There is evidence that the Indians were not the very first to America and that they constantly and brutally invaded each other. Vikings raided the Indians as early as 1002. The British Empire conquered the world.

The first 53 English Pilgrims at the inaugural three-day Thanksgiving celebration with Chief Massasoit and 90 of his braves enjoyed fellowship and gratitude together.[189]

Unlike many nations, America has a conscience. America is still actively doing its best to rectify its past dealings with American Indians, blacks, and other groups more seriously.

Texas fought a war of independence with Mexico in 1836 and became an independent republic. Texas voluntarily joined the United States in 1845. Hawaii and Alaska joined the union in the twentieth century, over 300 years after conflicts between American settlers and American Indians occurred. The biggest acquisition of American land came as a result of the Louisiana Purchase. America and France did not wage war over this land. As the name says, the French offered it for sale, and Jefferson legally bought it.

Evan Sayet says it best: "Americans are the exact opposite of imperialists. We don't even try to take over Canada. It's not that we couldn't. We have the world's greatest military. They have Celine Dion."[190]

Liberal argument: Trump is a nationalist, a populist, a Nazi, a fascist, and not a true American. Trump should not brag about our greatness because it hurts other people's feelings.

The facts: Frank Sinatra was "a piper, a pauper, a puppet, a poet, a pawn and a king."[191] Anyone can string gibberish together to create the illusion of something meaningful.

Trump proudly admits to being a nationalist. Nationalism is pride in one's country. This is not the same thing as white nationalism, a racist white supremacy movement. Populism is, by definition, the people. This is the opposite of being associated with the elites. Promos for *Caddyshack* described this as the battle between the slobs and the snobs.[192] A leader should be more in tune with the people than the elites, so being a populist is hardly pejorative. Nazis murdered 6 million Jews, rendering this comparison idiotic. The Nazis were National Socialists. Trump's critics are far closer to socialism than he is. He is a capitalist, the very antithesis of socialism.

Fascists are authoritarians. They murder political opponents. Trump repeatedly saw parts of his agenda stymied by liberal judges. He did not shoot the judges. He insulted them and accepted their decisions. Sometimes he appealed their decisions to higher courts, which is the height of staying within the confines of a constitutional republic. Those who have their feelings hurt by Trump are victims of their own fragility.

The coronavirus pandemic provides the best example of Trump as anti-authoritarian. Chapter 13 covers this in painstaking detail.

Liberal argument: America is a racist, homophobic, sexist nation to this day. Look at the cold-blooded murder of George Floyd.

The facts: America provides billions of dollars in aid to people of all races and ethnicities around the globe. George W. Bush's administration provided 15 billion dollars annually to help fight AIDS in Africa.[193] America is the leader in combating sex trafficking and other forms of human trafficking all around the globe. America also twice elected a partially black president named Obama with the help of millions of white votes.

The Republican National Committee's last few chairs included a gay Jewish man (Ken Mehlman), a black man (Michael Steele), and a woman (Ronna Romney McDaniel). Two of the leading Republican 2016 presidential contenders were Cuban-American Hispanic men (Florida Senator Marco Rubio, Texas Senator Ted Cruz). For a brief period, a black man led the 2012 (businessman Herman Cain) and 2016 (neurosurgeon Ben Carson) GOP presidential races. Trump's cabinet contains a significant number of minorities at the highest levels.

Our private sector has scores of multimillionaires and billionaires who are minorities.

In Muslim Middle Eastern nations, gays are thrown off of rooftops, and women are stoned to death. In America, gays hold pride parades, and liberal women hold marches on anything and everything.

As for Mr. Floyd, he was a victim of a barbaric murder. Minneapolis Police officer Derek Chauvin had his knee on Floyd's neck for a horrifying eight minutes and 46 seconds. Three other officers stood by and refused to stop it. Floyd was not resisting arrest, but Chauvin ignored his cries of being unable to breathe. Floyd's murder was heinous, but if Americans were racist, they would have turned the other way. Opinions of the case would have divided along racial lines. Instead, all four officers were condemned by Americans of all races. When videotape of the killing was released, the four officers responsible were arrested and indicted on charges up to and including second degree murder. Americans of all stripes wanted justice for Floyd and grieved for his family. This united reaction shows that America is the exact opposite of a systemically racist nation. Americans overwhelmingly condemn racism. Of vital importance are allegations that Floyd and Chauvin both worked security at the same nightclub. If a grudge existed, that would make Chauvin's motive revenge, not race. That could up the charges against Chauvin to first degree murder. Minnesota does not have the death penalty, but the federal government does. Federal charges in these kinds of cases are not uncommon. Lastly, only two of the four officers charged are white. One is black and another one is Asian. Floyd's murder was sickening, but it may not have been racial at all.[194]

Liberal argument: Western civilization led by American culture is not superior to any other culture. All cultures are basically equal. America needs to be more like Europe and submit to greater global globalization.

The facts: America leads the world in medicine and medical technology. The entire world's wealthy leave their own countries to be treated in American hospitals. American law includes two of the noblest ideas ever conceived, the presumption of innocence and a right to due process. Any indigent defendant receives a lawyer at taxpayer expense. Our Fifth Amendment to the Constitution protects individuals against self-incrimination.[195]

Our athletes are the envy of the world. America repeatedly wins the most medals at the quadrennial Olympic Games. America invented the internet and took the lead in keeping it free from government restrictions. Americans invented the automobile (Henry Ford) and the airplane (Orville and Wilbur Wright). We are a leader in space exploration. America's military took the lead in freeing 50 million women in Afghanistan and Iraq from subjugation.

> **Liberal argument:** America is the most violent nation on Earth. All we care about is ourselves.
>
> **The facts:** American might has done more than anything or anyone else to preserve peace on Earth. Our soldiers stationed in Europe have prevented Europe from being invaded since 1945. Our soldiers on the Korean Peninsula have preserved the Korean War Armistice of 1953. Our military delivers food and medical supplies to impoverished areas around the globe. We liberated Afghanistan from the Taliban, who were harboring al-Qaeda and using it as a base to attack our country. Later we liberated Iraq from the tyrannical rule and despotism of both Saddam Hussein and al-Qaeda's Zarqawi.

When ISIS tried to take over the Middle East, our military decimated them. We did not seize the Iraqi oil. We did not even charge Afghanistan or Iraq for the billions of dollars we spent freeing their peoples. We spent our money and sacrificed our soldiers to save their lives and preserve world peace. Our Navy keeps the world's seas free at our own individual expense.

ISIS grew on the remnants of al-Qaeda and attempted to establish a caliphate. They captured large sections of Iraq and Syria because of Obama's premature withdrawal from Iraq. Soon after getting elected, Trump reversed course on the failed Obama ISIS policy. General Mattis led U.S. forces to the destruction of the caliphate and of all major territory held by ISIS. Destroying the remnants of ISIS allowed American troops to finally withdraw from Syria.

America is the greatest, most powerful nation in history. No nation has ever had so much power and used it for so many good, noble purposes. If America is such a terrible nation, why do millions of people all over the world try to legally and illegally come live with us? The American people have freedom of speech, freedom of religion, and the right to maximize their God-given potential.

House Speaker and 2012 vice presidential candidate Paul Ryan gave the best articulation of America and American exceptionalism: "America is the only nation founded on an idea, not on an identity. . . . That idea is a beautiful idea. The condition of your birth does not determine the outcome of your life. Our rights are natural. They are God given. They are not coming from government."[196]

CHAPTER 8

Jews and Christians
Don't Blow Up Airlines

Judeo-Christian Values
Are American Values

Although I am a proud conservative Christian, I am not a theologian or a preacher. Believe in whatever religion you choose to believe in or no religion at all. This chapter is about history. It is not a sermon. It is about our American Judeo-Christian biblical roots expressed in our ongoing natural law and ethics.

It was an especially bold move when newly inaugurated President Trump decided it was finally time to enforce the Jerusalem Embassy Act (JEA).[197] The JEA officially called for moving the United States embassy in Israel from Tel Aviv to its capital, Jerusalem.

Virtually all nations have their embassies at their capital, but Israel had been held to a different standard. Trump's three predecessors all promised to move the embassy and then every six months signed a waiver allowing for delay. These delays by waiver had been occurring since 1995. Trump acknowledged Jerusalem as the capital of Israel.

Trump pledged to move our embassy for three reasons: (1) to mend our relations with ally Israel that had become strained under Obama, (2) to quickly enforce a foreign policy position to establish future peace and stability, and (3) to recognize the country that lights the torch as the birthplace and spiritual mother of America's own Judeo-Christian origins.

Trump's move was hotly contested by almost every country in the highly anti-Israel United Nations and by many America liberals (sadly, by many liberal Jews). Many other Americans in the Jewish and Christian communities rejoiced at Trump's decision.

As Ohr Hatorah's Rabbi Finley often states, there are undeniably two sides of the Israel argument: "1) Israel had a historical, sociological, legal right to return and exist OR 2) Arabs also have a right to object to what they see as an illegal occupation since Israel's founding in 1948."[198]

This discussion cannot even be addressed without honoring that both arguments exist. This is not a commentary on the validity of the arguments, just that they are made. There is no need for anyone to accept both arguments as valid. I support the former argument, not the latter. If a person does not acknowledge that both arguments exist, walk away. If you are interested in going deeper into the controversy, I highly recommend liberal Jewish law professor Alan Dershowitz's *The Case for Israel*.[199] He begins each chapter making the best case the Palestinians have on each issue and then refuting it.

For the purpose of this chapter, modern-day Israel is geographically where both the Old (Torah) and New Testaments (the Bible) come from.

There is sound logic as to why many Americans rejoiced over the embassy move. On the secular front, Israel is the only democracy in an area of dictatorships. Many of these dictatorships are hell-bent on destroying the West. Irrespective of any religion, Israel merits our support as an ally because of our shared democratic values. On the religious front, Americans know that our system of American ethics comes mainly from Jewish and Christian religious documents.

Our Founders built our nation and its guiding documents on ethics most largely influenced by Judeo-Christian principles. Leftists try to debunk this fact for their own more morally relativistic political agendas. If Judeo-Christian ethics aren't American and America is not good, then America should throw in the towel and abdicate its role as a beacon of morality.

When left intact as the wellspring and immutable keystone of American goodness, God's sustaining and eternal presence is painfully difficult for the left to alter.

The left loves to state that the Founders were deists and therefore not bound by any influences of biblical ethics. On the contrary, deism to this day is accepted as a part of Christianity. Fifty of the 56 Founders were Christians.[200] This is a matter of public record. For those seeking skeptical comfort, our Founding Fathers were also dedicated to good old-fashioned rational thought. The Founding Fathers were a perfect synthesis of reason and religion. Rationality and Christianity lived in harmony, not conflict.

Benjamin Franklin's protégé Thomas Paine was a deist committed to rationality. Paine also stated, "I believe in one God, and no more; and I hope for happiness beyond this life. I believe in the equality of man; and I believe that religious duties consist in doing justice, loving mercy, and in endeavoring to make our fellow-creatures happy."[201] This sounds like a fairly Judeo-Christian influence on this ethical man of reason.

Beyond the Framers, it was obvious that government wanted religious rights to be protected and freely practiced for the mostly Christian majority of the American people. This is why God was mentioned four times in the Declaration of Independence (God, Creator, Supreme Judge of the World, and Divine Providence) and over 200 times in our state constitutions. The power was best left to the states, but America was never anti-religious or nonreligious. Religion was welcomed and inhabited a significant role in the public square.

While it's not black and white, the United States is more of a Judeo-Christian culture than the media, academia, Hollywood, and your angry new age yoga friends (with their constitutional rights intact) believe. Many of them dismiss our nation's Christianity as an antiquated, repressive, patriarchal, overcontrolling religion of white European males.

Yes, we are a nation of Judeo-Christian ethical and moral lineage. No, it is not required by our government that you believe anything (or nothing). You are totally free to practice your faith or nonfaith.

The Heritage Foundation's Mark David Hall explains the dichotomy perfectly: "America did not have a Christian founding in the sense of creating a theocracy. Its founding was only deeply shaped and influenced by Christian moral truths. More importantly, it created a regime that was hospitable to Christians, but also to practitioners of other religions."[202] Our Founders were devout orthodox Christians who consciously drew from their religious convictions to answer most political questions.

Technically, then, America is not a Judeo-Christian nation, but it is undeniably a country shaped by Judeo-Christian morality and ethics. You don't have to believe in Christianity to honor that our ethics are generally exceptional. Good works and a code generally based on Judeo-Christian ethics pretty much sum up a Judeo-Christian nation. The Ten Commandments and the Golden Rule are codes of ethics. Charity and good works (like spreading freedom and giving foreign aid, for example) are motivated by ethics.

Being a Judeo-Christian nation that cannot be called Judeo-Christian is exactly why the separation of state and religion works. Lacking an official state religion doesn't abolish the fact that we still see our society as religion based.

The Founders were concerned with the all-powerful state, having just left the often-power-abusing and rights-abusing Church of England and European Catholicism in their rear mirror. Americans wanted no rules from government greater than their right to individual freedom. A lot of thought went into where we are today.

In 1791, the First Amendment provided a clause that prevents any church from devouring the state by prohibiting the federal government from making any law "respecting an establishment of religion."[203] In 1868, the Fourteenth Amendment extended religious freedom by preventing states from enacting laws that would advance or inhibit any one religion.[204] Establishing the role of religion, freedom of religion, and separation of church and state was a long, arduous process.

The Pilgrims are a great example. Puritan Christian Protestant Pilgrims risked their lives fleeing religious oppression to come to the United States. America was greatly influenced by their fierce need for both political independence and religious independence, but let's not glorify the Puritans. They did bring faith-based ethics with them, but the Spanish were already here. The Pilgrims, even after fleeing oppression, later practiced fierce religious intolerance toward Catholics and Quakers. Prior to the Pilgrims, the Spanish Catholics even slaughtered French Huguenots at Fort Caroline on future American soil.

It wasn't until 1635 that Roger Williams founded Rhode Island as the first colony with no established church.[205] He was the first to grant religious freedom to everyone, including Quakers and Jews. In hindsight, the Puritans actually recreated a microcosm of European-like religious intolerance that the Founding Fathers fought against.

This matters because regardless of whether or not we have a state religion, we remain tied to one of the noblest philosophies of all time. That philosophy enabled America to spread more good than any other country. Our religion-based ethical codes and our resulting good deeds are far from coincidental. They are inextricably linked. America's track record reflects good things done just as our ancient Jewish forefathers and foremothers did. We have through America's ethics and actions spread goodness. We liberated others suffering through oppression and economic hardship. America itself played a major role in expanding the number of global democracies from 30 in 1974 to 117 in 2018.[206]

Our Founders knew that the government they created could not remain neutral. The government has an obligation to prevent a self-imposed national state-sponsored religion, including secular humanism. Society should be set up to win while practicing goodness, and the Founders succeeded. Americans utilized mostly biblical ethics without a state religion similar to the ones they fled. It was an act of pure genius.

The government knew that to protect the freedom of individuals, it had to keep intact their rights to practice their faiths or not. Keeping church and state separate allowed states to do as they saw fit while respecting the First Amendment. The government does not have the constitutional authority to prohibit the free exercise of religion or protect anyone from being offended. Its only duty is to ensure the free exercise of religion under the First and Fourteenth Amendments.

Liberal argument: The Constitution mandates the separation of church of state. America is a secular nation, not a Judeo-Christian one. Our construction was founded on secular principles.

The facts: As explained in great detail in this chapter, this is false. The Constitution prohibits one official state religion but absolutely allows religions of all kinds in the public square. America's Founding Fathers were religious Christian men who derived our Constitution from long-standing Judeo-Christian principles, ethics, and values. America is currently a very religious country. Seventy-seven percent of Americans are Christians.[207]

Liberal argument: We live in a pluralistic society now with many different religions and are no longer a Christian nation. Government has a responsibility to create and sustain an environment of neutrality so that no citizen is offended by the religious speech of another.

The facts: Again, the overwhelming majority of Americans are Christians. The environment of neutrality already exists. We are all free to practice our religion of choice or no religion. Nothing in the Constitution protects people from being offended. Being injured is a legal problem. Being offended is an internal personal problem.

Liberal argument: Prayer should stay out of schools and the public forum as our nation has progressed.

The facts: Mandatory prayer has already been ruled unconstitutional. The Supreme Court ruled in the 1962 *Engel v. Vitale* case that state governments could not force students to pray in school.[208] As usual, the progressives have taken things too far in the other direction. They are now trying to ban voluntary prayer.

If a group of religious students want to hold a private service on school grounds, they should have the same rights as those wanting to form a bowling club, chess team, or social justice group. Students are no longer required to even say the Pledge of Allegiance, much less stand for it. Those who recite it but omit the words "under God" cannot be sanctioned in any way.

The rest of the pledge is compatible with every religion. When a relatively unknown basketball player claimed that the pledge violated Islam, this was quickly debunked. NBA superstar Hakeem Olajuwon is a proud Muslim and a proud American. He clearly stated that nothing in Islam prohibits pledging allegiance to the American flag.[209]

Liberal argument: To be religious is to publicly repress the rights of those who want to not be religious.

The facts: This is a case of projection by those wanting everyone to be secular. Theists do not go around attacking atheists. There is no wave of theist on atheist violence in America. Atheists are totally free to be atheists. There is not one legal case in America where an atheist had his or her right to be atheist violated. Anti-religion activist Michael Newdow brought his case to the Supreme Court in 2004 and lost by a 5–3 margin (which likely would have been 6–3 had Scalia not recused himself). Reciting "under God" in the Pledge of Allegiance was not deemed to be an endorsement of any particular religion.[210]

A Bet Din can declare a convert to Judaism not legally Jewish if the person's conversion fell short of Halachah (Jewish laws and practices). The Bet Din has zero right to declare that a defendant driving 80 miles per hour in a 30-mile-per-hour-zone is innocent. The defendant can claim that he or she had to race home in time for the Sabbath, when driving is forbidden. This does not excuse speeding under American law.

Liberal argument: Sharia law is a right protected under the Constitution.

The facts: Plenty of religious faiths have communities with their own religious courts in the United States. Religious Jews have a Bet Din (house of judgment) consisting of Jewish religious and legal scholars that adjudicate matters of Jewish law.[211] American courts have given significant deference to these religious courts but with one major caveat: American law supersedes religious law. No religion may engage in any practice in America that violates American law.

The problem with Islamic Sharia law is that it allows some customs (such as female genital mutilation and honor killings) that are outlawed under American law. All religious law must conform to American law, or it cannot be practiced in America. The Constitution gives American law supremacy over religious law.

Liberal argument: Islam is a religion of peace and should be protected even if the risks outweigh certain gains.

The facts: This is a deeply controversial issue where many conservatives are split. Pamela Geller and Robert Spencer have argued that the Koran itself promotes violence.[212] By contrast, Dr. Zuhdi Jasser is an American Muslim and Koranic scholar. Dr. Jasser has explained that certain tractates in the Koran are deliberately taken out of context by radical Muslims

> to justify the killing of Jews, Christians, and other
> non-Muslims. Dr. Jasser also explains that these
> tractates promote peace when they are understood as
> intended. Muslims who kill infidels are violating Islam
> and the Koran, not adhering to it.[213] Risks versus gains
> is a false argument. American Muslims are free to
> practice their religion, provided that it does not hinder
> anyone else choosing to live differently.

If Muslims want a footbath at airports, that is reasonable. Their praying privately before a flight does not harm anyone else. Conversely, a Muslim cab driver refusing to pick up a passenger carrying alcohol (prohibited under Islam) is committing a violation. The cab driver is trying to subjugate a non-Muslim to Islamic law. The concern over Islam is that its basic tenet is submission.

Muslims have every right in America to personally submit to their God, Allah. They have zero right to force a non-Muslim to submit. The Constitution makes this clear regarding every religion.

> **Liberal argument:** Republicans are fascists and
> neo-Nazis who impose their religion on others.
>
> **The facts:** This argument is too silly to spend time on.
> Republicans do not belong to any one single religion.
> There are Jewish Republicans, Muslim Republicans,
> Hindu Republicans, Sikh Republicans, atheist
> Republicans, and Wiccan Republicans.

Liberal argument: Both the Republican and Democratic Parties are pro-Israel.

The facts: This is no longer the case. The parties have in fact switched. In the 1950s, the Republican Party deserved its reputation as a home for White Anglo-Saxon Protestants (WASPs). William F. Buckley came along and weeded the anti-Semitism out of the mainstream conservative movement.

Buckley took on Pat Buchanan point by point and marginalized him and his ilk to the fringes.[214] They remain there to this day and are known as the alternative right, or alt-right for short. Since Buckley, the GOP has remained an overwhelmingly pro-Israel party.

The Democrats have gone in the other direction. While they have not completely become an anti-Israel party, there is rising anti-Israel sentiment in their ranks. The old guard faces a challenge by newcomers who are overtly hostile to Israel to the point of outright Jew hatred. Congressional freshmen Alexandria Ocasio-Cortez (AOC), Ilhan Omar of Minneapolis, Minnesota, and Rashida Tlaib of Detroit, Michigan, are a serious cause for concern among Jews. So is New York political activist Linda Sarsour, who has plenty of influence on the left.

Progressive Jews are in an especially tough bind. Many progressive events such as the 2018 Women's March (organized by Sarsour) banned progressive pro-Israel groups from participating.[215] While Obama never displayed overt anti-Semitism, some of his policies made Jewish Democrats very uncomfortable.[216] The 2015 Iran deal in particular fractured the previously united Democratic Jewish community.

The pro-Israel plank in the Democratic Party platform used to be a formality. In the last two presidential election cycles, it has provoked floor fights among Democratic delegates. The plank has been severely weakened with significant pro-Palestinian language.[217] Time will tell if Democrats become an anti-Israel party or if a leftist intellectual weeds out anti-Israel sentiment on the left as Buckley did on the right.

Liberal argument: America and Israel are both apartheid states.

The facts: Under South African apartheid, whites had privileges denied to blacks. It was the textbook definition of racism. America and Israel are the very definition of pluralistic societies. Israel allows religious freedom. Arabs make up 20 percent of Israel's population and have full civil rights. Arabs also make up 20 percent of Israel's government.

In the Israeli Knesset (legislature), Arabs hold a significant bloc of votes, especially during left-wing Labor-led governments.[218] On social issues, Israel recognized legal gay marriages from other nations before America did. Global leftists love to romanticize the Palestinians, but gays fare poorly in the Gaza Strip and in most Arab Muslim lands. Gays are often thrown off of rooftops in those areas.

Israel is the only Middle Eastern nation and culture where gays have full equality and civil rights under the government.

> **Liberal argument:** The world hates America because we support Israel.
>
> **The facts:** This is exactly backward. Islamists do not hate America because we support Israel. They hate Israel because it reminds them of America. Islamists refer to America as the "Great Satan." Israel is only "Little Satan."[219] Islamists see themselves in a jihad (holy war) between Islamic culture and Western culture.

This war has existed since the seventh century but intensified after the Crusades. This hatred of the West explains why Islamists would carry out terror attacks on nations that have nothing to with Israel but support the United States. France has frequently shown hostility toward Israel, but France's support of the United States (tepid as it is) made it fair game for multiple Islamist terrorist attacks.

Many on the American left see Israel as a burden. If Israel ceased to exist, or if America stopped supporting Israel, America would be left alone. Nothing could be further from the truth. Eliminating Israel would give America's enemies more time to focus on destroying America. In the same way the West Bank and Golan Heights are buffers for Israel, Israel is a buffer for the United States.

Again, Islam is based on submission. Israel and the United States refuse to submit to Islam and are standing in the way of a regional (and eventually global) Islamic caliphate. Islamists hate us because they reject the Judeo-Christian biblical Torah values on which America was founded. Leftists and liberals complain that

American pluralism and religious freedom do not exist. Ironically, Islamists hate us because they know those freedoms in America absolutely do exist.

Part III

SAFETY AND SECURITY

CHAPTER 9

Freedom Is Not Free, Might Does Make Right, and Reluctant Interventionism Is Just

Strong Military and Foreign Policy

Today's newer American generations try to simplify our complex world and seek an idealized world peace. We should just let other people live and let live. It almost seems like 9/11 and all our battles against other forms of global tyrannical expansionism never happened. The next battle will happen. The only question is when.

No sane person likes war. As William Tecumseh Sherman stated aptly, "War is hell."[220] Even the most just wars (conflicts and wars that are morally or theologically justifiable after all nonviolent options are exhausted first) are hell. Of course they are. It's war.

War inherently involves death. No lucid person left or right is pro-death. This dark, aberrant claim of loving war is often thrown around with impunity by the left. The left cites Eisenhower's warning of a military-industrial complex as the core evidence.[221]

Our military actions do admittedly create revenues (profits are good). It's the one sector our failing big government can't screw up (as much). A standing army is necessary for our American national and global security. The Constitution calls for it as needed. The investment in military might contradicts the mostly broken Keynesian economic fallacy that government spending stimulates growth. The military does create real goods, jobs, infrastructure, weapons, and services. Unlike most government programs, defense spending is not completely lost money. Defense as a government program remains an unavoidable necessity in an extremely unstable world.

Let's face facts. Unless you are 75 or older and born before the end of World War II on September 2, 1945, you've only been part of America as the world's number one superpower. You may take this for granted.

The daily comforts of U.S. world dominance makes it pretty easy to make an armchair call for giving global peace a chance. It's easy to say that our military budget should be cut and that we should surrender our dominance. Just kick back as our voluntary professional soldier army works (and gets injured and dies) around the clock maintaining America's reluctant interventionist role as the most moral superpower to influence domestic and global security.

You probably have also never experienced firsthand the global world-threatening horrors of fascism, communism, or socialism. Unless you lived in Hawaii in 1941 or in New York, DC, or Pennsylvania on 9/11, you've never been under foreign attack on domestic soil, as so many other countries painfully endure on a daily basis.

You have, though, seen the increasing threats of terrorism, including radical Islamic terrorism. These isolated incidents across our great nation are increasing, but to label them radical Islamic terrorism is now a racist hate crime. Don't spend too much time pondering that growing evil. In our defense, who should think constantly? This is why your tax dollars pay for national security. Thanks for pitching in, by the way.

If you insist on getting involved in the politics of foreign policy and commenting on it, you'd better get educated first or those rights you love so much could be affected.

Although we are now over 330 million Americans strong living in a radically different world, war and violence have not changed as much as we think since our humble beginnings. Tyranny is tyranny, and death is death. Looking back remains key to understanding our military to this day.

After the signing of our Declaration of Independence, American soldiers knew it was kill or be killed. If they did not die in war, they would be executed for rebellion. Our Declaration stated clearly that when a people is subjected to a long train of abuses aimed at absolute despotism, it is their right and their moral duty to change the government.

This duty is higher than one's own personal survival or selfish interest. It may, in fact, require the sacrifice of one's own life. This is why the Declaration concludes with these noble words: "We mutually pledge to each other our Lives, our Fortunes, and our sacred Honor."[222] For our first Americans, the call to fight was clear. Its reasons were just, and they did it. That was our military beginning. Since our Revolutionary War, we began tough and remain tough today.

Most people are not military or defense historians. They operate in more of the larger slogans of what our country does. Foreign policy slogans get thrown around in oversimplified reference to the past and present. We're told that "Freedom is not free," "Speak softly and carry a big stick,"[223] and "Might makes right."[224] These are good places to start on why America has a big military and must remain vigilant in its own defense.

"Freedom is not free" is not just a country song about patriotism. It is a serious remembrance of the cost of freedom. Our unplanned role of protecting our freedom and world freedom has been extremely costly in lives and money. America has suffered nearly 3 million casualties and spent about $10 trillion.[225] That money has been well spent as America leads the charge fighting evil forces throughout the world (and after 9/11, even at home). Our cost of freedom is great and a burden we shoulder reluctantly as a great ongoing sacrifice. We take it on daily with honor and loss.

President Theodore Roosevelt said that America should "Speak softly and carry a big stick." These great words mean exactly what they say. If you stay militarily large and defensively strong, tyrannical regimes will respect you. At the very least, they will fear you. If you don't, they won't. Obama experimented with the opposite of the Roosevelt approach, naively hoping we could all just get along.

Before Trump was elected, scholar Frederick W. Kagan spoke on this very topic at an American Enterprise Institute foreign policy conference. It was said that Obama's prince-bowing attempt at globalization and overly accommodationist foreign policy had possibly set America back over two decades on the international stage.[226] During his two terms, Obama tried to get America to surrender its role as the world's leading superpower.

Trump came in and quickly returned the United States to its former position of a respected global military power. Never let bullies bully. Deliver a quick punch on the snout or a hard threat that a punch is coming if they don't back down.

The slogan inherently means staying big and best positioned with a strong, large, ever-ready military force. This is to protect our own citizens and others around the world from being denied divinely given natural rights. The witness of history, as well as our own commonsense, bears simple testament to this fact: When America's armed forces are powerful, focused, and feared, the globe is a better place than when America is weak, unprepared, and vacillating.

"Might makes right" is tossed about in the news with leftist criticism of U.S. military actions as bullying. Might makes right has been taken out of context and misused. Anyone who wins (for any self-justified reason) can claim the mantle of being right. Conservatives know that this is not how our moral constitutional country has used its power. We are good and just in war. We fight evil forces with good when appropriate. Americans are willing to quickly toss off the restrictive shackles of moral relativism, atheism, nihilism, and radicalism. Socialists, fascists, communists, and "Islamofascist" terrorists cause human suffering across the world. Thank God we are not afraid to fight when necessary.

President George W. Bush created the brilliant term "Axis of Evil"[227] in his 2002 State of the Union speech. This was aimed at the tyrannical regimes of Iran, Iraq, and North Korea. In his simple patriotic manner, Bush labeled evil by its true name. Bush made clear that after 9/11, truly evil people must be aggressively defeated. Great power and democratic principles must be utilized by good people whenever necessary to protect the oppressed. Bush effectively made the distinction between the good people of the community of nations and the evil oppressive governments terrorizing these innocent people.

The "bad guys" cowered, and many of them paid dearly for their attacks on 9/11. Bush's own big stick was more than a fierce military. He also simply called the dynamic for what it was. He endured huge criticism, as does every president who must choose war over popularity. It was his job to honor our constitutional principles. When attacked, go on offense. He did.

Problems remain across many regions to this day. Bush could have even justifiably attacked more nations. The Pan-Islamic religious extremist nature of the terrorists' nationality organizing the attack cast a wide web. This was proven by Obama's aggressive use of predator drones. Obama faced great criticism in the Middle East and from civil libertarians by eliminating terrorists threat by threat with intensity across the entire region.

War by its nature is messy and far from perfect. America over time mostly gets it right. We kick ass, leave, and do not seize lands, slaves, concubines, or money on the way out. We always won. Then came Vietnam.

The progressive left and liberals are always quick to point to Vietnam's failure rather than its significant successes. The false Vietnam narrative is that the United States, by fighting the global threat of communism, abused its power. They insist that a large military intervention in other parts of the world for security is wrong and ineffective. The left is totally wrong.

Under Nixon, the United States was decisively winning the Vietnam War. The bombing campaign got the Vietnamese back to the table at the Paris Peace Talks. This victory was celebrated as VV (Victory in Vietnam) Day on January 23, 1973. When we won, the United States backed up the victory with the Paris Peace Accords. The agreement stated, "Should the South require any military hardware to defend itself against any North Vietnam aggression, we would provide replacement aid to the South on a piece-by-piece, one-to-one replacement, meaning a bullet for a bullet; a helicopter for a helicopter, for all things lost—replacement."[228] Communist tyranny had been halted by those accords.

Three months after Nixon's Watergate resignation, Democrats won a landslide victory in the November 1974 midterm congressional elections. They immediately used their new majority to defund the promised piece-for-piece military aid. Democrats broke the commitment America made to the South Vietnamese in Paris to provide whatever military hardware the South Vietnamese needed in case of aggression from the North. Democrats of the 94th Congress caused the United States to break its word. In 1975, President Gerald Ford appealed directly to those members of Congress in a nationally televised evening joint session. He begged Congress to keep the word of the United States. As he spoke, many members of Congress walked out of the chamber.[229] War-weary baby boomers balked on the commitment. As a result, Vietnam fell and suffered greatly.

The real loss of Vietnam was not the U.S. withdrawal, but liberals breaking America's promise. They wished that evil would just go away. It didn't. Luckily for America, liberals lacked the power to replicate their Vietnam mistakes in Iraq.

Liberals constantly cite Iraq as the one example that undeniably proves that our military polices are bad, abusive, and wrong. They insist that George W. Bush wrongly and maybe even illegally invaded Iraq. Again, the liberal narrative is false. Bush launched Operation Iraqi Freedom after Saddam Hussein violated 17 UN resolutions demanding that he comply with international weapons inspections. UN Resolution 1441 explicitly authorized the use of force to remove Saddam Hussein from power if he did not comply. He refused to comply, and Resolution 1441 was enforced.[230]

After losing as many people on 9/11 as we did at Pearl Harbor, we were on the offensive. Saddam Hussein was not responsible for 9/11; he absolutely was responsible for funding global terrorism. He paid $25,000 to the family of every Palestinian suicide bomber.[231]

Had Saddam succeeded in taking over Kuwait in 1990, Saudi Arabia was his next target. For the next 13 years, he remained an expansionist threat to the region and the world. The 2001 Global War on Terror launched by George W. Bush gave America the right to pursue terrorists and anyone harboring, financing, or supporting them in any way.

Bush operated on the intelligence we had and went after the Middle East issues aggressively. War is imperfect. Some things went wrong with postwar Iraq reconstruction in the early years before General David Petraeus's surge turned things around.

One Gulf War II myth that keeps getting repeated is that there were no weapons of mass destruction (WMD) in Iraq. This is a lie. We found traces of WMD in 2005, which the liberal media down-played.[232] The rest of the WMD are most likely in Syria. Even if there were no WMD (of course there were), the correct response is, "Who gives a damn?" The Iraq War was never about WMD, despite the desperation of liberals to make it so for political reasons. It was about removing a genocidal madman from power. The Iraq War was absolutely just. The laundry list of reasons is long. Saddam Hussein had countless murderous human rights abuses of his own people and over a decade of defying global sanctions. The cheers of freed Iraqis prove to this day that the world is a better place when oppression is removed (provided that intervention also represents the main purpose of American foreign policy, the advancement of American interests).

Leftists claim that America is an imperialist nation and a global threat, abusing our powers through our military dominance. This is supposedly proven by the Iraqi and Vietnam wars. The claim is pure hyperbolic garbage. However, this fiction is told and sold far too often in our schools, our media, and Hollywood. Truth gets drowned out.

The exact opposite American narrative is true. We are not passive, but as the world's referee, we still prefer peace to war. America has never been an aggressor lacking a conscience. America has often openly tried to roll back to several isolationist periods under pressure of its peace-preferring citizenry. Trump got elected on a platform of noninterventionism for a nation war weary after 15 years and two Middle East wars.

World events have constantly made American isolationism impossible for our country and its deep, natural-rights-based values system. It is hard when you're so blessed to ignore the suffering of others.

If the United States ever abdicated our superpower role, those with lower standards of freedom and less noble values would quickly fill the resulting power vacuum.

Communism has sadly proven this point well by murdering millions. There's no nation powerful and noble enough that can afford to take on our role. As the expression goes, it's a dirty job, but someone's got to do it. So we do it (although Trump has deviated from traditional conservative Republican orthodoxy on this position, time will tell if this is a permanent party shift or a brief shift solely connected to his administration).

Another false claim is that America uses our powers for financial gain in lieu of actual conquest of other lands. When we leave an area, we take no booty. We hold no lands except when a base should remain for access and stability for ongoing security reasons. Russia, France, England, Portugal, Spain, the Turks, the Mongols, the ancient Greeks, the ancient Romans, and others all raided and seized countries in ancient times. We don't. We strike back when we must. We come to the aid of allies when we must. When we intervene, we protect the oppressed and then leave. When we must, we play referee to help others avoid war whenever possible.

The creation of the United States could have been the beginning of a great conquest over the world had America's foundation not been so built on ethics and values. The liberal claim of America as a power-abusing bully is taught in our schools and throughout Hollywood. Nothing could be further from the truth. The liberal distorting of history is deeply offensive to those who fought and died for America. If it were true, then the entire North American continent would be America. Mexico and Canada exist without the slightest threat from the nation between them.

Military history as part of understanding foreign policy must be required in academia. College students are now calling for the removal of CAPITAL LETTERS for certain sentences so as not to be triggered. It takes a strong stomach to look war and evil in the face. Our youth must become educated to prevent their irrational hostility toward a professional volunteer army.

Why deal with reality when someone else will stare down, fight, and even die battling evil for you? Much can be learned by the study of war and its causes. The undeniable existence of evil is why we conservatives still stand for a strong ever-watchful military. As much as it may trigger some liberals to accept, real evil exists and always has.

Unlike many other issues that trigger liberals, with this one there is no safe space to run or hide. Radical Islam, an aggressive China, an apocalyptic Iran, a crazy North Korea, and a duplicitous Russia require constant American vigilance.

Americans still have the same courage as we did in 1775. We still prefer to run to the fight (for other people's freedom as well as our own). Whenever necessary, just, and unavoidable, Americans are willing to emulate our Declaration of Independence and pledge to each other our lives, our fortunes, and our sacred honor for what we believe in.

God bless our troops, our veterans, and our fallen soldiers everywhere.

Liberal argument: On the world stage, America is hated. We need to join the world community.

The facts: To quote Dennis Prager, "The world doesn't hate America. The left does."[233] It drives the left bonkers, but the world loves America. They love our culture. They want to drink Coca-Cola, eat Big Macs, and watch our trashiest television shows. In the 1980s, Eastern European nations under Soviet control secretly watched episodes of *Dallas*. They thought oil baron J. R. Ewing represented the American dream.[234] They love that we can make fun of our leaders. One German late-night television host patterned himself after David Letterman, even down to throwing his pencil at the cameraman.[235] The previously mentioned Russian obsession with blue jeans and Beatles' tapes, the Japanese prime minister's love of Elvis Presley and Graceland,[236] and Iraq's Saddam loving Sinatra[237] all had one common thread. This love of America and American culture is the rule, not the exception.

After Saddam was deposed in 2003, many Iraqi locals approached American soldiers and hugged them. Iraqis proudly displayed purple-stained fingers showing that they had voted.[238]

This world community the left keeps referring to is fictional. It never existed. Many of the wealthier European nations have utter contempt for the poorer ones. Britain passed Brexit for the express purpose of getting the hell out of the European Union.[239] European nations that once embraced foreign immigrants are now demanding an immigration cessation. In most countries, immigrants fail to assimilate. This leads to culture clashes as citizens of Nation X demand that immigrants of Nation Y get out and return to their Nation Y.

For example, the Middle East consists of 22 Arab-Muslim nation-states refusing to accept that one Jewish state of Israel has a right to exist.

There has never been a world community. There have always been nations with different needs, ambitions, and levels of aggression. The United States is the global parent who keeps these children (more often than not) from killing each other.

Liberal argument: Terrorism is a result of an arrogant U.S. foreign policy. Diplomacy is the best way to deal with terrorism.

The facts: There is a time for the soft power of diplomacy and a time for hard military power. Diplomacy is fine when both parties have something the other side wants. The stuff desired is called stuff. The best form of diplomacy is trade. Trade exists when each side has stuff for the other side. When a nation values stuff, they do not resort to war. After the Cuban Missile Crisis, the danger that the United States and the Soviet Union were going to blow up the world lessened over time. Neither side wanted to die. This made diplomacy possible. Reagan and Gorbachev eventually traded stuff. The Chinese worship stuff. They want to buy everything. We smartly sell it to them. The problem occurs when they try to steal our stuff rather than pay for it. Nevertheless, that issue is not going to be resolved through invasions or nuclear weapons.

The mullahs in Iran detest stuff, especially American stuff. They do not want to buy stuff. They want to blow stuff up. This makes them tougher to reason with. With Iran, diplomacy is useless. Forcibly removing the mullahs and replacing them with a pro-Western government is the only viable long-term solution. It is not our fault that they keep chanting "Death to America."

Diplomacy is worthless unless it is backed up by the credible threat of force. The best example of failed diplomacy came by way of former Secretary of State John Kerry. The Iran deal gave Iran everything it wanted, required nothing of the country, and had no enforcement mechanisms. Far from arrogant, U.S. foreign policy under Obama and Kerry went way past humble humility into embarrassing groveling weakness.[240]

Full weakness was on display when African Islamist terrorist group Boko Haram kidnapped young female children. First Lady Michelle Obama was ridiculed for her hashtag diplomacy. She held a sign that read #BringBackOurGirls.[241] This accomplished nothing. There was no force to back it up, and Boko Haram knew this. Force can work without diplomacy. Diplomacy cannot work without the valid threat of force.

The notion that we can mind our own business and be left alone has been proven false. We did not enter World War II until Japan bombed Pearl Harbor. We did not begin the Global War on Terror until we were attacked on 9/11.

We need to keep our focus on domestic issues and on foreign policy. Americans are used to multitasking. We can walk and chew gum simultaneously. Fixing the healthcare system does little good if all our saved patients get blown to kingdom come. All the jobs in the world will not help people if terrorists blow up the roads we use to drive to our offices. Various presidents from LBJ to Clinton to Obama and even Trump got elected on a promise to focus on the domestic scene. In every presidency, foreign events occur unexpectedly. Foreign policy will always supersede domestic policy because foreign policy issues are more likely to involve time-sensitive life-and-death matters.

Liberal argument: A smaller military is needed. We need to keep our focus at home on domestic issues.

The facts: The Heritage Foundation published a 2018 review that should be a serious cause for concern:

> The active component of the U.S. military is two-thirds the size it should be, operates equipment that is older than should be the case, and is burdened by readiness levels that are problematic. In the aggregate, the U.S. military posture is rated "marginal." The 2019 Index concludes that the current U.S. military force is likely capable of meeting the demands of a single major regional conflict while also tending to various other engagement activities. However, it would be very hard-pressed to do more than that. It certainly would be ill-equipped to handle two nearly simultaneous major regional contingencies.[242]

Liberal argument: The U.S. military does more harm than good. It is out of control and used primarily for the agendas of big business and right-wing politicians.

The facts: Most American wars have started under Democratic presidents. World War I happened under Woodrow Wilson. World War II happened under FDR and President Harry Truman. The Korean War happened under Truman, and the escalation of our special forces in Vietnam began under JFK. The bulk of the Vietnam War happened under LBJ. If harm was done, it was Democrats who did it. To be fair, most, if not all, of these presidents got the big decisions right with regard to keeping us safe. Back then, politics truly did stop at the water's edge. Democrats sincerely were willing to, in the words of JFK, "pay any price, bear any burden, meet any hardship, support any friend, oppose any foe to assure the survival and the success of liberty."[243]

After Vietnam, Democrats became an anti-war party. Pro-defense Democrats like Connecticut Senator Joseph Lieberman were drummed out of their party.[244]

In the past two decades, Republican presidents have waged war. Bush Senior led the Gulf War I in 1991, and his son led Gulf War II in 2003. What is lost on liberal critics is that both Bushes received congressional authorization for their wars. Bush the elder received his authorization from a Democratic Congress. Bush the younger received authorization for Gulf War II by key Senate Democrats. Most of these Democrats turned against the latter war only after deciding that they wanted to run for president and needed anti-war Democratic primary votes.[245]

The big business argument mainly focuses on oil and defense companies. The main company constantly attacked for the Iraq War is Halliburton. At the time he was selected by Bush the younger to be his vice president, Dick Cheney was the CEO of Halliburton.

The argument that this link proves corruption makes no sense. Most of these critics have no idea what Halliburton actually does. The response is usually "something with oil." Look it up on your own time, and you will see that Halliburton had a unique skill set that made it overwhelmingly qualified to take the lead in Iraqi reconstruction. Halliburton had only one major competitor, the French company Schlumberger. We all know that liberals worship France, but France was against the Iraq War. Why should a French company be rewarded with a lucrative reconstruction contract when it was Americans on the front line fighting the war? If Americans are taking the risks, we sure as hell deserve the benefits.

Without the American military, secure areas could soon turn back into war zones. American troops stationed in Germany, South Korea, and elsewhere around the globe are helping preserve peace. When we had troops in Iraq, that nation was on the road to a functioning form of democracy. Iraq had a constitution and three separate elections. When Obama pulled our troops out of Iraq, ISIS came in and began slaughtering innocents in an attempt to plunge Iraq into civil war. When Trump returned troops back to Iraq, ISIS was smashed, and Iraq was again on the slow path to functionality.[246]

Liberal argument: We invaded Iraq for its oil, and no weapons of mass destruction (WMD) showed up.

The facts: I have already covered Iraq in careful detail. If we invaded Iraq for the oil, we would have kept it. We did not even charge Iraq for the costs we incurred. We took 100 percent of the risks, and Iraq kept 100 percent of its oil. As for WMD, the liberal argument is a lie that has already been debunked. Screaming that the sun is blue and the sky is yellow does not make it so.

> **Liberal argument:** Global warming, not terrorism, poses the greatest threat to the United States.
>
> **The facts:** Anyone who believes this is already dead from the neck up. There is no need to rehash climate change, which was discussed in great detail in Chapter 3. Radical Islamists have murdered people all around the globe. They have bombed New York, Bali, Madrid, London, Paris, Mumbai, Russia, and Israel. Not one person anywhere in the world has ever died or even been physically injured as a result of climate change. If an injury existed, that person would bring suit in our lawsuit-crazy country. Not one ambulance chaser has even tried to bring such a lawsuit. It would get tossed out because no plaintiff would be able to prove that he or she has valid standing.

Al-Qaeda murdered more than 3,000 Americans by flying planes into the World Trade Center and the Pentagon. Boko Haram burned Nigerian children alive. Radical Islamists committed terrorist attacks all over the world and continue to do so. Other acts in the United States were radical Islamic terrorism despite liberal desperation to find an alternative theory. This includes the Boston Marathon bombing,[247] the Fort Hood shooting (Obama labeled it workplace violence),[248] the San Bernardino shooting,[249] and the Orlando, Florida, Pulse nightclub shooting. (Pulse is a gay bar, but the shooter was a radicalized Muslim. Liberals focused on the gay angle while ignoring the Islamist angle.)[250]

Trump reversed the Obama focus from climate change back to radical Islam. The terrorists are still trying, but our counterterrorism methods have improved. In May 2020, a young Islamist with al-Qaeda ties tried to carry out an attack at a naval base in Corpus Christi, Texas. Thankfully, Navy security forces killed the attacker before he could kill a single American.[251]

Polls consistently show climate change ranking at the very bottom of voter priorities.[252] Climate change is mostly a hobby for rich white liberals. Most Americans do not see climate change as affecting their daily lives. It is an abstract concept that frankly is quite boring. Radical Islam is easy to understand and believe because radical Islamic terrorist attacks actually happened. The murderers are real, and their victims are real.

Try finding one living terrorist victim who worried about climate change right before being shot or bombed. Climate change is an easy hobby to pursue when you live in a wealthy neighborhood with private security. Forget global terrorism for a moment. Before radical Islam, good old-fashioned crime was an issue. In many neighborhoods, crime is still a serious problem. Go to Chicago, Detroit, Baltimore, and DC. Approach inner-city blacks in the worst neighborhoods of those cities overrun by drugs and gangs. Try to find one person in those neighborhoods concerned about climate change. They will look at you like you are crazy. They will be right. If they get angry and try to shoot you, try defending yourself with a tree branch. It will not end well for you.

Liberal argument: The world is innately good. It's Americans who make it bad, especially the white ones.

The facts: The world consists of nations. Nations consist of people led by leaders. Some nations have mostly good leaders, whereas other nations, not so much. What is beyond dispute is that many world conflicts have absolutely nothing to do with the United States.

African countries kicked European colonialists out only to tear themselves apart internally. Libya went to war with Chad. Ethiopia fought with Eritrea. Eight hundred thousand Hutus and Tutsis hacked each other to death with machetes in Rwanda. Liberia had a brutal civil war. Iran and Iraq spent eight years killing each other. Then Iraq invaded Kuwait and threatened to invade Saudi Arabia next. Syria seized northern Lebanon. Mexicans complain about being turned away at their northern border by America while simultaneously shooting Guatemalans who approach Mexico's southern border.[253] Ireland and Northern Ireland spent decades killing each other until America brokered a lasting peace agreement. The same is true between Israel and Egypt and between North and South Korea. China keeps threatening to take over Taiwan. Russia gobbled up Crimea and wants to annex Ukraine and then reconstitute the entire former USSR.

On some days, the world is a brutally nightmarish place. The only thing keeping it from completely falling apart is American resolve. This resolve exists because we have the strongest, best, toughest, and yet still most ethical military the world has ever known.

CHAPTER 10

Guns for (Almost) Everyone

Criminals by Definition Do Not Obey Laws

We Americans own an estimated 357 million guns and counting.[254] Part of the reason we have so many guns is because we can. We are a rich country and can therefore afford to buy them (37 percent of gun owners have at least five guns).[255] We also hold a deservedly tight grip (thus the phrase "cold dead hands") on this right to preserve our individual liberty granted in the Second Amendment.

Don't come in my house, steal my stuff, or hurt my family. Let me hunt. If federal or state power just happens to get hijacked by crazed zealots, at least I have a fighting chance to defend myself. It's really that simple.

Our government has checks and balances to prevent it from going crazy. We citizens have our checks and balances on them, including free speech, free elections, and guns.

As for guns and their role, John Locke described the right of self-defense as a "fundamental law of nature. It is an unalienable right every bit as essential to human liberty as the right to speak."[256]

Self-defense is a natural right we have as Americans. For that right and others, "freedom is not free" applies. Sadly, criminals and mentally ill people pierce our heavily regulated gun industry and justice system and do bad things.

When it comes to protecting our rights, conservatives see the sadder realities of a free life for what they are. Liberals are much more willing to toss away rights if the ruling elites' vision demands such sacrifice.

The conservative view of guns comes from a cold stare into the eyes of the problem. The twin threats are crime and the possibility of government overreach. Rational action is necessary even though gun violence is highly emotional. We conservatives see the realities, grieve, and then take rational but limited (whenever possible) action. As hard as it is to deal with the realities of death and violence, we must painfully hold course. We as a nation must constrain ourselves. We cannot run around emotionally and strip away liberties every time life's painful realities reappear. The American pro-gun argument represents the need for constraint more than almost any other domestic policy argument for this very reason.

Our foundational power permitting gun rights and ownership comes immediately under attack every time emotions are triggered. The left and mainstream media avoid the hard reality of human nature and the high costs required to protect our rare brand of domestic freedom. Politicizing and stoking emotions are a way of trying to wish pain away.

Human nature is inherently flawed. The liberal left refuses to accept that it can't be perfected by more regulations or the removal of rights. If nothing remains for the left to transform or change, then the hollowness of the Democratic platform loses its legs. Hysteria then replaces conscious rational policy based on practical solutions.

Don't expect this debate to ever go away. Like abortion and euthanasia, the gun debate revolves around matters of life and death. If good people treat questions of life or death lightly, they are no longer good or ethical. A good, compassionate democratic nation values human life. This is why we are free and moral.

Some arguments that relate to life itself should never end. However, do not enter the ongoing fight of the deeper issues of our Second Amendment unprepared. Arm yourself well with the facts before jumping in.

If guns are the real problem, why haven't they gone away? For starters, banning guns is political suicide. Too many American voters support gun ownership. Despite what the liberal media may try to tell you, public attitudes and the case for individual gun ownership remain as strong as ever.

Beyond that, limiting guns will not increase individual security. As unpopular as it is in some circles to say, an expansion of private gun ownership in our society is the answer.

"Speak softly and carry a big stick" also applies here. The issue is one of human nature and reality. Bad people (some mentally ill) with guns exist. Good people with guns exist. More good people with guns means less gun violence. This is true in the military and remains true at home.

The Second Amendment says: "A well-regulated militia, being necessary to the security of a free state, the right of the people to keep and bear arms, shall not be infringed."[257]

Again, our Constitution is a charter of negative liberties. Freedom from government itself is its undeniable mandate. The ability to not be meddled with and to protect the right to life, liberty, and the pursuit of happiness is foundationally secured by a right to own guns.

Although our Second Amendment liberties may not be easily taken away, they are often highly amended by new laws. America already has over 20,000 pages of strict regulations beyond our basic rights to own guns. Guns and who can have them are more severely restricted than most people are even aware.[258]

There is not one American law that allows offensive gun use unless you are a police officer or a soldier. Private citizens using guns offensively rather than defensively are criminals. Criminals, if convicted, go to jail and can even face the death penalty. Justice itself and societal ethics remain our greatest form of gun control.

The idea that lawful gun reduction reduces crime remains a liberal fantasy. In England, where it's almost impossible to get a gun, a woman is three times more likely to be raped than in America.[259] Sixty percent of in-home burglaries in England take place while people are at home. In America, the number of in-home burglaries is only 13 percent.[260]

Criminals respect guns and seek to avoid facing them. Homicide rates do not increase with gun ownership. They decrease. Sixty-seven percent of gun owners list self-defense as their primary purpose of gun ownership.[261] More guns in the hands of law-abiding citizens means less crime. Defensive gun uses outnumber criminal uses.[262]

National Review's John R. Lott, Jr., the president of the Crime Prevention Research Center, is the author of *More Guns, Less Crime.*[263] He started out intending to write a book supporting gun control until overwhelming evidence forced him to reject his own original hypothesis. That is real science.

Gun ownership crosses all strata. No race or religion of people is more likely or less likely to own guns. Defending one's family is a universal human value.

Sadly, this right to self-defense often involves death. Every lost innocent life is a tragedy and a horror. Passing counterproductive laws and removing freedoms from innocent Americans will not bring back those we lost. It will only make more innocent people more vulnerable. American democracy is one of the most prosperous experiments in the world. Our government allows free markets. Our superior justice system holds the ethics in place. Guns are the citizens' part of our freedom equation. Tread lightly before trying to drastically change a 244-year-old experiment that has been largely successful.

Liberal argument: There is no individual right to own guns. The Second Amendment references a militia and is a collective right.

The facts: This is false logically and also false based on evidence. Logically, the Second Amendment is part of the Bill of Rights. The First Amendment and the Third through Tenth Amendments deal with individual rights. It defies logic that in an individual Bill of Rights, the Second Amendment alone would be a collective right. Its position right after the First Amendment shows how important an individual right it is. As for evidence, this issue does not require a liberal evolving Constitution or guesswork. The Founders explicitly stated gun ownership as an individual right. Founder James Madison's *Federalist Papers* settles the issue. Gun ownership is not to protect the government but for the people to protect themselves from their government. The Revolutionary War militia consisted of private citizens in their own homes, not a collective army sharing one roof.[264]

Liberal argument: Nobody is trying to ban guns. We just want reasonable restrictions. Australia reduced the number of guns and reduced crime.

The facts: Liberals love buzzwords like *reasonable*, *sensible*, *smart*, and other words that they render meaningless. They define reasonable as anything they declare reasonable simply because they say so. Australia did not engage in gun control. They engaged in gun confiscation on a massive scale. America is a much larger nation than Australia with millions more guns. Gun confiscation in America is unenforceable. Also, the Australian gun buyback had no discernible effect on gun violence, because crime was already decreasing several years before the buyback.[265]

Plenty of liberal politicians use gun control as a fig leaf on the step to gun confiscation. One tactic is imposing exorbitant taxes on guns, bullets, and other parts. Another bullying tactic is threatening banks and insurance companies not to do business with the National Rifle Association (NRA). Insurance companies are pressured not to provide policies to gun owners who face mounting legal costs from defending themselves using a gun.

The most underhanded move came when Eric Holder engaged in the "Fast and Furious" gun-tracking program. The federal government released guns and had them transferred to Mexico. The goal was to track those guns and then arrest the people who committed crimes using them. Naturally, the government lost track of the guns. Over 200 innocent Mexican civilians and an innocent American border guard named Brian Terry were murdered in 2010 with those guns.

A decade after Terry's death, the liberal media still refuses to find out who specifically ordered the program. Holder was held in civil and criminal contempt of Congress for refusing to answer that question. Obama blamed George W. Bush, as was his habit. The purpose of the program was to show an increase in crime and blame it on gun owners. It spectacularly backfired, revealing government incompetence instead.[266]

Liberal argument: Republicans are in the pocket of the NRA. They care more about money than dead children.

The facts: The NRA is a collection of several million citizens. The NRA is no different than any other lobbying group. People join the organization because they philosophically agree with the organization's goals. Republican politicians accept money from the organization for the same reason. There is no evidence that a Republican member of Congress ever held an anti-gun position until being bribed by the NRA into reversing course. Bribery is a crime. Flip the argument on its head. Congressional Democrats rake in millions of dollars from anti-gun groups. Is that corruption? They take money from people they agree with to promote policies they agree on to best represent citizens who agree with them. This is not corruption, and it is not a threat to democracy. It is the very citizen activism that is at the heart of our system. The left resents the NRA because it makes their case better. This is because, to the horror of liberals, many Americans agree with the basic fundamental right to own a gun.

Liberal argument: Hunters do not need assault weapons. We can ban assault weapons and still preserve the Second Amendment.

The facts: The Second Amendment has nothing to do with hunting. It has everything to do with helping private citizens protect themselves from their government. Most liberals have no idea what an assault weapon actually is. The reason for this is because there is no such thing. It is a fictional term. The most common attempt at an explanation is guns that look scary. Fully automatic weapons have for the most part been banned since 1935. A ban on several semiautomatic weapons was passed into law in 1994. It had no effect on crime and was allowed to expire in 2004.[267]

Before spouting off about guns, politicians should be asked to prove that they know what they are talking about. We could probably fool enough liberals into demanding an outright ban of the deadly Russian-made CL-635 Fire-Spreader. The ban may pass, but it would serve no purpose because the CL-635 Fire-Spreader is completely fictional.

Liberal argument: Too many innocent people are being killed. We need to reduce the number of guns so that we can reduce crime and innocent gun deaths.

The facts: Liberals vastly and dishonestly overstate the number of gun deaths in America. Liberal studies often include people defending their homes to kill criminals. Self-defense from bad guys is the primary purpose of a gun to begin with! The biggest inflation of the numbers comes from guns used to commit suicide.[268] While suicide is an absolute tragedy, there is zero evidence that a reduction in guns will reduce the number of suicides. We absolutely should spend money on suicide prevention, and we do. Every life is precious. If people are determined to end their lives, very little will stop them. Gun control certainly will not.

Liberal argument: We need to have a waiting period. California has a 15-day waiting period. If you need a gun right away, you are up to no good.

The facts: This is false. During the 1992 Los Angeles riots, a violent mob was prepared to burn down Korean grocery stores. The Koreans who had guns successfully defended their stores. Some blacks hung signs on their own stores that read "black-owned businesses."[269] This did not stop the mob from burning those businesses down as well. During the worst of those riots, the mob was going to burn down a convalescent home with plenty of infirm elderly patients unable to escape. Two 19-year-olds with semiautomatic weapons defended the nursing home to protect people they did not even know. The mob retreated, and the nursing home was saved. Liberals will argue that the LA riots were a special situation and not the norm. Those special situations are the very reason waiting periods are a horrendously dangerous policy prescription. Once an aberration, riots have become far more frequent in recent years. Chapter 12 of this book is dedicated to our recent "riot first culture."

> **Liberal argument:** If you are in danger, just call the police. Don't take the law into your own hands.
>
> **The facts:** Government, including law enforcement, has failed us time and again when it comes to potential mass killers. The FBI was warned specifically about the Parkland shooter twice but did nothing. Broward County Sheriff's deputies were called to the home of the Parkland shooter at least 39 times after 2010. An armed Sheriff's officer was present during the shooting and did nothing.[270]

The FBI dropped the ball in other recent catastrophes as well. The Fort Lauderdale airport gunman told the FBI that he was being mind controlled by the CIA before his rampage.[271] The Pulse nightclub shooter was on the terrorist watch list for two years and then taken off the list before he murdered in the name of Islam.[272] A 2014 report concluded that the FBI failed to act on warning signs over the would-be Boston marathon bombers.[273] The Obama administration even banned the phrase "radical Islam" from its government handbook.[274]

Not all government employees are corrupt or incompetent. Some of them are loyal, capable, and overwhelmed public servants. Try calling 911 in Chicago. The Chicago Police Department is stretched so thin that in the worst neighborhoods it will only respond to the most violent of crimes. Lower-level but still serious felony crimes could leave innocent Chicago citizens waiting for hours, if the police even show up at all.[275]

There are plenty of illegal guns in Chicago, but until the Supreme Court stepped in, the Windy City had a total ban on private citizens owning guns.[276] It obviously failed. If liberals want to place their blind faith in government (which they seem to do), fine. Do not risk the rest of our lives.

Liberal argument: Civilized societies do not require guns. Americans have become barbaric.

The facts: The first thing German Chancellor Adolf Hitler did to the Jews was mandate that their guns be confiscated.[277] As for why so many Jews voluntarily complied, it's because they trusted their government. The unimaginable is precisely that until it happens. Jews in Poland who stockpiled weapons lived longer and took down many enemies.[278] If more Jews had guns during the Holocaust, there still would have been dead Jews. There just would have been many more dead Nazis. Liberals will again claim that the Holocaust is a highly unusual situation. Again, those unusual situations are precisely why private citizens should own guns.

During the pre–Civil War slave era, the South banned blacks from owning guns. This made it easier to control them.[279] Liberals will naturally argue that this kind of gun confiscation would never happen in America today. They insist that the idea of our American government confiscating the guns of private citizens is pure paranoia. The liberals again have it backward. It's not that government liberals are against doing so. It's that they can't. They would if they could.

Liberal argument: We at least need some gun-free zones in certain areas such as public schools. There have been too many school shootings.

The facts: According to the Crime Prevention Research Center, so-called gun-free zones have been the targets of nearly 98 percent of all mass shootings.[280] This is why they are often fittingly referred to as *soft targets*. All a gun-free zone does is tell the criminals of the world that the area is unarmed. It's bad enough to go on vacation and leave the front door unlocked. Most people would not be stupid enough to go on the internet and announce it.

Liberal argument: There are too many white right-wing crazies with guns. Can we at least put them on a government watch list?

The facts: Almost all mass shootings end up being a person who falls into one of three categories: a leftist, an Islamist, or a mentally ill individual. There have been plenty of examples of leftists attacking conservatives based on political hatred. Right-wing violence in America is for the most part another statistical aberration. When asked for examples of right-wing violence, most liberals point to Oklahoma City bomber Timothy McVeigh or abortion clinic bomber Eric Rudolph. They did their acts of evil over 20 years ago. In the twenty-first century, right-wing violence borders on myth. Left-wing violence actually happens on a consistent basis. For ideological reasons, the liberal media distort this truth. Conservatives can be trusted with guns because they have spent their lives around them and know how to use them responsibly. Liberalism is also far more emotion based than conservatism. When one is emotional, one is far more likely to make irresponsible decisions and take reckless actions. These same emotional liberals then project their own lack of self-control on conservatives who possess the discipline that comes with learning about how to properly use guns. As Evan Sayet brilliantly said, "Let's compromise. Nobody should be able to own a gun if they have a criminal record, a psychiatric record, or a Barbra Streisand record."[281]

Liberal argument: President Obama made it tougher for mentally ill people to get guns. President Trump repealed that Obama regulation. Trump made it easier for mentally ill people to commit mass shootings.

The facts: This is misleading. One of the few areas of broad consensus is that mentally ill people should not have access to guns. The problem with the Obama regulation is that it allowed people to be declared mentally ill without a hearing. Your neighbor could report you as acting crazy, and then the feds would come in and seize your guns. You would absolutely have a right to appeal but would not have your guns returned to you until you won your appeal. In the interim, lacking any evidence, you would be stripped of your constitutional rights and property.[282]

The presumption of innocence is one of the bedrock principles of the American legal system. Obama wanted to make it easier for people his government deemed crazy to be subjected to harassment, detention, and confiscation of their guns. These so-called crazy people were just conservatives who disagreed with Obama on policy matters and attended Tea Party meetings.

The Obama administration had a history of using government power to target political opponents.[283] Without private gun ownership, there is no telling what he and Holder could have done. All Trump did was restore law and order by repealing a dangerous power grab. It is easy for liberals to support such a power grab when they are not the ones being targeted. Next time (hopefully never), it could be them.

Liberal argument: Doing nothing is not the answer. At least do something!

The facts: This might be the most vapid of the arguments. It puts hysteria over reason. Sometimes doing nothing absolutely is the answer. If the proposed solution makes matters worse than the existing problem in its current form, then yes, doing nothing *is* the answer. Part of the frustration with the American political system is that it seems that nothing ever gets done. The political term for this impasse is *gridlock*. This gridlock is actually the system working just as intended. President George Washington wanted the Senate to cool down the passions of the House, similar to putting cream and sugar into hot tea to cool the tea.[284] It is better to be too slow to act than to act in haste.

The American people have repeatedly voted for divided government. The moment it seems that one party wins control of the White House and Congress, the next midterm election sees the president lose partial or total control of Congress. The voters are patient in most cases. When they demand action be taken, Congress seems to be able to move rapidly (by congressional standards). If no action is taken on gun control, this is because enough voters want no action taken. They already suspect that the proposed solutions will fail to make matters better. This suspicion is rational, justifiable, and accurate.

Whenever Democrats aggressively push gun control, they get punished at the polls. The elections of 1994, 2000, 2004, 2010, 2014, and 2016 featured gun control as a prominent issue. In every single one of those elections, Republicans won overwhelmingly. When Democrats keep quiet about gun control, they fare better. Clinton abandoned the issue in his 1996 reelection campaign. Obama took hard-left stands on many issues but stayed quiet on gun control. It was the one area where he publicly deviated from leftist orthodoxy. He personally believed in it but grasped the cold political reality. He lacked the votes. Democrats now refer to gun safety rather than gun control. Voters have not been fooled.

As much as it bothers liberals to hear this, it is not the NRA that prevents gun control laws from being passed. It is the voters. The NRA is just the messenger. This is one case where you dare not try to shoot the messenger. This messenger is heavily armed.

CHAPTER 11

Every Nation Secures Its Borders

Immigration

Over 1 million legal immigrants are granted American citizenship annually.[285] Much of this happens because of chain migration. The average immigrant sponsors 3.4 family members.[286] Regardless of what you hear about detained children at our borders, Americans value family. Our originally predominantly European country as of the last Census was 61 percent white, 18 percent Hispanic, 13 percent black, 6 percent Asian, and 2 percent fitting into other categories.[287] This does not count 22 million illegal aliens (with around 8,000 more illegal aliens attempting to enter every day).[288] In New York City public schools alone, 176 different languages are spoken.[289]

Our Framers' original vision of America being a melting pot of immigrants protected by natural law and freedom already works via legal immigration. I could just end this chapter here, but won't.

The core immigration arguments boil down to three main parts: (1) political power and votes, (2) the use of near-slave-wage labor coveted by certain business factions and its long-term economic effects, and (3) security.

Conservatives generally want America's legal system upheld to protect our security and our middle and lower classes. Forget the wants momentarily. What do conservatives and Republicans believe?

The right is opposed to illegal immigration. We support our already existing policies. This is especially fair to Cuban-American immigrants, who took five to seven years of their lives to qualify for and then pledge to become uniquely American beside us. Unfairness is when 22 million aliens sneak in illegally and use all the benefits of our country (cash aid, housing vouchers, food stamps, free education for 10 years) to get an amnesty fast pass to jump the line.

Republicans believe that general policies of amnesty only encourage more illegal behavior. Trump broke from Republican orthodoxy by offering Democrats a compromise. He offered "Dreamers" (people who were illegally smuggled into America as children who are now young adults) a pass in exchange for the border wall.[290] Trump's offer was rejected by Democrats hell-bent on keeping the Dreamers as a campaign issue.

As for harming the economy, there are many studies that show damage to the wage rate supply and demand. American workers in Miami with a high school education saw their wages fall by up to 30 percent after the 1980 Cuban Mariel boatlift refugees arrived.[291] Supply and demand are undeniable. New workers willing to work for less reduce overall wages. Mass immigration as we are now facing has always caused problems. In 1975, even Democrat Governor Jerry Brown fought against allowing post-Saigon Vietnamese refugees into California on the grounds that the state already had enough poor people: "There is something a little strange about saying, 'Let's bring in 500,000 more people' when we can't take care of the one million Californians out of work."[292] Even California back then knew the economic truths of flooding the market with low-cost workers.

Republicans believe that our nation of immigrants is a nation of laws first. The Trump administration's zero-tolerance policy simply means obeying the law. Coming to America without a visa is not a soft crime (whatever that is). It's a crime, just as murder, theft, rape, extortion, bribery, and evading taxes are crimes. This is not about adding laws. It's about rolling back politicized programs and court decisions misinterpreted to support liberal desires to control the vote with more Hispanics.

Several easy solutions can support legislative changes to support our laws. Some solutions include a border wall, e-verify, and a working visa tracking system (on November 26, 2018, key lawmakers approved a plan to double the number of visas for temporary seasonal guest workers).[293]

Hard power through votes is the big enchilada. Hispanic people are the largest minority in the United States. Only Mexico has a larger Hispanic population than the United States. In 2016, Hispanics made up 11 percent of the electorate, up from 10 percent in 2012. There are an estimated 55 million Hispanics in the United States comprising over 17 percent of the population. Hispanics comprise 30.5 percent of people in Arizona, 38.6 percent in California, 47.8 percent in New Mexico, and 38.6 percent in Texas.[294]

Hispanic legal immigrants decisively support Democrats when they arrive. The overwhelming majority of first-time immigrant voters vote Democrat. If Democrats can capture these immigrant votes, the American Electoral College could be almost permanently dominated by the Democratic progressive agenda. Democrats in their 2016 DNC party platform publicly stated their plan to give all of them citizenship.[295] Someone has been spending over $1 million a day for the massive infrastructure of southern border marchers seeking amnesty. We have a clear picture that it's not the Republicans.

Costs and profits matter. An illegal immigrant will work for $4 per hour in America rather than $1 per hour in Mexico. Letting the immigrant do this illegally may sound like an act of benevolence. Wrong. This is pseudoslavery, not compassion. Why are the same liberals so obsessed with a $15 minimum wage even condoning this? It's morally mind-boggling.

Illegal immigrants, according to CBS News, presently make up 53 percent of hired farmers, 15 percent of construction labor, 9 percent of production, 6 percent of transportation, and 5 percent of the overall American workforce.[296] According to the Pew Hispanic Center, illegal immigrants also make up 20 percent of the nation's cooks and almost 30 percent of its dishwashers.[297] Mexican restaurants are not the only culprits here. In recent years, the federal government sanctioned McDonald's, Sizzler, and Krispy Kreme for hiring illegal immigrants.[298]

When it comes to hiring illegal immigrants, the ethical question appears cut and dry. It's illegal (by definition!) to break the law, but Americans are addicted to cheap labor. Liberals insist that it is vital to American farms and the overall economy to keep good people from other countries working in near-sweatshop-like conditions. Mexicans have been reduced to today's cotton pickers, and it's just wrong. Let the wage markets collapse and come to the adjusted market. Let the winners win and the losers lose. If we really are a compassionate nation, let wages rise to take care of our new legal immigrants and our own unemployed.

This deeply moral issue is not talked about nearly enough. The American dream is not to come here and sleep in a one-bedroom apartment with eight people and make one-third of the minimum wage. Democrats want those votes, so they do what is best for Democrats. Is it really acceptable to rob 10 or 20 years of an immigrant's life so that his or her children can come here? Don't the parents also merit the same opportunity to take an English class on tape, then legally immigrate, get a GED, and have a real life themselves? Why do we sign off on the current exploitation system? Do immigrants not deserve the entire fullness of the American dream? Aren't we also robbing them of finding a way in their own countries to innovate, fail, or succeed? Aren't we doing this by trapping them here as pseudoslaves at one-third of the minimum wage so that avocados and lettuce are cheaper? Do you believe in the power of the individual or do you not? Don't prostitute decades of a person's life in exchange for the next generation. Enabling them into that life is unfair, exploitative, and cruel.

America can take the hit by letting go of those who have come here illegally. Release 5 percent of our workforce in exchange for a legal country. Liberating immigrants from low-wage abuse is worth higher prices on our goods. This is really caring for a people as opposed to using and abusing them. Let's not glamorize this trap. Our big businesses may fail. Restaurants may have to create better menus, tighten their belts, and market more. You may have to clean your own house.

American farming and the agricultural industry have been on the decline since 1950. As of 2000, only 3 million people work on farms. An estimated half of them are illegal immigrants.[299]

According to the Pew Research Center, roughly 6.1 million Americans were out of work in October 2018. On the other side of the ledger, there were roughly 8.1 million illegal immigrants working in the United States.[300]

Fox News host Tucker Carlson deftly pointed out an illegal immigration irony. As swarms of potential future illegal immigrants march toward our borders, the rallying cry of the open-borders left came from the progressive labor's United Farmworkers Union. When Cesar Chavez said, "*Si, se puede,*" he meant something very different: Yes, we can . . . seal the borders.[301] Chavez hated illegal immigration. He was a proud Hispanic Mexican and a leftist, but he fought to keep illegal Mexican immigrants out of this country. He understood that peasants from Latin America will always work for less than Americans will. This is why employers prefer them. Chavez knew that. "As long as we have a poor country bordering California," he once explained, "it's going to be very difficult to win strikes."[302]

Chavez led a 1969 march down the center of California to protest the hiring of illegal immigrant produce pickers. Chavez's life is a reminder of how much and how quickly the left has changed.

Until recently, most Democrats agreed with Chavez. He opposed unchecked immigration because he knew it hurt American workers. He was right.

In his groundbreaking book, *The Enemies Within,* Trevor Loudon explains how and why communists invaded the American labor movement. This infiltration caused organized labor to mortgage their souls and undermine their own movement by switching from being anti-illegal-immigration to pro-illegal-immigration. Leftist politics bordering on communist took precedence over workers' rights.[303]

Democrats have stopped caring about those workers and about the middle class. Democratic votes and big business pseudoslavery are the priorities. Anyone who thinks differently is labeled a xenophobic racist. The solution is to fight against illegal immigration because it is the right thing to do.

Uphold our laws. Stop using immigrants for votes. Protect immigrants from themselves. Stop protecting businesses addicted to cheap labor. Stop the immorality of selling illegals a false American dream that illegal labor is best for everybody.

One final issue regarding immigration receives far too little attention. Most of the focus is on economics, but security is a serious concern. We all know the security arguments about protecting America, but what about protecting the illegal immigrants? These people are human beings, and illegal immigration puts many of their lives at risk. Being exploited for cheap labor is horrendous enough. Illegal immigrant women are much more likely to be sexually assaulted than American women.[304]

Plenty of sexual predators prey on illegal immigrant women for this very reason. Illegal immigrant women and children are far more likely than their American counterparts to be used for sex trafficking and other forms of dehumanizing activities. Sometimes it is criminals from their own nations who bring them to America for promised jobs and then turn them into sex slaves upon their arrival. A crackdown on this evil requires a crackdown on illegal immigration. The lives of good, innocent people depend on it.

There are lots of reasons to care. The vast majority of Americans actually do.

Liberal argument: Undocumented immigrants do the jobs Americans won't do.

The facts: They are illegal immigrants, not undocumented anything. An honest conversation starts with using honest language. Are there jobs Americans refuse to do? Even if we were a nation of snobs and this were true, this issue can be solved. We can create special immigration pools for qualified farm and service industry skilled immigrants, but for at least minimum wage. This is certainly better than a diversity lottery. We can be creative. Americans can figure out just about anything. Let's not fool ourselves into thinking that this problem is unsolvable.

The free markets will work as they always have in every sector. For a short time, items may be twice as expensive. Some businesses thriving on cheap labor will fail. Maybe some Democrats won't get elected until they come up with a real political platform. This sure beats granting amnesty to exploit Hispanic lettuce and avocado plantation workers just trying to get ahead.

The challenge is that the free market cannot correctly raise wages while the flow of illegal immigration holds wages down. The bigger question for big business and agricultural firms is what will happen to them if we uphold our laws and stop wage repression. American citizens would absolutely take those jobs. America can take the hit. We'll innovate and find better ways to farm.

Keep in mind that most Americans are used to a reasonably good economy over the course of their lives. Recessions are normally brief hiccups between multiyear booms. When the economy is doing well and citizens are making money, illegal immigration tends to get a pass. The COVID-19 pandemic changed all of this. America went from having the greatest economy in our lifetimes to a calamity not seen since the 1930s Great Depression. A staggering 40 million people filed for unemployment benefits in March and April 2020. One out of every four able-bodied workers became unemployed or drastically underemployed. With so many Americans out of work, the idea of allowing illegal immigrants to take any jobs at all is intolerable. If the American economy collapses, there will be no jobs for anyone, citizens or immigrants. With so many Americans desperate to feed their families, those working adults absolutely would do whatever it takes to survive. They would pick fruits and vegetables in a heartbeat, provided that they were not being paid the slave wages given to illegal immigrants.

Liberal argument: Undocumented workers who enter America should be immediately granted amnesty.

The facts: Since liberals obsess over fairness, force them to answer how this is fair to the millions of immigrants who come here legally and spent years properly going through the immigration process. It must be noted that many illegal immigrants are Hispanic, whereas a large plurality of legal immigrants are non-Hispanic. Giving favorable treatment to Hispanics just for being Hispanic is the very textbook definition of racism. Even if we accepted amnesty as legitimate (of course it isn't), can we at least agree that immediate amnesty is a miserable idea?

Can we at least pretty please have immigrants vetted first? Perhaps the guy with outstanding warrants in Mexico for drug trafficking and murder can rank lower on the desirability scale than the Mexican schoolteacher who wants to be a housemaid. Is this too much to ask? At the very least, before granting amnesty, can we force Democratic politicians to go on record and justify why this is necessary? Of course, it is about votes. Democrats should be forced to be honest and say that before an election, not right after it.

> **Liberal argument:** Undocumented immigrants have a right to all education and health benefits that citizens receive (financial aid, welfare, Social Security, and Medicaid) regardless of legal status.
>
> **The facts:** Liberals are constantly focusing on what people can get. Their entire life is about demands. Focus on what people should give. It's long past time to get back to JFK's maxim of "Ask not what your country can do for you. Ask what you can do for your country."[305]

Illegals already receive free medical care. Nobody is ever turned away from an emergency room based on being indigent. However, illegals should not receive top-shelf HMO or PPO care including dental care until every American has those benefits. Taxpayers should not be providing illegals with free liposuction, tummy tucks, rhinoplasty, or LASIK eye surgery.

Social Security is not a welfare program. That money is earned through decades of work. One of the main problems with illegal immigration is that illegals do not pay into the Social Security Trust Fund. Whether this is the fault of the illegals or their employers is irrelevant. If an illegal paid Social Security for 30 years, then yes, he or she should be eligible to receive benefits.

America is a rich nation, but many Americans are the furthest thing from rich. The 2020 coronavirus pandemic shattered millions of Americans economically. The number of Americans harmed physically was dwarfed by those who had their financial livelihoods threatened. State and local governments were strained. Left-wing blue state governors exacerbated problems by putting their ideology over commonsense. Gavin Newsom announced that California had a budget deficit of $54 billion, the largest in state history. He warned of massive budget cuts to police, firefighters, and even emergency medical workers on the front lines of the COVID-19 battle.[306] He simultaneously announced that illegal immigrants would be eligible for unemployment and other stimulus funds.[307] This violated federal law and the California Constitution. Congressional Democrats led by Pelosi repeatedly tried to get payments to illegal immigrants in several federal stimulus packages. Every dollar given to someone who has zero right to be in the United States is a dollar not spent on suffering American citizens.

There are potential proposals worth looking at. One idea is to give amnesty to any illegal immigrant (provided that the person does not have violent felonies in his or her background) who serves two years in the U.S. military. This is a job 99 percent of Americans refuse to do, which is why we are so blessed to have the 1 percent who do serve voluntarily. Most Americans would support this proposal, especially if there was the slightest chance that the draft would ever return. Anyone who loves America so much that they are willing to possibly fight and die for it deserves amnesty.

As for "free" everything else, the answer is no. Nobody is entitled to anything. This does not deserve further explanation.

Liberal argument: Trump is a nationalist, populist, xenophobic, anti-Muslim bigot who does not care about children, immigrants, or amnesty.

The facts: Chapter 13 of this book is dedicated to Trump. As for being a nationalist and a populist, he happily and unapologetically admits to being both of those things. His life history on immigration and race relations is discussed in great detail in Chapter 13. Until then, a word to the wise (and not so wise): don't attack the guy you need to persuade to let illegals into the country he runs. It's about as sensible as attacking the CEO of a company you wish to work for or do business with. You need Trump to like you. He doesn't need you. He has done just fine for more than seven decades without you. Accept the fact that his reasons for wishing to deny illegal immigrants entry are completely valid, even if you disagree with his policy. If he says it is about national security, accept that he believes this, even if you believe his concerns are overblown. Attacking what is in his heart is counterproductive. Flies. Honey. Vinegar. Enough said.

Liberal argument: The wall is not a priority or necessary. Walls are immoral. Walls don't work.

The facts: These are four separate vapid arguments.

When liberals say the wall is not a priority, what they mean is that it is not a priority to them. The wall is certainly a priority to many Trump supporters who voted for him specifically because he promised to build a wall. A president's priorities are whatever he says they are. Trump said a border wall was a priority during the 2016 primaries, the general election, and after he was inaugurated.

As for the wall being necessary, that is subjective. For those who want unlimited illegal immigration to rig future elections (Democrats), the wall is a hindrance. For those who want to stop illegal immigration and future vote rigging (many conservative Republicans), the wall is necessary. For those who consider national security more important than climate change (conservative Republicans), the wall is necessary.

Whether walls are immoral or not is irrelevant. What matters is what is legal. Feelings cannot and must not be allowed to replace codified laws. What matters is what works.

Of course walls work. Sometimes these walls are totally moral as well. The Israeli wall has drastically reduced the number of successful Palestinian suicide bombings. Palestinians dig tunnels, and Israelis blow up those tunnels. There is zero dispute that the wall has saved Israeli lives.[308] The Berlin wall was immoral. It kept East Germans under the iron fist of Soviet Communism. It prevented West Germans from seeing their East German brethren.

The Berlin wall was designed to keep people in, not out. It was meant for subjugation of one's own people, not to discourage foreigners. Foreigners try to flee communist countries, not run toward them. The Berlin wall was morally horrendous and legally quite effective. It worked.

If walls failed to work, liberals wouldn't be so hell-bent on preventing one from being built. They oppose it because walls work exactly as intended. Rich liberals live in gated communities with private security and armed guards precisely because they know those walls work. Never let hypocrisy get in the way of a phony emotional liberal argument.

Liberals including House Speaker Nancy Pelosi previously voted to have walls erected along the southern border and at one time called for their extension. Democrats changed their position and opposed walls only after Republican President Trump supported them. Their motive is to deny Trump and Republicans a political victory. This is cynical politics at its worst. Pelosi's longer-term motive is to increase the Democratic voter base. Her own views are open-borders compatible.

Liberal argument: America is a nation of immigrants.

The facts: America is a nation of *legal* immigrants. More important, it is a nation of legal immigrants who have wanted to assimilate. The Irish, the Italians, and the Jews literally have helped build this country. Proud to be Irish, Italian, and Jewish, many of them still live in Irish, Italian, and Jewish neighborhoods and strongly cling to their ancestral cultural heritages. They are simultaneously proud to be American and fly American flags.

Leftist community organizers need to teach a portion of illegal immigrants some public relations skills. Demanding entry into the United States while waving Mexican or other Central American flags is miserable public relations. Iranian mullahs chant, "Death to America!" Should we let them in as well? During the Vietnam War protests, a slogan about America was "Love it or leave it."[309] At the very least, we should be able to say, "Love it or stay in your own damn country." America is not perfect, but we are far better than the nations from which illegal immigrants are fleeing. Otherwise, they would not be flooding here. This is not ethnocentrism. It's reality.

> **Liberal argument:** Immigration is good for America.
>
> **The facts:** This could be true or false. It is certainly not automatically necessarily true. Immigrants often work for lower wages. This is great for employers but terrible for American employees who see their wages depressed.

The biggest falsehood told about immigrants is that they want to be American. Many of them do, but many of them detest American culture. Pretty much everyone can agree that Albert Einstein was a positive addition to America. The famous physicist represented the best of immigration.

Ilhan Omar represents the worst of immigration. She escaped a civil war in Somalia and came to America as a young refugee with her father. She lived in Minneapolis and in 2018 became one of the first two Muslim women along with Tlaib ever elected to Congress. She could have become an American success story, but she squandered the goodwill she received by repeatedly spitting on her adopted home country. She is under FBI investigation for financial fraud. She is facing accusations of visa fraud for lying to immigration authorities so that she can remain here under false pretenses. She was married to three different men in three years, one of whom was her brother. Potential crimes aside, she has repeatedly attacked America as a racist nation while making bigoted remarks herself. She has launched vitriolic attacks on Jews and made anti-gay remarks. Whenever she is accused of wrongdoing, she attacks her accusers as racist, sexist, bigoted, and Islamophobic. She was the keynote speaker at the 2019 Council on American Islamic Relations (CAIR) dinner. CAIR has known ties to radical Islamic terror groups.[310]

Einstein was great for America. Omar is terrible for America. Truly making immigration good for America requires carefully screening immigrants. The politically correct liberalism that allows people like Omar into America is more than just foolhardy. It's downright dangerous.

For immigration to be good for America, it is necessary to focus on quality rather than the liberal approach of quantity.

Liberal argument: Migration and immigration are different from those seeking asylum. Denying asylum is immoral.

The facts: Again, morality is subjective. Laws are codified. The asylum process has been abused. It should only be for people truly fleeing government oppression. If their government is trying to murder them, they may have a legitimate case. Americans generously gave asylum to Cubans because they were fleeing the murderous Communist Castro regime. If Cuba ever becomes a democracy, automatic asylum may be reconsidered.

Asylum is not for people escaping gang violence, domestic violence, or poverty. If your spouse is abusing you, call the police. If gangs target you, call the police or demand action from your government. If your police and government are too weak or too corrupt, then get a better government! It is not America's responsibility to take in everybody just because their government sucks. If your government is trying to murder you, that is serious. If your government is doing a lousy job growing the economy and giving you the life you want, vote your government officials out.

At the very least, don't come to America and vote for the same policies that screwed up your own country. It's bad enough that New Yorkers move to Florida, people from Massachusetts move to New

Hampshire, and Marylanders louse up Virginia. We don't need this problem on an international scale.

> **Liberal argument:** It is cruel to separate children from their parents.
>
> **The facts:** It is cruel for illegal immigrant parents to separate themselves from their children and abandon their children by trying to come to America separately. That is child abuse. For the families who come together, separating them is the only humane thing to do. Illegal immigration (liberals still can't figure this out) is illegal. It is a crime. The children are innocent victims, but it is their own parents who are victimizing them, not the U.S. government.

The parents are taken to detention centers for adults. Taking children to these detention centers would be cruel. Democrat FDR did this to Japanese Americans in one of the most shameful horrors in American history.[311]

If an American parent commits a crime such as burglary, robbery, or anything else, he or she is taken to jail. The children are not taken to jail. That would be insane. So yes, the children are separated from their parents when the parents commit crimes. Sometimes the children are put in foster care. However, America is not going to start imprisoning American children just to keep them united with their parents. Because liberals are obsessed with equality, the least we can do is treat the children of illegals the same way as we treat the children of Americans when their parents commit crimes. This is, to use another liberal buzzword, the epitome of fairness.

The real solution to the immigration problem can be taken from a quote normally associated with healthcare. An ounce of prevention is worth a pound of cure. Rather than allowing the entire 7 billion people on Earth to overwhelm the American border, America should take as many steps as reasonably possible to help other nations prosper. We already give plenty of nations foreign aid. Is it too much to ask that we check on where the hell that money is going? It is much cheaper to help Mexico thrive than it is to import every poor Mexican. The issue is not if they are good or bad people. Many of them are probably great people. That does not give them a legal right to be Americans.

Most important, most immigrants (with all factors being considered equal) would rather stay in their own nation. Most people do not want to give up their family, friends, and earthly possessions to trek thousands of miles around the globe to a land they know nothing about. They do not want to risk starvation, disease, and death to come to a land where they do not know anybody and do not know the language, culture, or traditions.

These people do not really want to come to America. They want the American quality of life in their own nation with their own friends and loved ones. If liberals truly want to make this a better world, they need to lead by example. They can donate as much money as possible to foreigners to keep them happy where they are. The American government can then match those donations. Or not.

Liberal argument: It is racist for conservatives to refer to immigrants as dirty, diseased, or criminals.

The facts: The concept of the "great unwashed masses" has nothing to do with whether they brush their teeth or wash their faces. Anyone who takes a redeye flight from Los Angeles to New York or vice versa will feel dirty and grimy when the plane lands. The trek from a foreign nation to America is even longer and far more arduous. The issue is not hygiene, but public health.

America has rigorous health standards. Children are required by law to be immunized or be expelled from public schools. Other nations are much poorer than America. These nations frequently lack the technology and financial ability to maintain the same level of preventative medicine as America does. Diseases America eradicated still exist in other countries. Obama put America at risk by allowing in people with Ebola.[312]

The Chinese government got thousands of its own people infected with the coronavirus. Many Chinese people went to Italy without knowing they were infected. That led to thousands of Italians dying.[313] Illegal immigrants are not given health screenings when they cross the border. They escape into the general population. They could be perfectly healthy, but anything short of an American medical professional evaluation is substandard. The COVID-19 pandemic is deadly.

The same liberals who demanded that Americans stay in quarantine lockdown at home also demanded that we allow illegal immigrants to come here and roam free. Sanctuary cities are more than just illegal. They are a Petri dish for diseases. The worst COVID-19 outbreaks in America occurred in sanctuary cities, where local politicians openly thwarted federal immigration officials from enforcing laws. Los Angeles since 2018 has seen a rapid spread of typhus, tuberculosis, and other plagues that America eradicated over a century ago.[314]

Crime is also a major legitimate concern, despite liberal attempts to wish it away. Illegal immigration is illegal. Illegal immigration is a crime. By definition alone, every single illegal immigrant is a criminal because he or she is guilty of the crime of entering America illegally. This does not necessarily make them bad people. People who steal groceries to feed their families are criminals. So are murderers. Reasonable people can agree that murderers are bad people, whereas a grocery thief may be a good person in a desperately bad situation. Morally, the grocery thief could be a sympathetic figure deserving compassion and empathy. Legally, the grocery thief broke the law. So did the illegal immigrant.

Most Americans are far more concerned with violent crime. Most illegal immigrants are not violent criminals. This is not good enough. This is as hollow as saying that not all Palestinians are suicide bombers. In both cases, the number should be zero. Liberals will argue that it is unfair to lump all illegal immigrants in with the brutal violent ones. Many of them were horrified at the murder of Kate Steinle[315] by an illegal immigrant. The problem with the broad-brush argument is that there is no way of knowing in advance which illegal immigrants are murderers and which are just trying to feed their families. The only thing they have in common is that the murderer and the hardworking family man both entered America illegally. The only effective solution is to ban them both. In the same way that other nations have inferior health standards, they also have substandard law enforcement methods of cracking down on their own criminals.

America had an almost complete cessation of immigration from 1924 through 1965.[316] The president of the United States has the constitutional authority to ban all immigration (legal and illegal) from everywhere at any time. The Supreme Court upheld the Trump travel ban of 2017.[317] The more liberals obsess with flooding America with immigrants and encouraging the flouting of laws, the more severe the backlash and calls for immigration restrictions will be. Modest immigration can be a benefit. If the only choices are total overwhelming immigration and a complete cessation of immigration, Americans will opt for the latter.

CHAPTER 12

Violent Anarchic Mobs Are Bad

The Decline of Law, Order, and Civility

Americans have always been for the most part a peaceful people. As the expression goes, we settle our differences with ballots, not bullets.[318] Our politics are described as coarse, but we are quite civil compared with other nations. The British repeatedly insult each other on the floor of the House of Commons. Asians are considered exceedingly polite, but Far East legislatures have been known to break out in fistfights that rival any Major League Baseball bench-clearing brawl. In olden days, American senators were known to physically beat each other with their canes.

Nowadays, Congress is a model of civility. "Will the gentleman yield? My esteemed colleague has a point of order regarding the gentle lady across the aisle." Senator McConnell is not a likely candidate to engage in fisticuffs with a fellow senator.

Over the last few decades, political violence has been more common in America. In the 1970s, Bill Ayers and his Weather Underground committed a series of political bombings.[319] Timothy

McVeigh bombed a federal building because of hatred of his government.[320] Unabomber Theodore Kaczynski committed several bombing murders over a period of time.[321] Ayers was on the left and very politically active. McVeigh has been described as being on the right, but he was not very political. Kaczynski's politics were incomprehensible. He was sentenced to life in prison but spared the death penalty because the jury was convinced that he was seriously mentally deranged.

Different people with different explanations would lead people to conclude that political violence comes in all forms and that both sides do it. This is as simplistic as it is wrong. Two groups stoke the flames of most American political violence (exempting cases involving mental illness): Islamists and leftists. There is no epidemic of conservative Republican violence in America.

The liberal media allowed their bias to deliberately distort the truth. Episodes involving conservatives are amplified or invented out of thin air. Liberal violence is downplayed, excused, rationalized away, or altogether ignored.

The Sierra Club, an environmental group, had a board member who sank several ships in the name of protecting Mother Earth.[322] The Earth Liberation Front (ELF) committed terrorist attacks in the name of a green society.[323] In addition to ELF, there was the Animal Liberation Front (ALF). Forget the sarcastic alien from Melmac.[324] ALF did in the name of animal rights what ELF did for the environment.[325] Bombs were set, and innocent people died. These groups are all on the political left.

Political violence accelerated rapidly when Obama assumed the presidency. He was a community organizer. The term *community organizer* sounds harmless. Communities are good. Being organized is good. Helping a community get better organized has to be a good thing, right? People were led to believe that community organizers are charitable people who stand in line and serve homeless people at soup kitchens. Community organizers are political agitators. They are professional protesters. They get people to yell, "No justice, no peace!"

Al Sharpton is a community organizer. He bills himself as a civil rights activist, but MLK preached nonviolence. Sharpton's rhetoric on more than one occasion caused violent riots. When a Jewish driver accidentally killed a black youth, Sharpton racialized what was a tragic car accident. Sharpton's words fired up a black mob that murdered an innocent Jew named Yankel Rosenbaum.[326] Sharpton never apologized for his words or for the result. Rosenbaum had nothing to do with the black child's death. Rosenbaum was not even American. He was an Australian student minding his own business. Then he became a murder victim.

Obama and Holder turned their administration into Sharpton on steroids. Hungarian billionaire George Soros, a hardcore leftist and convicted felon in France in absentia, played a significant role.[327] Obama provided the power of the federal government and worked the pliant media (his Deputy National Security Advisor Ben Rhodes openly bragged about his own expertise in manipulating the media).[328] Holder as the top law enforcement officer used the law to reward friends and punish enemies. Soros provided the money. Together this triumvirate did everything they could to promote leftist violence and create the false image of right-wing violence.

Early in the Obama administration, members of the New Black Panther Party stood outside voting booths with guns and billy clubs.[329] Their purpose was to intimidate whites from voting, and they had some success. None of the New Black Panthers ever went to jail for this.

Another action that occurred during the early Obama years was something called the *knockout game*. The goal was to go up to a random stranger and try to knock him or her out with one punch.[330] These acts were dismissed by Obama and Holder as random violence rather than connect an obvious pattern. The knockout game proponents were overwhelmingly black. The victims were mostly nonblack. If the roles were reversed, hate crime charges would certainly have been filed.

Even if one accepts that the knockout game was organic (debatable), well-coordinated leftist groups committed other serious acts of violence.

Occupy Wall Street (later shortened to just Occupy) consisted mostly of white leftists and anarchists who wanted to overthrow the capitalist system and replace it with socialism, communism, or nothing at all. They took over various parks and other areas around the United States and refused to leave. They did this in mostly liberal areas like New York and San Francisco.[331]

Occupy knew that liberal politicians would at best knuckle under to their demands and at worst even sympathize with them. Occupy burned buildings, injured innocent people passing by, and even turned on each other and committed numerous sexual assaults and other violent crimes. The media desperately tried to downplay Occupy and declare the group nonpartisan, but Occupy members were leftists acting badly in blue states and blue cities.

Red areas of Texas did not see an Occupy presence. This is another example of why private gun ownership has its benefits. Occupy members deliberately targeted areas where they would have free reign without fear of retaliation.

Other organizations that began before the Obama era but received outsized attention upon his election were Code Pink and La Raza. Code Pink was an anti-war group led by leftist activist Medea Benjamin. Its most famous member was Cindy Sheehan, who became a celebrity for cursing out a Republican president.[332] When she was no longer useful to advance leftist causes, her former friends turned on her, and she disappeared from the public eye. La Raza means "for the race." More specifically, it means, "For the race, everything. Outside the race, nothing."[333] They are a Hispanic separatist group. Both Code Pink and La Raza have committed acts of violence over the years.

With Code Pink mainly representing white women, Occupy representing white men, and La Raza representing Hispanics, one major group was missing. The first black president and his radicalized attorney general (Holder became famous during the Clinton years for defending Puerto Rican terrorist group FALN)[334] needed a black separatist group as well. Obama and Holder pushed the narrative that blacks were in fear for their lives from whites. When a Hispanic named George Zimmerman killed a black man named Trayvon Martin, the liberal media even invented a new term to exacerbate racial tensions. Zimmerman was the first person to ever be declared a "white Hispanic."[335]

Obama and Holder had nothing to do with Martin and Zimmerman fighting. They had everything to do with pitting black citizens against white police officers. Obama's anti-cop bias showed early on when he falsely claimed that a white police officer "acted stupidly" for detaining a black professor who was a friend of Obama.[336] The officer followed proper procedure, and Professor Henry Gates was justifiably detained.

Following that episode, Obama's inherent biases led to him advancing the narrative that white cops killing black youths was an epidemic. Officers needed better training. Obama never looked at the case facts. The police officers were guilty until proven innocent.

In some cases, the officers did overreact. Eric Garner's death in Brooklyn was completely avoidable. He was selling loose cigarettes, which for some reason New York leaders consider the greatest threat to humankind. He was placed in an illegal chokehold, yelled, "I can't breathe," and died. The officers were severely and deservedly punished.[337]

In other cases, the officers acted well within their rights. In Ferguson, Missouri, Mike Brown robbed a liquor store and then tried to murder a police officer. Brown was bigger than the officer, who killed Brown in self-defense to save his own life. Rumors spread that Brown had his hands up in the air yelling, "Hands up, don't shoot." That never happened, and the original person making that allegation recanted.[338] It was too late. A newly created leftist group fanned the Ferguson flames, and it was burn, baby burn.

The new group was called Black Lives Matter.[339] When others responded that blue (police officer) lives mattered, that was called racist. Even people insisting that all lives matter were called racist. Black people were being targeted more than other races, or so the media kept telling the American people.

Black on black violence in Chicago and other cities was ignored. The fact that most blacks who were killed lost their lives to other blacks was ignored. The fact that some of the police officers killing blacks were black themselves was ignored. The narrative had to be white police officers murdering black youths. The Obama administration pushed this fictional narrative. The liberal media slavishly and obediently ran with this fictional narrative. The American people and race relations in general paid the price for this fictional narrative.

One other group that sprung up late in the Obama years was Antifa, which was short for "anti-fascist." Antifa was a collection of leftists and anarchists who were less white than Occupy but less black than Black Lives Matter. Antifa declared that violence was perfectly acceptable as long as the person being attacked was a fascist. Antifa defined fascism as pretty much anything its members disagreed with.[340] All conservative Republicans and Tea Partiers were fair game. Antifa attacked, the media declared them apolitical, and Obama and Holder had another weapon with which to bludgeon innocent conservatives. The goal of the Obama administration was to render conservatives too terrified to participate legally in the political process. They had a scary amount of success.

At least Obama and Holder had an endgame. The problem with Black Lives Matter, Occupy, and Antifa was incoherence. For the most part, these groups had no discernible objectives. They were angry. They wanted stuff. They wanted change. They could never articulate what that meant.

While led by hardcore leftists, many members of the rank and file of these groups had no clear policy objectives. Wanton destruction of property and injuring people were not the means to an end. It was the end in and of itself, destroying things for destruction's sake.

There was no violent conservative equivalent. Conservatives just wanted to be left alone. They wanted to stop being punched by strangers.

A reasonable question many people asked regarding the violence was "Why? For what reason were these people tearing apart a country most of us love?" The sad reality is that many of these community organizers turned domestic terrorists did not love this country. From early on through a combination of media, public schools, and leftist politicians, they were taught to hate America and everything we stand for. They wanted to tear America down, and Obama, Holder, and Soros were happy to help them.

All three of these men believed in a global world without borders. America needed to be more like every other country. If the people could not be peacefully persuaded, then force would be necessary.

Hillary Clinton, who had her own radical past, was supposed to continue America on this path. Trump winning the election temporarily stopped the left's plans. However, the next generation of radicals has already mobilized. Senators Harris of California, Warren of Massachusetts, Booker of New Jersey, and Gillibrand of New York all desire to continue the Democratic Party's lurch toward hardcore leftist community organizing violence. Holder continues to agitate.

One of the main reasons to support conservatism is because conservatives will stop this violence in its tracks. Liberals exacerbate the violence. Some liberals are afraid of the rioters and need their votes. They are too weak to stop them. Other leftists are far more dangerous. They deeply believe in the cause and approve of the violent methods.

The reason the left engages in political violence is because it works for them. They have the media on their side. Conservatives eschew such violence because it collides with their ongoing commitment to the constitutional process. Republicans are the party of law and order. They have to obey the law. Democrats are the party of fairness. If something is unfair, they can rationalize violence in the name of enforcing fairness.

The violence will stop when the political price of violence outweighs the benefits. Nothing forces a political party to change tactics and strategy like losing multiple elections. The violence will stop when law and order conservatives win elections and forcefully stop it.

Liberal argument: Blacks are only 12 to 14 percent of the population but make up 50 percent of the prison population. This is because of systemic white Republican racism.

The facts: Blacks, particularly young black men, are committing 50 percent of the crime. Many liberal scholars opine that the legacy of slavery and Jim Crow still exists, even though it has been abolished in law and in the hearts of most Americans. The principal present-day problems facing the black community are due to a combination of failed liberal policies and self-inflicted wounds.[341]

The biggest self-inflicted wound facing blacks is, as previously stated, a 72 percent out-of-wedlock birthrate.[342] Far too many black children have the deck stacked against them through no fault of their own. However, it is not conservatives encouraging Americans to have unprotected sex. Conservatives have repeatedly tried to introduce abstinence into sex education classes. Liberals have ridiculed abstinence until after marriage as unrealistic. Liberal welfare policies have trapped blacks in a never-ending dependency cycle. Chapter 4 dealt with this, so reiteration serves no purpose.

There was not one single case of Tea Party violence. Allegations that Tea Party members spit on black congressmen were proven false. There was one video of one man speaking in a loud voice to one black congressman. The Tea Partier spoke excitedly, causing spittle to fly out of his mouth. He did not deliberately spit on the congressman. This was clearly accidental.[343] Spitting while talking is a bigger embarrassment for the person doing it (and is also now potentially deadly thanks to the coronavirus). Far from being racist, there were black Tea Partiers, Hispanic Tea Partiers, and other Tea Party groups all over the world. The movement inspired Nigel Farage, who spearheaded the Brexit movement.

Liberal argument: The Tea Party was a racist violent conservative movement.

The facts: The Tea Party movement had nothing to do with racial issues, foreign policy, or social issues. It was a movement solely dedicated to fiscal issues. The TEA in Tea Party stood for "taxed enough already." Unlike their leftist counterparts, Tea Party members had clear objectives. They wanted lower taxes and lower government spending. They wanted the government to bring back fiscal sanity and prevent America from going bankrupt. Tea Party rallies were peaceful. Tea Party members cleaned up parks rather than litter them. They would thank police officers rather than attack them. They did not set office buildings on fire. They ran for political office and won many seats. They worked within the system.

The Tea Party was about taxes, which are race neutral. When the IRS sends a refund check, it has no idea about the recipient's nationality. The left deliberately tried to paint Tea Partiers as racist to discredit the movement and intimidate its conservative participants into withdrawing from politics. Obama's government even had the IRS (led by Lois Lerner) target Tea Party groups for ideological reasons[344] to bully those political opponents into submission. Trump's election was the only reason the targeting stopped.

> **Liberal argument:** Political violence is nonpartisan.
> Both sides do it.
>
> **The facts:** Leftist violence against conservatives
> exploded exponentially after Trump was elected.

A leftist Sanders supporter shot Louisiana Congressman and House Majority Whip Steve Scalise. The man wanted to kill as many Republicans as possible. Scalise and two other congressmen were on a baseball field practicing for the annual House baseball game. The man even asked if the players at practice were Democrats or Republicans. Told they were Republicans, he began firing. Capitol Hill police quickly acted, saving Scalise's life.[345] After several surgeries, Scalise is still recovering from his injuries.

Republican Kentucky Senator Rand Paul was nearly beaten to death by his neighbor. Paul suffered several broken ribs and still has trouble breathing to this day. Liberals desperately tried to dismiss this incident as a gardening dispute. The neighbor was a leftist angry with Paul for his votes and his beliefs. Paul was clearly beaten up by a leftist over ideological differences.[346]

Democratic Congressman Eric Swalwell's district is in northern California just outside of Democratic Congresswoman Barbara Lee's Oakland district. Swalwell's 2018 opponent in the general election was Rudy Peters. Two months before the election, a man came up to Peters and started cursing anti-GOP and anti-Trump rage. The man then tried to stab Peters, who was lucky that the switchblade malfunctioned.[347] Swalwell did not know the attacker and publicly condemned the attack two days later. Nevertheless, this was another example of liberals violently attacking conservatives.

Numerous GOP headquarters at the county and state levels have been vandalized. The North Carolina GOP headquarters was firebombed with Molotov cocktails.[348] In February 2020, Jacksonville, Florida, turned into the Gaza Strip. A young leftist drove a van into the Duval County GOP voter registration booth.[349] There is no conservative equivalent to this barbarism leftists have adopted from Islamists.

Several Republican senators have been chased out of restaurants by screaming liberal mobs. Trump's press secretary, Sarah Huckabee, was asked (not so politely) to leave a restaurant by the leftist owners. They bragged about how they treated her on social media.[350] Florida Attorney General Pam Bondi had people come up to her and scream in her face.[351] There is no conservative equivalent.

On the rarest of occasions that a conservative may try to mimic the worst liberal behavior, mainstream conservatives quickly condemn the bad behavior. When liberals engage in violent behavior, most liberals stay silent until polls show that voters dislike it. Swalwell (belatedly) speaking out was a rare exception.

Some liberals encourage violence and then deny doing it. Angry leftist Los Angeles Congresswoman Maxine Waters shouted to her supporters, "Let's make sure we show up wherever we have to show up. And if you see anybody from that (Trump) cabinet in a restaurant, in a department store, at a gasoline station, you get out and you create a crowd. And you push back on them. And you tell them they're not welcome anymore, anywhere." Only a liberal could rationalize those comments away as nonviolent.[352]

As for liberal media reporters, they and their supporters desperately want to apply racial motives to a conflict that is clearly ideological. They hate Trump's guts. Like most members of the liberal media, they seem to despise all Republican presidents. If Trump's behavior is beneath the dignity of the office (a legitimate conversation to have), then surely the behavior of his media critics also deserves scrutiny. They crossed the line from journalists asking questions to openly hostile crusaders engaging in anti-GOP filibusters.

Liberal argument: Trump foments violence at his rallies toward minorities in the crowd and during his press conferences at minority reporters.

The facts: Liberal agitators purposely infiltrate Trump rallies for the express purpose of causing disruptions and provoking violence. They do this because they know the liberal media will always side with the liberal agitators. At one event, Trump in a clearly joking manner suggested that maybe the liberal disruptor needed to get punched in the face. The entire audience knew he was joking. Plenty of liberal politicians speak about Trump in far worse terms. That one rally was the only time Trump ever made that joke. At all subsequent rallies, when agitators acted up, Trump told the crowd to handle the situation peacefully. He kept emphasizing that the agitators must be handled peacefully.

Since taking office, Trump has been labeled a racist, sexist bigot. When he retaliates, he is criticized further. CNN's Don Lemon even told his audience that a president facing such criticism is supposed to shut up and just "take it."[353] This is liberal nonsense. Nobody is required to sit back and allow people to assassinate their character.

Liberal media types keep insisting that Trump is stoking violence against the media. They insult him. He insults them back. His supporters enjoy chanting "CNN sucks."[354] This is not violence. It is freedom of speech. There is a difference between insulting somebody who is provoking you and trying to murder him or her. The media even tried to connect the murder of Saudi pseudojournalist Kamal Khashoggi to Trump's attacks on CNN.[355]

The Crown Prince of Saudi Arabia either murdered or ordered the murder of Khashoggi at the Saudi Arabian Consulate in Turkey.

A Middle Eastern Arab killed another Middle Eastern Arab in another Middle Eastern Arab country. The liberal media insisted this was somehow the fault of an American president who is neither Middle Eastern nor Arab. This is insanity.

Trump referred to members of the media as "the enemy of the people."[356] What he should have said is that they are the enemy of half the people. They clearly are. They are liberals who hate conservatives and refuse to accept that conservatives have a right to win elections and govern. April Ryan[357] and Jim Acosta[358] are not impartial journalists. They are liberal advocates. They should be hosting opinion shows, not doing hard news. Their race or ethnic backgrounds are irrelevant. Liberal bias knows no color or gender.

Ryan is a hypocrite on the issue. She demands that all her questions of Trump be answered. She shouts at him without consequences. Ryan is less supportive of the First Amendment when the tables are turned. When a young male reporter quietly tried to cover Ryan's remarks at a speaking event, Ryan's security team physically accosted the reporter and removed him from the room by force.

Acosta physically seized the microphone back from a young female press aide who was trying to hand it to the next reporter. Acosta's boorishness led Trump to temporarily remove Acosta's press pass. Nobody is entitled to a press pass, and no president is required to hold press briefings.[359] The Constitution only requires that the president provide Congress with an annual State of the Union. This used to be submitted in writing. Now it is a full-blown speech with pomp and circumstance.

When not fomenting violence, liberal agitators posing as neutral journalists are engaging in projection. They repeatedly accuse Trump and other conservatives of right-wing violence that is completely mythical.

Two openly hostile journalists pushing this mythical violence narrative are Yamiche Alcindor and Weijia Jiang. Alcindor is black (as is Ryan), and Jiang is Chinese. Both of them play the race card against Trump in almost every press conference. They turn serious coronavirus pandemic briefings into their own personal grievance forums.

When U.S. Surgeon General Jerome Adams lovingly referred to one of his relatives as "Big Momma," Alcindor went on the attack. She insisted that his language was racist. Adams is black and replied that he spoke that way in his black household with love.[360]

Jiang flies into a rage every time Trump criticizes China. She bellowed that his reference to COVID-19 as the "Chinese virus" was a slur against Chinese people. Sane people understand that the virus came from China. When Jiang angrily asked Trump about his role in the origins of the virus, Trump properly told her to "Ask China." She erupted at him and asked if he said that to her because she is Chinese. He has repeatedly said the exact same thing to reporters of all stripes.[361]

Jiang once tried to get Trump to condemn an anonymous administration official who allegedly called the coronavirus the "Kung flu" to her face. She insisted that this was a racist slur. When Trump asked her which official said it, she refused to answer. She has never answered, which means that she very well may have made up the entire incident.[362]

Jiang and her colleagues regularly claim a spike in violence against Chinese Americans since the coronavirus came on the scene. Naturally, this is all Trump's fault. After 9/11, George W. Bush was blamed for a spike in violence against Muslims. In both cases, the charges were liberal hysteria with no factual basis. Americans know the difference between the Chinese government leaders and the local Chinese restaurant owner selling beef fried rice and egg rolls.

Kaitlan Collins is another leftist agitator who frequently tries to pile on. She came to Jiang's defense and tried to insinuate that Trump was a racist who was stoking violence. Collins herself has a documented history of anti-gay remarks.[363]

The very people accusing Trump of promoting racism and violence are often the ones doing it themselves.

Trump is not responsible for third-world dictators in their own countries who imprison or kill media members. For those who do not know, the sainted media darling Obama did try to have journalists imprisoned. Their sin was disagreeing with him. Holder personally tried to have Fox News reporter James Rosen tried as an unindicted coconspirator.[364] Holder resented being compared to Torquemada, but if the dictator apparel fits, wear it.

> **Liberal argument:** It is unfair to blame liberal politicians for a few bad actors.
>
> **The facts:** It is not a few bad actors. When a random Republican nobody has ever heard of says something offensive, every Republican in America is forced to disavow the comments. The liberal media constantly target Republicans in a game of guilt by association. The reverse is not true. There are two main issues to keep in mind with this guilt-by-association tactic. The first has already been addressed. Conservatives are quick to condemn bad actors and marginalize them. Liberals are far too slow to do so, if they do so at all. In the worst cases, liberals support the bad actors. The second issue is far more serious. Conservative bad actors are usually private citizens. Provocateurs exist on both sides. However, conservative columnists do not have access to the U.S. military. At best, they may have a few large bodyguards who are only necessary because of liberal violence. Liberal bad actors are frequently members of our government. On a weekly basis, a liberal House or Senate member makes inflammatory remarks as they ramp up their presidential campaigns.

Observe the behavior of the leaders of both political parties. The heads of the Republican National Committee have been calm, normal, pleasant people. Ronna Romney McDaniel is a polite Midwesterner from Michigan. Her predecessor, Reince Priebus, was an equally polite Midwesterner from Wisconsin.

Democratic National Committee leader Tom Perez repeatedly screamed and cursed in public and often dropped f-bombs at rallies.[365] His predecessors both had a nasty streak. Debbie Wasserman-Schultz yelled and screamed.[366] Howard Dean said, "I hate Republicans and everything they stand for." Dean's name is synonymous with rage.[367]

Once Perez dropped his f-bombs, it became trendy for formerly normal members of Congress to turn into verbal street thugs. Senator Gillibrand does whatever the polls tell her is popular in any given week. She immediately started dropping f-bombs under the policy of no Democratic presidential contender left behind.[368]

It is not about cursing. People sometimes curse. It is about overall civility and which political ideology lacks it. Conservatives are the ideology of civility. Liberals are the ideology of violent rage. No amount of liberal media spin will change this. Pointing out the bad behavior is not the problem. The behavior itself is what needs to change. If the American left wants to be treated like human beings, they need to start acting like human beings. Taking every step to prevent leftists from physically harming conservatives just for being conservatives would be a really good bare minimum.

As for the protesters, their argument is undone by their own words. It is the left that excoriates people for staying on the sidelines. A common refrain is that people who see evil and do nothing to stop it are complicit in that evil. One police office murdered George Floyd, but the other three officers who refused to stop the killing were also arrested. Standing by and watching criminal behavior is criminal behavior. The protesters knew that rioting was taking place. They did nothing to stop it. Many protesters actively helped the rioters escape detection. Other protesters did nothing either way. The protesters are right that the rioters exploited the protests to riot. The protesters are wrong in allowing the riots to happen unabated. When virtually every single major leftist protest eventually turns violent, the violence is the trend. The very concept of mostly peaceful protests is offensive. Picture a husband who is kind to his wife 28 days out of every month but physically beats her the other two or three days. That relationship is not mostly peaceful. It is abusive and violent.

Liberal argument: The George Floyd protests were mostly peaceful. It is unfair to lump the few violent rioters in with the mostly peaceful people protesting injustice. Black lives matter.

The facts: This is two separate arguments that are both morally bankrupt. The protesters are focusing on black citizens being murdered by white police officers. While every life is precious, the number of these incidents is statistically miniscule. Black-on-black homicides are the norm. Black children and black police officers are being murdered by young black men. Of all the ways black people will lose their lives, death at the hands of a white police officer is below virtually every other possibility outside of climate change. White people killing black people on any level is a statistical anomaly, not a trend.

As for the protesters, their argument is undone by their own words. It is the left that excoriates people for staying on the sidelines. A common refrain is that people who see evil and do nothing to stop it are complicit in that evil. One police office murdered George

Floyd, but the other three officers who refused to stop the killing were also arrested. Standing by and watching criminal behavior is criminal behavior. The protesters knew that rioting was taking place. They did nothing to stop it. Many protesters actively helped the rioters escape detection. Other protesters did nothing either way. The protesters are right that the rioters exploited the protests to riot. The protesters are wrong in allowing the riots to happen unabated. When virtually every single major leftist protest eventually turns violent, the violence is the trend. The very concept of mostly peaceful protests is offensive. Picture a husband who is kind to his wife 28 days out of every month but physically beats her the other two or three days. That relationship is not mostly peaceful. It is abusive and violent.

Language and behavior must remain consistent for intellectual honesty and reasonable discussion to exist. Nowadays when a police officer subdues a suspect, crowds gather around with their cellphones looking for the slightest impropriety. The citizens go out of their way to get involved. It is the height of hypocrisy for protesters to carefully monitor law-enforcement officers while turning a blind eye to rioters. Ask protesters if they filmed rioters and looters and turned that evidence over to law enforcement. The generation that films everything else seems to stop filming when it truly matters. It takes zero courage or character to stand up for people you agree with and stand against people you disagree with. Standing up for right always and against wrong always is real honorability and a far harder task.

Even TV sitcom characters understand this. The highly underrated series finale of Seinfeld saw the gang witness a mugging and do nothing to stop it. Jerry, Elaine, George Costanza, and Cosmo Kramer were all sentenced to one year in jail for their callous indifference. The George Floyd protesters will not be jailed or fined, but at the very least they do deserve a scolding. They let their cities burn. The rioting required their apathy to succeed. They are guilty of indifference, which everyone from Edmund Burke to Martin Luther King Jr. warned against.

Part IV

TRUMP

CHAPTER 13

Facts Trump Feelings and Deeds Trump Words

Results Trump Everything

Some of you may be wondering why President Donald J. Trump is discussed at the end of this book rather than at the beginning. At the risk of angering his many supporters (myself included), President Trump is the least important part of this book. This is not meant to denigrate him in any way. This is a book about ideas. Mr. Trump is a snapshot in time. In the blink of an eye, he will be an ex-president. Long after he is out of office, these ideas will still be debated. Trump is a human being. Humans come and go. We are nothing more than a mere blip in time.

The next question is a reasonable one. If we humans are insignificant in the ultimate big picture, why discuss Trump at all? He must be mentioned because he is the current president of the United States. At this moment in history, he is the most powerful and therefore most relevant person in the world. Heading into the 2020 election, every American political issue connects to him. He is the chief executive, the chief diplomat, and the commander-in-chief.

He is also presiding over one of the most consequential presiden-
cies in American and world history. In 2019, he was cruising toward
reelection. He had a booming economy and a fractured opposition.
He was exonerated in the Russia probe and acquitted in a frivolous
impeachment trial involving Ukraine that most Americans found puz-
zling. Democrats hoping to succeed him held debates, and each debate
brought fewer viewers. By the time former Vice President Joe Biden
stumbled his way to the nomination, fellow Democrats were already
openly discussing replacing him at their convention. The February
2020 impeachment consumed Democrats and bored everybody else.
Trump was riding high, and more important, so was America. Then,
in early 2020, the Chinese government unleashed hell on the world.

The COVID-19 coronavirus crisis was more financially devastating than the 2008 financial crash and killed many more Americans
than the September 11 attacks of 2001. The country just shut down.
By March 2020, Americans everywhere had to quarantine. Going
outside for a walk or to work was considered a dangerous activity.
Trump's reelection and the fate of the country depended on his ability to navigate the American people through this horrendous period
in time. His personal style was irrelevant to all but his most hardened
critics. The man who came into office vowing to end wars was now a
wartime president against "the invisible enemy" coronavirus. History
and the 2020 electorate would judge him by how he handled coronavirus. The only thing that mattered was coronavirus policy, more
specifically the results emanating from his coronavirus policy.

For far too many people, a rational discussion of his policies
is impossible. His gargantuan personality casts a shadow over the
issues of the day. There are legitimate reasons to criticize Trump.
This country was founded on the idea that civilians have the right to
criticize their leaders without fear of being put to death. However,
the worst criticisms of Trump are unfair, unjust, and false. His presidency should be judged based on his job performance, not his personality. It is not possible to discuss his record without thoroughly
debunking the craziest liberal attacks on his character.

> **Liberal argument:** Trump is a racist who allied with Charlottesville extremists and has a history of racism. Trump said that there were "very fine people on both sides" of the Charlottesville conflict.[369]
>
> **The facts:** Charlottesville is a defining Holy Grail for the Trump as racist narrative. It is also based on a total outright lie.

Trump's "very fine people on both sides" comment had nothing to do with Charlottesville, Virginia. He was referring to the debate over Confederate statues.[370] His comment was completely truthful and accurate. Not everyone against removing Confederate statues is a racist. Many people want to preserve history. Without history, we cannot learn how to be better in the future. Not everyone in favor of removing the Confederate statues is a leftist zealot or social justice warrior. Many people are genuinely hurt by images they see as racist. The liberal media took Trump's comments about the Confederate statues debate and falsely claimed that he was referencing Charlottesville.

Trump is often accused of unfairly painting with a broad brush. This time he did the exact opposite. He concluded that many of the leftist protesters were not violent Antifa members. They were mainstream liberals peacefully protesting against white supremacists and confederate statues. On the other side of the spectrum, many of the protesters on the right were not white supremacists, KKK members, or neo-Nazis. They were mainstream people on the right who were peacefully protesting their right to bear arms and preserve statues representing American history.

To lump the peaceful protesters in with the violent ones is completely unfair. Trump was totally right in saying that there were good people on both sides. There were. Trump did not show solidarity with right-wing bigots. He defended free speech for people of all ideologies, and speech itself is not automatically tantamount to violence. The disagreement over Confederate statues was an important free-speech issue, and Trump was totally right to recognize that good people on both sides could disagree on a solution.

It was the left and not the right that caused the Charlottesville violence. Contrast Charlottesville with Orange County, California. On one Sunday, right-wing nationalists scheduled a rally in Orange County. Leftists decided to hold a counterrally one day earlier. The leftist rally on Saturday had a much larger attendance than the right-wing Sunday rally. The left successfully ridiculed the right without a drop of blood being shed.[371] This was the absolutely proper way to conduct political warfare.

In Charlottesville, the leftists decided to schedule their rally at the exact same time in the exact same place as their right-wing counterparts. Right-wing nationalists frequently bring guns to their rallies. Normally, this does not lead to any violence. The right-wingers do not shoot each other. The guns are for self-defense, which is their legal right under the Second Amendment and in the state of Virginia after the age of 18. Their message, no matter how repugnant, is protected speech under the First Amendment.

By deliberately heading toward the right-wing rally with weapons of their own, leftists provoked the inevitable violent confrontation.[372] One person died because leftists refused to follow the Orange County example of protest.

Another debunked myth of Trump bigotry involves his very first press conference in 2015 announcing his presidential run. Liberals keep insisting that Trump called all Mexicans murderers and rapists. This is false. What he said was that Mexicans bring drugs and crime. He then ad-libbed "and some, I assume, are good people."[373] Trump clearly could have been more artful. He should have started by saying that most Mexicans coming into the United States are good people. Despite this, some of them *do* bring drugs and crime. He has earned the benefit of the doubt because of his lifetime of generally respectful behavior with friends, employees, business partners, and political supporters, as well as the fair treatment he has displayed toward Hispanics in real life.

Trump has been attacked for engaging in racially discriminatory practices with regard to renting apartments in his many buildings. Those accusations were lobbed against his late father, who is no longer alive to defend himself.[374] Donald Trump was fresh out of college at the time. Blaming him for his father's possible sins is as valid as blaming the pro-Israel former California Governor Arnold Schwarzenegger for his late father's support of Nazis.[375] Nobody in their right (or left) mind would blame Chelsea Clinton for her father's or mother's many misdeeds (crimes).

The caricature of Trump as a racist is nonsensical. He spent his life as a New York City real estate developer. For all its flaws, New York is the least racist place on Earth. Conducting business requires getting along with people who speak over 100 languages. Private citizen Trump repeatedly hired minorities to top positions in the Trump organization.[376]

Two of his first four winners on *The Apprentice* were minorities.[377] Before running for president against a Democrat, he received civil rights awards from Democrats.[378] He socialized with them. Hillary attended his wedding to Melania. Hillary's daughter, Chelsea, and Trump's eldest daughter, Ivanka, partied in the Hamptons together. As president, Trump continued his pattern of hiring minorities to top positions. Former UN Secretary Nikki Haley, Transportation Secretary Elaine Chao, Education Secretary Betsy DeVos, and Housing and Urban Development (HUD) Secretary Ben Carson were all his personal choices. Haley, whose family hails from India, is now even mentioned as a serious 2024 presidential contender. Trump knew they were minorities when he hired them. Outside of Rachel Dolezal,[379] Ray Finkle, and Lois Einhorn,[380] gender and race are hard to disguise.

> **Liberal argument:** Trump is a sexual predator who cares nothing about women.
>
> **The facts:** Trump is no angel. He has been a serial adulterer. He cheated on his first wife, Ivana Zelnickova, and his second wife, Marla Maples. Rumors have been swirling that he committed adultery on his third wife, First Lady Melania Knauss.[381] LBJ publicly bragged that he had more extramarital affairs than JFK.[382] Adultery falls under what Catholics call peccadilloes. Consenting extramarital sexual relationships are immoral but have not been illegal since the Salem witchcraft trials. Most people would not sentence any president to death as John Proctor faced in Arthur Miller's *The Crucible*.[383]

The *Access Hollywood* tape nearly cost Trump the presidency. He joked on a radio interview that he went up to random women and grabbed them by the (kitty cat).[384] This is one example where Trump's verbally bad behavior works in his defense. He was a frequent guest of shock jock Howard Stern, who called Trump a "great guest."[385] On one program, Trump bragged about having unprotected sex with scores of married women during the 1980s. Given that Trump was putting his life at risk of contracting AIDS, Trump cavalierly referred to his 1980s sexcapades as his "personal Vietnam."[386]

Trump was also a guest of Oprah on her wildly successful television program. Did Trump make crude remarks on her program? Of course not, which tells us something about him. He is a very media-savvy guest who knows how to adapt to various hosts. He spoke in filthy tones with hosts discussing filthy topics and in a serious, sober manner with dignified hosts like Oprah.

Stern's listeners did not tune in to hear Trump's views on tax policy and trade. Winfrey's viewers did not care to hear about Trump's
bowel movements. Trump's talent with the media propelled him to
his own television show and then the White House. It is highly
possible that Trump, like many men, bragged about sexual exploits
that never occurred.

Liberals then point out that Trump faced multiple allegations of
improper behavior toward women. This narrative falls apart under
close scrutiny. These women all testified in the court of public opinion rather than a court of law. In a court of law, lying under oath is
a crime. Allegations made in official depositions subject accusers to
discovery. Any materially false statements would subject the accusers
to severe penalties. Not one woman went to court with a criminal
complaint against Trump.

The most public of Trump's accusers was Stephanie Clifford
(Stormy Daniels). She filed a civil complaint against him, not a
criminal complaint. She lost in court and was ordered to pay Trump's
legal costs. Her being a stripper and a porn star did not invalidate
her claim. Her own words did her in. She stated in a *60 Minutes*
interview that her alleged sex with Trump was completely consen-
sual.[387] She specifically stated that she was not a victim. This begs the
question of why she sued to have her nondisclosure agreement invalidated. If Trump cheated on Melania, that would again be immoral
but legal.

Clifford was also served poorly by having an attorney who seemed
more interested in enriching himself than his clients. Mentioning
his name serves no purpose. He had numerous default judgments
against him. He is a long-time Democratic operative who learned
bare-knuckle politics from Chicago Mayor Rahm Emanuel, one of
the very toughest political street fighters. Emanuel's understudy even
announced in 2018 his intention to seek the 2020 Democratic presidential nomination and oust Trump from office before backtracking
and announcing he would not run. He has since been indicted on

multiple counts of defrauding clients, including Clifford. He was convicted on several counts and sent to prison, with more charges pending.[388]

Accusations are not evidence. Trump's accusers have credibility issues of their own. The reason many powerful men lost their jobs during the #MeToo era is because they were guilty. Harvey Weinstein, Kevin Spacey, Al Franken, Matt Lauer, Charlie Rose, Eric Schneiderman, and many others got caught.[389] The women said it, and those men did it.

Men are not the only ones crossing the line. First-term Democratic Congresswoman Katie Hill[390] was caught having sexual relationships with her staff members of both genders. A photo showed her naked and cutting a female staffer's hair. Another photo showed her completely naked while smoking a bong and sporting a Nazi Iron Cross insignia tattoo on her thigh. Her ex-husband was accused of leaking the photos and violating revenge porn laws, but Hill admitted that the photos were authentic. Hill claimed that she was being persecuted because she was bisexual, but House rules prohibit any congressperson from having sexual relations with any staffer. Hill responded by lashing out at Trump and Republicans, but they had zero power to remove her. Her fellow Democrat Nancy Pelosi forced her out. Speaker Pelosi acted toward Hill exactly as she did with former Democratic New York Congressman Anthony Weiner. Like Weiner, Hill threw stones from a glass house, rendering her impossible to defend. Hill continued lashing out at Republicans after resigning, but voters were not fooled. She became so politically toxic that her California congressional seat north of Los Angeles flipped back to Republicans in a May 2020 special election.[391] Hill was forced out because she was guilty.

Trump and his Supreme Court Justice nominee Brett Kavanaugh survived because the serious (and some ludicrous) charges they faced were not backed by evidence even one time.[392] God help this country if due process of law and the presumption of innocence are ever revoked.

Liberal argument: Trump is a Nazi fascist dictator.

The facts: These accusations are too stupid to dignify and deserve to be given very short shrift. Hitler murdered 6 million Jews. Trump was never accused of murdering anyone. The left is far too cavalier with labeling every Republican as the face of genocide. Even removing the worst slurs, including Brownshirts and Hitler, still leaves the nonsensical accusation of Trump as a dictator. Dictators take their critics and have them shot to death. Temporarily suspending the press badge of one unctuous CNN correspondent is hardly dictatorial. Trump frequently calls the media (and other political critics) names. Arguments about his behavior and temperament are legitimate. Comparing him with people who imprison or execute political dissenters borders on the insane. When Democrats won the House of Representatives in the 2018 midterm elections, Trump had none of them killed. The charge itself offers yet another irony proving the utter lack of liberal self-awareness. The very people who accuse Trump of being a dictator and an imperial threat to democracy are the ones freely criticizing him every day without consequences. Trump does not eat babies either, despite the protests at numerous Wiccan conventions.

More important, Trump made a definitive statement that has never been refuted. When asked early in his presidency about Putin, Trump replied, "I've never met him."[393] In a world where more than 1 billion people own smartphones with advanced cameras, not one picture of Trump shaking hands with Putin ever surfaced. They met during his presidency, but no proof exists of their meeting before then. One picture from one person derails Trump's absolute claim. Trump's fiercest political opponents in the media and Congress produced nothing.

Liberal argument: Trump colluded with Russia to rig the 2016 election against Hillary Clinton.

The facts: This may be one of the least lucid lines of attack launched against any president. To accept the premise requires a total suspension of reality. Russian President Vladimir Putin is a cold-blooded killer who vaporizes his victims without a trace of evidence linking back to him. His specialty is secrecy. Trump worships publicity. His entire life since birth has been public. Again, private people do not emote in front of Oprah or chuckle on the radio with Howard. Trump spent his life making sure everybody knew what he was doing the moment he did it and that he did it better than everybody else. Trump and Putin are incompatible business partners.

After two years of investigating, the special counsel found zero evidence of collusion (which constitutional scholars and proud liberals Alan Dershowitz and Jonathan Turley accurately point out is not a crime anyway) by Trump, any members of his family, any members of his campaign, or any members of his administration.[394]

The Russia narrative's most preposterous aspect is the nature of the alleged election meddling. Liberals are convinced that the Russians meddled but cannot say in what form the meddling occurred. What did the Russians actually *do*? Not one voter has claimed in a court of law that specific actions by Russia affected his or her vote.

The Russia narrative is about revenge. Trump defeated Hillary and humiliated Obama. They retaliated by having Trump and anyone connected with him framed for crimes. Former Obama and Trump National Security Advisor General Michael Flynn was the first person framed. Before becoming a Fox News contributor (and therefore invalidated by many liberals who declare all Fox News employees invalid), Sara Carter was merely one of the best reporters in the business. On a daily basis, she produced mountains of evidence that pointed toward crimes committed by Trump opponents, not Trump.[395]

The Russia narrative is only half the story. The heads of various intelligence agencies and Obama administration officials spied on the Trump campaign. The plot was so elaborate that it defies believability, except that it happened. The goal was to blackmail General Flynn into rolling over and claiming that Trump colluded with the Russians to defeat the Hillary Clinton campaign. This would then trigger an impeachment trial that would remove Trump from office. In simple terms, the Hillary Clinton campaign hired people to manufacture research that would be given to Obama intelligence officials and administration members. They would use this research to build a case. The endgame was nothing short of the overthrow of a legally elected government solely because the losing side despised the guy who won.[396]

This was a case of pure projection. The very people accusing Trump were the same people who committed the very crimes they attributed to him. Political consultant Roger Stone,[397] campaign advisor George Papadopoulos,[398] and others were caught up by overzealous prosecutors obsessed with triggering an impeachment.

In May 2020, temporary Director of National Intelligence (DNI) Ric Grenell in his official capacity released a trove of unredacted documents that had been kept hidden for three years. These documents revealed the names of the people engaged in the illegal spying.[399]

General Flynn was released from prison when Attorney General
Bill Barr dropped the case. The judge in the case tried to sentence
Flynn anyway, but an appeals court cracked down on the judicial
overreach.[400]

Liberals pointed out that Flynn initially pled guilty. This was
because a crooked prosecution team threatened to throw his son in
jail as well.[401]

The main intelligence conspirators were former CIA Director
John Brennan, former FBI Director James Comey, and former DNI
James Clapper. The main administration officials involved in the
conspiracy were former UN Ambassador Samantha Power and former National Security Advisor Susan Rice.[402]

Obtaining the search warrants to begin the unmasking (spying) required lying to FISA Court judges. Exculpatory evidence was
deliberately never disclosed to the judges.[403]

One of the spying requests was even made by Biden. Obama
knew about the entire spying operation.[404]

In 2017, many Obama intelligence and administration officials
testified under oath privately that there was no collusion between
Trump and Russia. For three years after this, these same people went
on television and publicly said Trump did collude. They allowed the
entire investigation of Special Counsel Bob Mueller to go forward
while privately knowing that it was all predicated on a lie.

Each side accuses the other side of lying and spying. So how do
we know that the Trump people are telling the truth and the Obama
people are lying? Why should we just take the Trump people at face
value?

There are two answers to this very valid question. The first is the
pattern of behavior. The Obama administration had repeatedly been
caught spying on others throughout his presidency. They were caught
spying on foreign leaders, including German Chancellor Angela
Merkel.[405] They were caught spying on members of the U.S. Senate,
including Dianne Feinstein of California.[406] They were caught spying on reporters, including James Risen and James Rosen.[407]

Past as prologue is an indicator but not evidence. Only one man is collecting hard evidence. He is apolitical and incorruptible. Connecticut U.S. Attorney John Durham is a bulldog no-nonsense prosecutor who is investigating the entire Russia probe from the beginning.[408] He is a registered Democrat who once worked under Eric Holder. He is completely inoculated from partisan politics. He also can do one thing that nobody else trying to get to the truth can do: issue criminal indictments.

Inspector generals can issue reports. Congressional committee chairs can hold hearings where witnesses stall and run out the clock. Durham can have people arrested and sent to jail. He does not speak to the media. He does not leak to the media. Those who say what he is doing don't know and those who know (in this case only him) will not say anything.

The Obama conspirators attacked Trump and Barr, but they did not dare criticize Durham. He is expected to hand down criminal indictments. The louder the Obama conspirators protest on TV (some of whom are even employed by CNN as experts), the more we know that Durham is getting closer to the truth. Durham's rock-solid credibility means that anyone who gets indicted is finished.

The question is not if anyone committed crimes. It will be whether they roll over and offer proof that Obama was behind everything. The legacies of the last two presidents and both 2020 presidential contenders are on the line.

The collapse of the Russia hoax is just the beginning. All the liberal spin in the world will not stop a prosecutor with the law and the facts on his side.

Liberal argument: The people rejected Trump, as evidenced by Republican losses in the 2018 midterm elections.

> **The facts:** The voters largely validated his policies.
> In a midterm election, the party in power frequently
> suffers staggering losses. Reagan and Obama both
> won two presidential elections and got clobbered in
> both midterms. Trump partially defied the midterm
> curse. Republicans did lose the House, but they actu-
> ally gained seats in the Senate and held on to several
> key governorships. In major races where Trump and
> Obama campaigned against each other, Trump's can-
> didate won every single race.

In most midterms, presidents are politically radioactive.
Candidates do not want to be seen anywhere with them. In 2017 and
2018, scores of Republican candidates begged Trump to campaign
with them. This is highly unusual. In many key races, Trump rallies
boosted Republican candidates and provided them with the decisive
margin of victory. After nearly 20 years of voters being angry at election time, 2018 saw a large swath of happy voters. Trump was able to
successfully campaign in the midterms because he had successfully
governed in the two years leading up to them.

> **Liberal argument:** Trump was impeached for quid pro
> quo abuses with Ukraine. This proves his lack of fitness
> for office.
>
> **The facts:** The moment the Russia hoax collapsed,
> the Ukraine hoax was born. Democrats alleged that
> Trump pressured the president of Ukraine to investi-
> gate corruption involving Vice President Biden's son
> Hunter Biden. Failure to investigate the Bidens would

> result in Trump withholding financial aid to Ukraine. Republicans countered that the aid was never withheld. The Ukrainian president said he was not pressured. Trump released the full transcript of the phone call in question, and it revealed zero illegal behavior.[409]

The heart of the scandal involved a whistleblower CIA analyst named Eric Ciaramella. Ciaramella is a partisan Democrat, a never-Trumper, and a friend of Russia hoax conspirator and Trump enemy Brennan.[410] Ciaramella in 2018 would have been ineligible for whistleblower status. Just before he launched his 2019 accusation, Democrats changed the very definition of what a whistleblower is. Being a whistleblower used to always require firsthand knowledge of wrongdoing. The statute was changed to allow hearsay to be treated on par with actual knowledge of an event.[411] Hearsay does not hold up in a court of law, but impeachment is a political action, not a legal one.

Several Democratic witnesses all conceded that they had zero firsthand knowledge of any wrongdoing. These career diplomats claimed that Trump's foreign policy was counter to American interests and had to be thwarted. This turns the Constitution on its head. Foreign policy is whatever the president says it is. The diplomats work for him. He can fire them and every other executive branch employee for any reason at any time without explanation. Democrats were reduced to asking one witness if being fired hurt her feelings. Emotions and feelings are not a substitute for codified law. The Ukraine hoax was born for the same reason the Russia hoax was born. People who hate Trump wanted his legal election overturned because they hate him.

One witness was the ambassador to Ukraine, Marie Yovanovitch. Her impeachment testimony left her under a cloud of suspicion. She claimed to be a nonpartisan bureaucrat. Like Comey and others, she was a disgruntled ex-employee seeking vengeance on Trump for firing her.[412] Another witness was Lieutenant Colonel Alexander Vindman of the National Security Council (NSC). Trump fired him and his twin brother for insubordination after the trial. Vindman was personally escorted out of his government building by security.[413]

The main anti-Trump villain in the impeachment trial was Los Angeles Congressman Adam Schiff. Like Brennan and Comey, Schiff spent three years claiming he had evidence of Trump-Russia collusion. Privately, Schiff in 2017 admitted that he had no such evidence at all.[414] The pattern for Ukraine was the same. Schiff publicly attacked in front of the cameras, privately knowing that he had snake eyes for proof. Schiff was trying to invent a crime out of thin air, and his house of cards was collapsing. Trump was acquitted of the charges and rose in the polls. Realizing how politically toxic impeachment was, Pelosi tried to sideline Schiff and New York Congressman Jerry Nadler, a long-time Trump antagonist.[415] Impeachment was a ratings flop as daytime television viewers quickly grew bored. Schiff and Nadler were just not made for television. After receiving a flood of angry phone calls, CBS replaced impeachment coverage with episodes of their popular soap opera *Young and the Restless*.[416] The backlash has Schiff facing the fight of his political life to hold his congressional seat.[417]

Democrats were convinced that the impeachment trial of 2020 would be the main issue in the November election. Within days of the trial ending, the entire process was quickly reduced to a footnote. COVID-19 was the only political story, and Trump's response drove the narrative. Democrats console themselves by saying that Trump is forever impeached, but most Americans still have no idea why. He is also still in office. Justice prevailed, and there is nothing Democrats can do about it.

> **Liberal argument:** Trump's policies created misery, and if people are happy, it is because Trump inherited a great situation from Obama.
>
> **The facts:** Those two lines of attack are directly contradictory. Either times are good or they are not. Asking people if they are happy before deciding on a line of attack is disingenuous. Presidents get the credit and the blame for what happens on their watch. (Although somehow Bill Clinton gets credit for the internet boom economy of the 1990s without getting blamed for the 2000 dot-com collapse. He was responsible for neither. He was peripheral.) Trump's policy accomplishments through February 2020 were numerous. They are given short mentions to avoid redundancy.

Can we finally now get to Trump's policies? Yes. A multisourced summary of many of Trump's notable achievements follows:

The Economy

1. Consumer confidence reached an 18-year high.[418]
2. Business confidence soared because of reduced regulations that spurred hiring.[419]
3. Small business hiring hit an all-time high.
4. Gross domestic product (GDP) growth. Obama's economy, excluding the 2008 recessionary year, averaged 2.1 percent. Trump's economy has averaged more than 3 percent with an exceptional 4.2 percent GDP rate recorded in the second quarter of 2018. This is the best GDP performance in years.[420]

5. Employment/more jobs! More than 2 million jobs were cre-
    ated with a 3.9 percent unemployment rate benchmarking an
    18-year low (that's also just one-tenth of a point off an actual
    50-year low, the lowest point since 1969). Black and Latino
    employment rates all hit record lows. September 2018 non-
    farm payrolls rose by a better-than-expected 201,000. Wages,
    the last missing piece of the economic recovery, increased
    by 2.9 percent year over year to the highest level since April
    2009, (According to the *Wall Street Journal*, employee wages
    rose 3.1 percent, the highest in a decade.) The National
    Federation of Independent Businesses June 2018 report
    recorded 6.7 million nationwide job openings with 6.6 mil-
    lion Americans classified as unemployed, an unprecedented
    balance.[421] Under Trump, the labor participation rate hit its
    highest point in over six years. Wage growth rose more than
    3 percent for the first time in 10 years. The unemployment
    rate benchmarks remained under 4 percent for 19 months,
    the longest streak in 50 years. Five million Americans were
    lifted off of food stamps, and 5.3 million new jobs were cre-
    ated, inclusive of 600,000 new manufacturing jobs. Asian-
    American employment also hit its lowest level. Women's
    unemployment hit its lowest rate in 65 years,[422] and 8,764
    opportunity zones were finalized to promote new jobs and
    growth in lower-income areas.

6. Mortgage applications for new homes rose to a 7-year high.[423]

7. Regulations cut! Trump signed an executive order requir-
    ing that for every new regulation, two regulations must be
    eliminated. He exceeded his promise. This gutted Obama
    era regulations, increasing business confidence. Government
    regulatory activity slowed by an impressive 70 percent ver-
    sus Obama era levels.[424] New business regulations dropped
    drastically lower than Obama for the same period, turning
    off a spigot of new business regulations. Trump weakened
    overrestrictive Dodd-Frank regulations that were hindering

regional and community bankers from lending. Trump's actions strengthened consumer and business investment and borrowing.[425] This drove up bank share prices by 25 percent from 2017 to 2018. Higher share values and more lending meant more economic growth for local businesses.

8. More U.S. investment came as major businesses (Foxconn, Toyota, Ford, and others) committed to building and doing business in the United States, spurring growth.[426] Ford opened a new factory in Michigan and committed to keeping 1,000 jobs at home by 2023.

9. The 2018 Tax Cuts and Jobs Act passed by the GOP Congress and signed by Trump delivered considerable growth through all of 2019.[427]

10. The stock market skyrocketed 7,000 points in the days and weeks following Trump's election victory, followed by a surge of job-creating corporate profits. The Dow Jones Industrial Average topped 29,500 for the very first time on February 12, 2020.[428]

Energy Independence

1. Trump issued an executive order to promote energy independence and economic growth while also protecting coal and coal miner jobs. Trump positioned a new clean coal technology mine to open.[429]

2. Trump authorized the construction of the Keystone and Dakota pipelines.[430] The Dakota pipeline is up and running without harming the environment. Trump also gave half the government's 1.9-million-acre Grand Staircase–Escalante National Monument back to the state of Utah for multiple uses and further energy independence growth. This reversed the Obama EPA eminent domain land grab of more than

5 trillion acres, ending Utah's own Sagebrush Rebellion land use regulation challenges.[431]

3. Nonmetropolitan areas had new population growth for the first time since 2010.[432]

Individual and Constitutional Rights

1. **Supreme Court justices.** Trump placed constitutional conservatives Neil Gorsuch and Brett Kavanaugh on the high court.[433] The Trump administration appointed about 200 federal judges overall through May 2020 . He flipped a couple of appeals courts from liberal to conservative and has even made the notoriously liberal Ninth Circuit Court far less liberal.

2. **Promoting the Women in Entrepreneurship Act.** Trump encouraged the National Science Foundation's entrepreneurial programs to recruit and support women to extend their focus beyond the laboratory and into the commercial world.[434]

3. **Federal opposition to legalized marijuana.** Trump took action in the face of a severe nationwide drug addiction crisis. With 30 states now having legalized marijuana, a proposed amendment to the Controlled Substances Act allows federalism to prevail as the Founding Fathers intended and leaves the marijuana question up to the states.[435]

4. **Second Amendment.** Trump supported calls for mental health reform after the Parkland shooting as well as arming schoolteachers and employees if needed. With 79 percent of Americans in support of the Second Amendment as a constitutional right, Trump remains supportive of the Second Amendment.[436]

5. **Executive orders for religious freedom.** Trump created a White House Faith and Opportunity Initiative to reduce burdens on the exercise of free religion.[437] He also issued a

rule that healthcare workers may choose to refuse to provide services such as abortion or assisted suicide on the grounds of religious or conscientious objection.

Trade

1. **Renegotiated NAFTA.** Trump reached a new bilateral U.S.–Mexico trade agreement. Canada soon dropped its opposition as the agreement became trilateral.[438]
2. **Trans-Pacific Partnership (TPP).** Trump promised during the 2016 campaign to withdraw from this treaty on his first day in office. He kept this promise, preserving American jobs.[439]
3. **The Paris Climate Accord.** The United States withdrew from it because of its huge hidden costs, inefficiencies, lack of achievability, unenforceability, and lack of parity.[440]
4. **Obama's Cuba policy.** Trump reversed it by restricting travel to and trade with the still-communist-ruled island. The Cuban government responded with baby steps toward greater economic freedom.[441]
5. A successful trip to Asia built a strong coalition for stopping North Korea and convinced Asian markets to do business with the United States. Trade partners were told to focus on their own business at home, and the United States would do likewise.[442]
6. Trump signed a trade deal with China to end decades of trade losses to China.[443] He asked Congress to support the U.S. Reciprocal Trade Act to allow the president to impose tariffs on countries that unfairly cheat on trade.
7. The United States and Brazil signed a technology safeguard agreement in a joint security initiative as Brazil became a major non-NATO key ally for trade and security.[444]

8. Trump reached a breakthrough agreement with the European Union to increase U.S. exports.

Crime

1. Trump appointed the Task Force to Reduce Crime and ordered the Department of Justice (DOJ) to target MS-13 aggressively. He signed the Preventing Violence Against Federal, State, Tribal, and Local Law Enforcement Officer Act.[445]

2. Trump issued an executive order targeting drug cartels.[446] Trump's High Drug Trafficking Area Program benchmarks disrupted approximately 3,000 trafficking organizations since 2018.

3. Combatting human trafficking. Trump in 2018 declared January as National Slavery and Human Trafficking Prevention Month. He also signed a presidential executive order on enforcing federal law with respect to transnational criminal organizations and preventing international trafficking.[447]

4. Trump signed a criminal justice reform bill called the First Step Act, which reduced mandatory minimum sentences in certain instances and expanded on "good time credits" for well-behaved prisoners. First Step instructs the DOJ to establish a risk and needs assessment system to classify an inmate's risk and provide guidance on housing, grouping, and program assignment.[448]

Immigration

1. Trump reduced illegal immigration and took steps to continue this reduction.

a. He authorized 5,000 more border control agents and 4,000 National Guard troops for securing the southern border.

b. He quickly listened to the American people on the long-standing *Flores* agreement (the 1997 federal court decision that strictly limits the government's ability to keep children in immigration detention created under Bill Clinton).

c. He repeatedly offered the border wall to Congress in exchange for Dream Act exceptions (rejected by Democrats).

d. Border crossing arrests hit an all-time low as deportations hit an all-time high.

e. As promised, the border wall construction is underway.

f. He fought back against sanctuary cities.

g. He created the Victims of Immigration Crime Engagement Office to support and protect those harmed by such crimes. This office was explicitly called for through an executive order entitled, "Enhancing Public Safety in the Interior of the United States."

h. Homeland Security. Trump issued a waiver allowing further expedited construction of the southern border wall.

i. Trump announced his plan to create a new "fair, modern, and lawful" system of immigration.

j. Thanks to ongoing Trump pressure, Mexico agreed to substantially increase border troops by 6,000 National Guard soldiers. Shortly after, border apprehension under Trump's "Remain in Mexico" policy dropped positively by nearly 56 percent as Mexico apprehended over 140,000 people south of the border line.[449]

2. Trump's travel ban to increase national security was largely upheld by the Supreme Court.[450]

3. He created commissions on the opioid addiction crisis, declaring opioids a national public health emergency.[451]

4. Food stamp use fell to the lowest level in seven years, reversing the large Obama era escalation of citizen-weakening SNAP overdependency.[452]

Government

1. Trump reduced the White House payroll and executed a hiring freeze on all federal employees to downsize government as promised, saving taxpayers millions.[453]

2. Trump donates his personal presidential salary to various charitable causes.[454]

3. Gas prices hit their lowest levels in more than 12 years as a result of Trump freeing up more access to domestic reserves and reducing Middle East dependency.[455]

4. Trump issued an executive order for Americans to buy and hire American first.[456]

5. Trump signed a five-year postemployment lobbying ban for his appointees and going forward.[457]

6. Under Trump, the Labor Department announced millions of dollars for the Homeless Veterans Reintegration Fund to assist homeless veterans back into the workforce.[458]

National Security/Foreign Policy

1. Trump restored America's image as a military powerhouse and global leader. The National Defense Authorization Act of 2018 included spending increases and proposed pay increases for military members.[459] He reduced F-35 jet costs.[460]

2. North Korea. Trump designated it a terrorist state and then aggressively negotiated historic new relations. Trump got approximately 55 POW-MIA American soldiers' remains returned to be honored and buried.[461] He attended three summits with North Korea and increased U.S. pressure for North Korea to cease all nuclear weaponry and missile testing. Trump then created a cost-sharing agreement for troops deployed with South Korea on the border in a further show of support for South Korea while cutting a balanced-share agreement. Trump later met with Japanese Prime Minister Shinzo Abe in support of South Korea and trade. The North Korean vessel *Wise Honest* was seized for international and U.S. violations.

3. **Iran.** Trump decertified and withdrew from the Iran nuclear deal and restored sanctions on Iran.[462] His Treasury Department sanctioned 9 individuals and 14 entities under Iran sanctions and then labeled Iran's Revolutionary Guard a terrorist organization. He later announced his intention to bring Iran's oil imports to zero, further increasing pressure. Trump also revoked numerous waivers for Iran. Trump ordered the strike that killed top Iran Revolutionary Guard Qasem Soleimani.

4. **Syria.** Trump responded aggressively to Syria's use of chemical weapons while cautiously avoiding a full-scale war.[463] Per his prior campaign promises, Trump withdrew U.S. forces from Syria. After complications arose in an area packed with Turkish, Kurdish, Russian, Syrian, and Iranian-backed troops, he left 600 troops in northeast Syria to protect the economic stability of the region's oil fields. Syrians welcomed Trump's decision and his commitment to help modernize the fields, believing them a needed shield that would bring investments and an economic boom.

5. **ISIS.** Our military under Trump's orders smashed ISIS with the mother of all bombs (MOABs) in Afghanistan.[464] Trump pushed forward and hosted the Global Coalition to Defeat ISIS. He ordered the operation that killed ISIS leader Abu Bakr al-Baghdadi.

6. **China.** The relationship drastically changed after the COVID-19 pandemic, which will soon be covered in great detail. Prepandemic, Trump was already cracking down on China's unfair trade practices and intellectual piracy.[465]

7. **Russia.** Trump was much tougher on Russia than a colluding president would have been. He left in place sanctions imposed over Russia's invasion of Crimea in 2014, approved the sale of lethal weapons to Ukraine (something Barack Obama did not do), ordered missiles fired at Syrian military sites, openly targeted strategic operations and allies of Russia, and publicly threatened Russia (and China) about election meddling and currency manipulation.[466] The U.S. Treasury under Trump's guidance sanctioned six Russians and eight entities for illegal aggression toward Ukraine. Trump signed an executive order imposing sanctions on Russia for its use of chemical weapons in the 2018 attack on Russian double agent Sergei Skripal and his daughter.

8. **Israel.** Trump moved the U.S. embassy in Israel to Jerusalem.[467] Trump radically repaired the Obama era's damaged relations with Israel. On November 18, 2019, Secretary of State Mike Pompeo announced that the Trump administration was reversing nearly 40 years of doctrine and returning to the Reagan policy regarding Israeli settlements in the West Bank. These Israeli settlements would no longer be considered illegal.[468] Trump became the first U.S. president to fly directly from Saudi Arabia to Israel rather than go through Cyprus.[469]

9. **Africa.** Trump commenced policy statements challenging ongoing African violence and legal corruption as well as protecting the seizure of white farmers' lands. He was supported by the Zulu nation for doing so.[470]

10. **Venezuela.** Thanks to Trump pressure, more than eight European nations joined in recognizing Juan Guaido as Venezuela's legitimate leader. Trump later issued financial

sanctions against Maduro for blocking humanitarian aid. Trump revoked 77 visas, further pressuring Maduro's regime. The U.S. Treasury Department added further support for Venezuelan democracy by sanctioning 40 Maduro people and entities.[471]

11. **Yemen.** Hostage Danny Burch was freed after 18 months of captivity in Yemen. Trump brought home more than 20 American captives during his presidency.[472]

12. Trump signed an executive order to prepare and protect against future electromagnetic pulse (EMP) threats.

13. Trump visited the United Kingdom, France, and Ireland on the 75th anniversary of D-Day, reaffirming our ongoing commitment to our allies.

Other Trump Actions

1. **Department of Veterans' Affairs.** Trump signed the VA Mission Act. Veterans can now choose their own doctors, whistleblowers are covered, and the VA can finally terminate bad employees.[473]

2. **Education.** Trump sent much of education back to the states. He signed the Strengthening Career and Technical Education for the 21st Century Act. He reauthorized the Carl D. Perkins Career and Technical Education Act, a $1.2 billion program last overhauled by Congress in 2006. The new law allows states to set their own goals for career and technical education programs without the education secretary's approval. The law requires states to make progress toward those goals and makes other changes to federal career technical education law.[474]

3. **Healthcare.** Trump protected people with preexisting conditions and yet signed an executive order mandating agencies not to apply Obamacare penalties. He ended Obamacare

subsidies and got Congress to repeal the Obamacare mandate, effectively repealing the hated law. Obamacare was initially ruled constitutional by the Supreme Court as a tax. The
repeal of the Obamacare tax penalty allowed a federal judge
to finally strike down Obamacare as unconstitutional.[475]

4. **Media.** Through constant outright challenges to the media,
Trump got Americans to become more politically aware
of media manipulation. He used social media (with some
admitted downside) to bypass the biased media and commu-
nicate directly with the people.[476]

5. **Cleaning up the DOJ and FBI.** Trump fired and removed
government officials to try to depoliticize and restore trust in
what became a biased, corrupt justice system.[477]

6. **United Nations.** Trump reversed the Obama era EU-inspired
globalist vision while also seeking parity in UN and NATO
costs and obligations.[478]

7. Trump signed the Land and Water Conservation Fund law,
creating three new national monuments, two of which honor
civil rights leaders. This added 1.3 million acres of American
preserved wilderness.[479]

8. Under Trump, the Department of Health and Human
Services (DHHS) finalized a rule that drug companies must
disclose the process of medication on TV advertisements.
This protects our seniors. He awarded $107 million to 1,273
health centers across the United States to improve service
quality.[480]

9. Under Trump, the Department of Labor, DHSS, and the
Treasury Department approved health reimbursement
arrangements (HRAs), helping more than 11 million
Americans.[481]

10. With Trump tackling the opioid crisis, the Centers for
Disease Control and Prevention (CDC) reported drug over-
dose deaths dropped 5 percent (prepandemic). This was the
first decline in three decades.[482]

11. Trump signed an executive order modernizing influenza vaccines in the United States to promote national security and public health. He directed the DHHS to overhaul seasonal flu vaccine production and urge more Americans to be vaccinated.[483]

12. Trump issued an executive order protecting American monuments, memorials, and statues and combating recent criminal violence. He reaffirmed the 1964 law that our federal monuments be protected. Those committing damages exceeding $100 are subjected to a ten-year prison sentence and fine not to exceed $250,000. The renewed law and order act was created for the further containment of rioters, arsonists, and left-wing extremists. Those who carried out and supported these acts explicitly identified themselves with ideologies such as Marxism that call for the destruction of the United States system of government.[501]

13. Trump issued an executive order on building and rebuilding monuments to American Heroes. He announced the creation of the "National Garden of American Heroes" by July 4th, 2026 to defend "our great national story" against those who vandalize statues.[502]

The evidence is irrefutable. Trump's policies in his first three years in office were mostly successful. There was direct correlation between his policies and improved American prosperity, freedom, and security from January 2017 through February 2020.

Trump governed as a conservative, and conservatism works.

Then came the world-changing coronavirus. Lives were lost. The economy cratered. The stock market crashed. Unemployment skyrocketed. The country shut down.

Trump had to deal with a life-and-death public health threat that never existed before. Democrats now had plenty of new lines of attack against Trump, each one less truthful than the one before.

> **Liberal argument:** Trump failed to stop the coronavirus from coming to America.
>
> **The facts:** The American people did not blame FDR for Pearl Harbor. They did not blame George W. Bush for 9/11. They did not blame Trump for the coronavirus. The virus came from a lab in Wuhan, China, and rapidly spread from there. The Chinese government lied about the severity of the illness. The Chinese government allowed its citizens to travel throughout the world infecting people.

In late January 2020, Trump instituted a travel ban from China. He was immediately attacked as racist.[484] On March 12, 2020, he extended travel bans to Europe. The entire purpose of a travel ban is national security. Trump's first proposed travel ban came on January 27, 2017. That affected seven mostly Middle Eastern nations. It was focused mainly on radical Islamic terrorism, but the goal of protecting the homeland was the same. The very next day, Democrats sued to block the travel ban. On June 26, 2018, the U.S. Supreme Court upheld the 2017 travel ban.

Dr. Anthony Fauci stated that the 2020 Trump travel ban was vital to stopping the spread of COVID-19 in America. The travel ban drastically reduced the number of deaths.[485]

Democrats wasted 18 months trying to block the original travel ban. They would have blocked the 2020 travel ban with China. Because of the 2018 Supreme Court, they knew they were powerless to do so.

Trump's critics were against the travel ban. The travel ban was the key policy to slowing the spread of the virus.

> **Liberal argument:** Trump's policies exacerbated the spread of the coronavirus.
>
> **The facts:** Once the coronavirus arrived in America, several liberal policies spread the virus. Trump was against those policies. Many blue state governors and mayors support sanctuary cities. In addition to promoting mass numbers of illegal immigration, sanctuary cities frequently become giant homeless shelters. The homeless posed an increased health risk to themselves and others.

The first major coronavirus outbreak occurred around Seattle, a sanctuary city and hotbed of homelessness. The next major outbreak was in New York City, where homelessness is rampant under the permissive policies of leftist Mayor Bill de Blasio. Homeless encampments right outside of hospitals and nursing homes contributed to nursing homes becoming a death sentence for those confined in those medical institutions. By May 2020, one-third of all coronavirus deaths came from nursing homes. In the worst affected states, over half of all coronavirus deaths came from nursing homes.[486]

Trump has tried to crack down on sanctuary cities, and liberals blocked him every step of the way. Conservative areas do not have rampant homelessness. Liberal cities do, especially liberal sanctuary cities.

Trump gave broad latitude to governors to experiment with solutions. The key decision revolved around nursing homes. Conservative Florida Governor Ron DeSantis protected the nursing homes. He ordered that COVID-19 patients be banned from nursing homes. Liberal New York Governor Andrew Cuomo did the exact opposite. He mandated that nursing homes be used to shelter COVID-19 patients. DeSantis was right, and lives were saved. Cuomo was wrong, and nursing home patients died.[487]

Beyond liberal policies, bad personal behavior by many liberals helped spread the coronavirus. New York City is overwhelmingly liberal. So are the Hamptons on Long Island. NYC liberals violated quarantine orders and fled to the Hamptons, leading to a major outbreak on Long Island. These NYC liberals then fled to Rhode Island and did the same. Then they flew to (mainly south) Florida, spreading infection all along the way. New York's Cuomo put the lockdown orders in place. His own brother, liberal CNN anchor Chris Cuomo, traveled between both of his houses in the Hamptons while sick with the virus. Chris Cuomo (and other liberal governors and mayors) were on TV every night attacking Trump and shaming people to stay home while repeatedly violating their own advice.[488]

Florida and Louisiana are red states (although Louisiana has a Democrat governor) that became major coronavirus hotspots. However, it was outsiders who spread the disease, not locals. In addition to New Yorkers, Florida hosted two major events that brought global travel to the state. The Super Bowl was held in early February in Miami. Then came spring break and the annual mass influx of young people behaving recklessly. South Florida had the bulk of the coronavirus problems. Disney World in Orlando also receives global traffic. Louisiana saw a massive spike after the annual Mardi Gras revelry that ran through February 25, 2020. Many people from all over the country, including a lot of young people, come to Bourbon Street in the French Quarter.

Young spring breakers and Mardi Gras revelers are not all liberals, but demographically they are certainly by and large not conservatives. Neither are the NYC snowbirds.

Liberal argument: Trump had no plan to tackle the coronavirus.

The facts: Trump was far ahead of his critics. The left spent January and February obsessing over his impeachment. Trump on January 29, 2020, formed the White House Coronavirus Task Force. This task force featured some of the most competent and capable people in the history of public service. Trump's first task force appointee was the widely respected Dr. Anthony Fauci, the director of the National Institute of Allergy and Infectious Diseases. Dr. Fauci was universally praised for his role in dealing with the AIDS crisis of the 1980s. Vice President Mike Pence chaired the task force. The response coordinator was Dr. Deborah Birx, who has been the U.S. global AIDS coordinator for Obama and Trump. Surgeon General Adams and Seema Verma, the administrator of the Centers for Medicare and Medicaid Services, also played key roles. By any honest standard, Trump assembled the medical A-Team.[489]

From the get-go, the task force held lengthy press conferences complete with easily understandable PowerPoint slides. Fauci, Birx, and the rest of the task force clearly explained what they were doing, why they were doing it, and what actions needed to be taken by the American people. They answered questions from the media in a clear fashion. While the media in general treated Fauci and Birx respectfully (they fawned over Fauci and considered him infallible), they wasted valuable time attacking Trump whenever he spoke. The overall public perception was that the task force was succeeding. This led to rising poll numbers for Trump. Liberals responded by demanding that media outlets stop covering the coronavirus briefings. The same liberals who spent years screaming in favor of transparency were now advocating for censorship. Some liberal anti-Trump networks censored the briefings, but enough people still saw the briefings and found them to be informative and lifesaving.[490]

Liberal argument: Trump kept ignoring the science and the doctors.

The facts: Trump knows that he is not a doctor and has publicly said so. Fauci and Birx were both explicitly asked if Trump ignored their advice. To the liberal media's consternation, Fauci and Birx both said that Trump was very closely engaged with their work. He asked questions, understood the answers, processed the information, and largely accepted their expert recommendations. Fauci and Birx both said that the most important action was to "flatten the curve" and slow the spread of the virus. They recommended to Trump that he shut down the country, and he did exactly that. Fauci and Birx clearly said that every time they recommended a major course of action, Trump accepted their recommendation.[491]

Liberal argument: Trump left the states to fend for themselves.

The facts: This is false. Throughout his presidency, Trump sparred with liberal governors on a variety of matters. His biggest state executive pre-coronavirus antagonists were New York's Cuomo and California's Newsom. During the pandemic, Trump gave the governors everything they asked for. In several cases, he gave them significantly more than they needed.

Cuomo and Newsom both publicly admitted that Trump cooperated with them fully. He was in constant communication with them and responded rapidly to their requests. Trump's response was effusively praised by both Cuomo and Newsom. Cuomo added that in his telephone conversations, Trump repeatedly inquired about the health of Cuomo's elderly mother and his brother Chris.[492]

Trump did have public wars of words during the coronacrisis with Governors Gretchen Whitmer of Michigan and J. B. Pritzker of Illinois. Trump objected to both state governors using their respective powers to enact draconian restrictions not backed by science. As red states eased their lockdowns, Michigan and Illinois extended theirs. Protests erupted in Michigan over Whitmer's targeting of barbershop and salon owners for arrest.[493] Trump threatened to withhold federal aid but never followed through on this threat. While the threat angered the governors, Trump did it for the people of those states who wanted their lives back. Trump also threatened to crack down on states that kept churches and synagogues closed.[494] Democrats allowed marijuana shops to stay open as essential but deemed places of worship nonessential. This was clear ideological targeting, and Attorney General Barr warned against religious discrimination.[495]

The main request from blue state governors that Trump outright rejected were bailouts. Many of these blue states had billions of dollars of debt that existed long before the pandemic. Decades of liberal mismanagement and terrible policies caused the debt. Trump was totally willing to help states recoup losses specifically related to COVID-19. He was unwilling to give blue states one penny to bail out their prepandemic profligate spending. Leftist blue state governors tried to exploit COVID-19 to push a socialist agenda and spread the very policies that financially wrecked their states in the first place.[496]

> **Liberal argument:** Trump repeatedly refused to invoke the 1950 Defense Production Act (DPA).
>
> **The facts:** Whenever any Republican expands government, Democrats use it as an excuse to expand government even more. Once George W. Bush gave bailouts and stimulus money in 2008, Obama had an excuse to give even more money away. Bush's use of the intelligence agencies and FISA Courts to spy on terrorists gave Obama the excuse to spy on private citizens. Trump was against expanding federal power, even his own. Republicans knew that a future Democratic president could then invoke the DPA at will. Trump was deliberate and cautious in his use of the DPA rather than become a dictator, as his critics keep calling him.[497]

Trump took a far better approach. Rather than force the business community to build ventilators and masks, he asked them to do this. He appealed to their sense of patriotism. He provided them business incentives, including a ton of positive media coverage. When he hosted *Celebrity Apprentice*,[498] he repeatedly gave various companies glowing media. They received free marketing solely based on their friendship and business relationships with him. He did the exact same thing in the White House, and the companies responded positively to his overtures.[499] He chose the carrot over the stick, and this worked. He correctly chose the conservative pro-business approach rather than the liberal top-down government anti-business approach.

Liberal argument: Trump had no plan to fix the economy.

The facts: Trump's original task force began by focusing on the medical threat at hand. When the curve began to flatten (the entire point of the task force), the next step was to reopen the economy. Trump added very respected economic minds to the task force. Treasury Secretary Steve Mnuchin was added very early on. Mnuchin spoke to Pelosi several times a day. Pelosi herself said that Mnuchin played a key role in getting three rounds of vital stimulus relief passed.[500] Trump and Pelosi were barely on speaking terms. Although Mnuchin worked directly for Trump, he had Pelosi's trust. This allowed him to be an important intermediary. Mnuchin was every bit as important and effective as Hank Paulson was during the 2008 financial crisis. Another early task force hire on the economic side was National Economic Council (NEC) Director Larry Kudlow.

In April 2020, Trump created an economic task force that included various business minds. He included people who had criticized him, including Mark Cuban.[501]

A major lifeline to the small business community came in the form of the Paycheck Protection Program (PPP) set up through the Small Business Administration (SBA).[502] PPP loans helped save many small business owners from bankruptcy. The program was imperfect. Some large businesses, including Planned Parenthood, received loans meant for small businesses. Many large businesses who received PPP funds, including the Los Angeles Lakers, were successfully shamed into returning the money. While liberals and conservatives were united in outrage over the abuses, liberals put ideology first in giving a pass to Planned Parenthood. Planned Parenthood kept the PPP funds.[503] Nevertheless, the program was created from scratch. Trump created an entire successful new program faster than Obama could even create a healthcare website.

The Trump administration allowed an exception to the unemployment system. Independent contractors and self-employed people were now eligible for benefits. This was a lifeline to the many small business owners who work for themselves.[504]

Trump also constantly held roundtables with business leaders in various industries.[505] One day he'd sit down with executives from the restaurant industry. The next day it was pharmaceutical manufacturers. When the price of oil crashed to unprecedented levels, he sat down with oil executives. At all of these meetings, Trump did plenty of talking but also plenty of listening. He asked the executives to tell the American people who they were, what their companies did, and what they needed to get back on track. These roundtables were public. Some liberal networks again refused to cover them because they gave Trump positive press. They just could not stand the image of Trump as an effective leader. Invaluable ideas came out of these meetings. Business leaders, including Trump, tend to know more about business than anti-business critics who never ran a business.

For unsung heroes in so many different businesses, a simple pat on the back can be nearly as vital as a paycheck. Recognition matters. The left tends to look down on blue-collar workers. They also often dismiss people in supply-chain management as boring. Trump took hardworking Americans and made heroes out of them. After 9/11, Americans celebrated police officers and firefighters. During the pandemic, nurses and other medical personnel received balcony serenades. This is lovely, but they are all white-collar professionals. Trump invited truckers to the White House and feted them in a Rose Garden ceremony.[506] Imagine being a trucker working 14-hour days and feeling unappreciated. Then imagine standing next to the president of the United States telling your story. Anheuser-Busch made millions of dollars by telling Americans, "For all you do, this Bud's for you."[507] Thanks to Trump's understanding of the American spirit, truckers were given the greatest heroic celebration since Jerry Reed sang "East Bound and Down" in *Smokey and the Bandit*.[508] Trump got elected on a promise that the forgotten person would be forgotten no more. He meant this.

When people feel appreciated, they get fired up. Trump became the coach rallying his team. American manufacturers from automakers to beverage distilleries with no medical experience rolled up their sleeves and got to work making ventilators. They went from never making a ventilator to making America the ventilator capital of the world.[509] This was a direct result of the Trump Coronavirus Task Force and his business roundtables.

While the stock market is not always an indicator of overall economic health, it should not be dismissed either. The Dow Jones Industrial Average (DJIA) crashed in 2020 from a February 12 high of 29,551 to a low of 18,213 on March 23.[510] The nearly 40 percent drop in six weeks had companies and investors terrified (although the point swings were violent, the percentage drop was still not as bad as the 1987 crash). In 1987, Reagan and Federal Reserve Chairman Alan Greenspan prevented a financial breakdown. In 2008, it was George W. Bush's team led by Paulson that staved of collapse. In 2020, Trump had the steady hands of Mnuchin and Kudlow to calm the hysteria. By April 2020, half the losses were recovered as the DJIA settled in a 23,000–24,000 trading range.

Unlike the 2008 crash, the American business community bore zero blame for the 2020 pandemic. In 2008, bailouts were controversial. In 2020, Trump and even anti-business Democrats allowed for bailouts of big businesses who were harmed through no fault of their own. The rare bipartisanship on this issue led by Trump allowed even hated industries such as airlines to be given relief.

Every action Trump's critics say they would have done are either things he already did or wildly impractical leftist fantasies such as guaranteed income for all. Many of Trump's critics, including Obama, have never run a business and have no idea how a business operates. The business community does the hiring, and most businesses are small businesses. While there is a long road ahead, Trump proved his ability to solve this temporary economic shock.

> **Liberal argument:** Trump got people killed by recommending hydroxychloroquine.
>
> **The facts:** Hydroxychloroquine has been around for decades. It has proven effective at curing malaria. The only reason this drug became even the slightest bit controversial is because Trump mentioned it. This fits under the liberal "Orange Man Bad" illness known as Trump derangement syndrome (TDS). If Trump comes out against killing innocent puppies and kittens, a percentage of liberals will then be in favor of it. Trump favored hydroxychloroquine, so liberal Democrats *had* to reflexively be against it.

Democrats (naturally) denied this and insisted that they were following science and that Trump is anti-science. Well Trump did not just wake up one morning and declare himself a medical drug expert. He spoke to medical experts and listened to them. He observed results, which is exactly what an honest scientist practicing real science is supposed to do. The results showed him that the benefits outweighed the risks inherent in every drug.

The best result came from human testimonials. One powerful testimonial came from Michigan State Representative Karen Whitsett. She is a black woman and a Democrat with a district that represents parts of Detroit and Dearborn. These are among the least pro-Trump areas in the entire country. In March 2020, Whitsett came down with COVID-19 and rapidly declined. She was near death. When she heard President Trump mention hydroxychloroquine, she decided to give it a try. Trump is fond of asking, "What do you have to lose?" At that point, Whitsett had nothing to lose. She recovered and shocked the political establishment by crediting hydroxychloroquine—and Trump—with saving her life.[511] Rather than be glad she lived, Democrats censured her on the Michigan State House floor for praising a GOP president and obliterating their anti-Trump narrative.[512]

Liberal argument: Trump got a man killed by telling him to drink fish-tank cleaner.

The facts: Even by liberal Democrat standards, this is too ridiculous to give much credence. For the few liberals who believe the anti-Trump things they say, a reality check is necessary. Charles Cooke of *National Review* brought a healthy dose of sanity to this insane nonissue.

Trump never said the drug was a guaranteed cure. He simply said that early results seemed promising and were worth a greater look. Critics pointed to side effects, but every single drug has side effects. Hydroxychloroquine helped more people than it harmed. Early signs *were* promising. Trump was right, and his critics were wrong.

A woman in Arizona heard Trump mention the benefits of hydroxychloroquine. She found fish-tank cleaner in the pantry and gave it to her husband. The man drank the fish-tank cleaner because he thought it was chloroquine. Fish-tank cleaner is *chloroquine phosphate*, not hydroxychloroquine. For those of you thinking of cleaning your swimming pools with any chloroquine, don't. It won't work. For that, use chlorine.

Additionally, the Arizona man was persuaded more by his wife than by Trump. They had a contentious relationship that involved physical violence. After his death, police opened a homicide investigation. (His wife has not been charged. Opening up a homicide investigation is standard procedure.)[513]

Cooke's summary of the entire episode is perfect:

> We simply cannot run our country on the assumption that "I have high hopes for this drug currently in clinical trials and hope it will eventually be fast-tracked by the FDA and prescribed by a doctor" will be heard by reasonable people as "go into your pantry right now and eat fish tank cleaner if the ingredients look similar to you to a word you heard on television." Insofar as there is any advice to be disseminated here, it's "Don't eat industrial cleaning products," which one would hope is a lesson that most people have already internalized.[514]

Hopefully, liberal millennials and younger people who eat Tide PODS will also stop.[515]

Liberal argument: Trump got people killed by demanding that America reopen too soon. He put corporate profits over public safety.

The facts: This was liberals using their straw man false equivalency tactic. Anyone in favor of wanting to reopen the economy was a monster who at worst immorally wanted people to die and at best amorally were indifferent to people dying. Liberals overwhelmingly favored extending the lockdown. Conservatives overwhelmingly wanted the country to reopen.

The original purpose of the quarantine lockdown and the social distancing was to flatten the curve. The fear was that hospitals would become overloaded and strained to the breaking point. People who needed hospitalization would be crowded out and die before getting proper hospital treatment. Ironically, it is countries with socialized medicine where people die waiting for a doctor's appointment or a medical procedure. The U.S. capitalist healthcare system had never experienced rationing. Coronavirus pandemic actions were specifically put in place to prevent this occurrence from becoming a reality. Once the curve was successfully flattened, liberals needed to move the goal posts to deny Trump a success.

Flattening the curve became a complaint about a shortage of ventilators. Trump summoned American businesses to build ventilators. They rose to the challenge, and America had a surplus of ventilators. Then the liberal media complained about an inadequate supply of testing. Trump repeatedly pointed out that anyone who wanted a coronavirus test could obtain one at no cost. Liberals demanded that all 330 million Americans be tested, which was as impractical as it was illogical. A person could get tested at noon and then contract coronavirus at 12:05 p.m. People should get tested if they feel symptomatic. Mass hypochondria was unhelpful. Then Democrats went a bridge too far, even for them. The new metric was that the country could not reopen until there was a vaccine.[516]

Original projections for a vaccine were 12 to 18 months away. Trump's Food and Drug Administration (FDA) was fast-tracking drugs that would normally face bureaucratic hurdles. Even this accelerated timetable did not predict a possible vaccine until very late in 2020.

Red state governors began the reopening process while blue state governors and mayors extended lockdowns. The typical liberal justification was that they favored science while conservatives did not.

The choice of death versus money was insulting. It was sneeringly dismissive of the many people who were financially on the brink. Rich liberal celebrities let us know that they were trapped in their McMansions. Therefore, we were "all in this together" as we were trapped in our small homes. We did not have paid servants or refrigerators stocked with every different invented flavor of expensive ice cream.[517] We did not have people to fetch our groceries. In many cases, even affording the groceries was a challenge. Even for rich liberals used to basking in their own glow, the lack of empathy for the less fortunate was stunning. Many of these liberals who screamed at people to stay home were either retired, working remotely at home, or living off of their trust funds or entertainment industry royalties.

The choice of death versus money was disproven by the results. While liberals were clamoring for lockdowns, conservatives, including Governor Brian Kemp of Georgia, took the opposite approach, reopening their states earlier.[518] Some conservative governors, including Kristi Noem of South Dakota, never closed their states at all.[519] The results were predictable. The red states recovered economically far more quickly than the blue states without compromising public safety and health.

It was blue state governors issuing edicts that were as arbitrary as they were senseless, highlighted by Whitmer banning the purchase of certain gardening supplies.[520] This is authoritarianism. Liberal governors and mayors led by Eric Garcetti of Los Angeles and Bill de Blasio of New York City, threatened citizens with fines and arrests.[521] De Blasio threatened to round up and arrest Orthodox Jews holding a funeral for violating social distancing rules.[522] Trump used his power cautiously, while leftist mayors and governors brought their full government muscle down on their own citizens.

The choice of death versus money was also false. It was a horrendous choice between death and death. The deaths from coronavirus were heartbreaking. Unfortunately, many more people risked death from the lockdown. Being trapped at home led to many people suffering despair, depression, and dementia. Alcoholism and drug abuse rose. People who had gotten sober relapsed. There was a noticeable spike in suicides.[523]

Humans are built for human contact. We are not meant to be trapped alone, isolated from society. Other than the Unabomber, most of us do not want to be cut off from civilization. Online interaction is better than nothing, but it is far from sufficient. For many people, attending their church or even meeting their friends for dinner is a matter of survival. Having a couple of friends come over to watch the ballgame is a mental health issue. Conservatives understand that the slim possibility of a death from physical illness is worth the risk of a higher chance of death from mental despair and decline.

One last point about the coronavirus deaths is an issue that liberals are desperate to deny. While the number of nursing home deaths in New York was vastly understated, the overall number of coronavirus deaths was vastly overstated. Colorado became the first state to revise its numbers downward. To fix these discrepancies, coronavirus deaths have been divided into two categories: people who died *from* COVID-19 and people who died *with* COVID-19.[524] The former properly addresses causation, whereas the latter lets us exclude cases where the coronavirus is incidental to the death. A drug dealer who murders a fellow dealer in a drug deal gone bad may have had coronavirus, but the death was probably more a result of receiving strategically placed bullets.

Americans know that we will bounce back and defeat the coronavirus. Trump proved himself up to the challenge. The American people have always been up to any challenge.

The strong case for President Trump's reelection becomes even stronger when faced with the alternative.

Liberal argument: Trump is exhausting. People are tired of the drama. It is time to return America to stability and normalcy. America should vote for Joe Biden for president in 2020.

The facts: Biden has spent decades crafting an image as America's lovable uncle who says goofy things in an endearing way. He is "Middle-Class Joe" from Scranton, Pennsylvania, who rides the train to work with the regular folks. The liberal media who still worship Obama have done backflips to protect Biden in a bubble-wrapped safe space that would make even liberal arts college students blush. Once the facade is removed, the truth is undeniable. Biden is a totally unacceptable choice for president. He must be rejected for numerous reasons.

Biden is corrupt. He became wealthy without ever having held a private-sector job. He was elected to his local city council at age 25 and to the U.S. Senate at age 29 (he turned 30 before he was sworn in, or he would have been ineligible). He served in the Senate for 36 years, ran for president twice badly, and was rescued off the scrap heap by Obama to become vice president. Like Hillary Clinton, Biden turned his political career into a pay-for-play operation.

Much of this has been done through his ne'er-do-well son Hunter. The father cannot be blamed for his son's drug use, dishonorable discharge from the military, or impregnating a woman while carrying on a sexual affair with the wife of his own dead brother Beau (the good son).[525] The father should be blamed for using his influence to get Hunter a ton of high-paying jobs where Hunter had no qualifications and did no work.

The most famous of these companies was Burisma Holdings, a Ukrainian oil and gas exploration company. Hunter was paid over $83,000 per month for being a consultant despite having zero experience in the oil and gas industry.[526] Even Obama expressed concern that this would create the appearance of a conflict of interest. It appeared this way because it was. The Obama administration had

Ukraine foreign policy interests, in which Biden Senior played a major role. When the Ukrainian government began investigating corruption involving Burisma, Vice President Biden stepped in and blocked the investigation. He threatened the Ukrainian government that the Obama administration would withdraw foreign aid to Ukraine unless the prosecutor on the case was fired. Biden is on video laughing about this and admitting that the Ukrainian government fired the prosecutor and got its foreign aid money.[527]

This was bad enough, but it got worse. A new Ukrainian president got elected on a platform of ending corruption similar to Trump's vow to "drain the swamp." Part of this cleaning up of corruption meant continuing the investigation into Burisma and the Bidens. Because Trump discussed corruption with the Ukrainian president and because they were pursuing Biden, this telephone call was used as a basis to impeach Trump.[528]

The very thing Trump was accused of doing is exactly what Biden did.

This all means that Biden the elder twice tried to overthrow the Trump government. His attempt to frame Trump on Russia is evidenced by his signature on an unmasking request. His attempt to frame Trump on Ukraine is evidenced by his videotaped bragging of his own corruption and his attempts to conceal it.

On top of all of that, Biden began his lifelong quest for the presidency by committing plagiarism. His campaign kickoff speech in 1987 was heavily borrowed verbatim from British Labor leader Neil Kinnock. Biden dropped out of the race in disgrace.[529]

Biden is incompetent. Over the years, Biden has been compared to everyone from Barney Fife to Yosemite Sam. He is a bungler and a bumbler. After 40 years of elective office, try finding something he was good at. His comments on the 2009 swine flu pandemic were so riddled with errors that Obama had to sideline him.[530] Biden was reduced to ribbon-cutting ceremonies and funerals. FDR and Reagan changed the world. Try finding something big that Biden took the lead on and got right. His inability to even conduct an online town

hall had his aides and campaign staff cringing. Try naming one significant positive political accomplishment that Biden has ever been
responsible for. A blank piece of paper will suffice. More than a hand-
ful of Democratic power brokers quietly debated whether to try to
replace him, but their odds were slim. Every four years the media
plays up the possibility of a brokered convention, and that scenario
disappears every four years by Super Tuesday in March. Unless Joe
Biden's health concerns become a reality, he is the 2020 Democratic
presidential nominee whether Democrats like it or not.

Biden has a history of racist remarks. His own words tell the story:

You cannot go to a 7-Eleven or a Dunkin' Donuts unless
you have a slight Indian accent.[531]

I mean, you got the first mainstream African-American
(Obama) who is articulate and bright and clean and a
nice-looking guy, I mean, that's a storybook, man.[532]

He [former West Virginia Senator and KKK leader Robert
Byrd] was fiercely devoted, as you've all heard, to his principles. Even once he became power, he always spoke truth
to power, standing up for the people he proudly was part of,
and you've heard it many times today but it bears repeating
again, in defense of the Constitution he revered.[533]

Poor kids are just as bright and just as talented as white
kids.[534]

Well I tell you what, if you have a problem figuring out
whether you're for me or Trump, then you ain't black.[535]

Most of the time, Biden gets a free pass because he is a Democrat.
Whether it's a racist comment or just a stupid comment, Democrats
roll their eyes and then say, "Well, that's just Joe being Joe." On the
rare occasions when his own party calls him out, he claims that he
is being taken out of context. This means that he was taken literally.

To say that Biden is a racist would be unfair. To say that he has a history of racially insensitive comments is totally fair. If Trump or any other Republican made those comments, they would be politically skewered. Former Republican Virginia Governor and Senator George Allen was on a fast track to be president before one comment far milder than any Biden comments permanently derailed Allen's political career.[536]

Biden is battling cognitive decline. Even saying this causes liberals to go into angry self-righteous mode. Comedians and pundits spent years making fun of Reagan, Dole, and John McCain for being old. That was fine because they were Republicans. Well, Democrats get old too. McCain was 72 when he was defeated in his final presidential run. Dole was 73. Reagan was 69 when he was elected and 77 when he left office. Trump was the oldest person to get elected president at 70. Biden at 77 is older than all of them.

Plenty of old people are highly functioning. Former Mayor Michael Bloomberg, Senator Sanders, and Dr. Fauci are all 78, one year older than Biden. None of them show signs of cognitive decline. Sanders has crazy ideas, but zero problems expressing them.

This is not about malapropisms. Both Bushes were unfairly raked over the coal for fracturing their syntax. Former Vice President Dan Quayle was brutally ridiculed for mangling a couple of expressions and misspelling a word. Yogi Berra became a beloved figure because of his linguistic mistakes. This is not about speech impediments. Biden deserves credit for overcoming a childhood stuttering problem.

Cognitive decline is far more serious. Biden often forgets what he is saying midsentence. He strings individual words together that fail as a collective to form coherent sentences.

There was a time in history when such matters were never discussed. FDR's confinement to a wheelchair was a private matter. Times are different now. Americans want to know everything about their potential presidents. In 2016, Hillary Clinton's secrecy and evasiveness about her medical condition led to more questions. She was mentally sound but definitely suffered from a still-undisclosed physical illness. She had frequent coughing fits on the campaign trail and needed help standing up more than once.[537]

Biden's defensiveness over his age led to him engaging in bizarre behavior. He challenged questioners at his own town halls to push-up contests and boxing matches.[538]

Biden suffered from a pair of brain aneurysms in the 1980s. One of them did rupture.[539] For those who want video evidence, YouTube has plenty of videos of Biden appearing confused and befuddled.

This is not an "absent-minded professor" joke. Biden needs to release his complete medical records. Liberals in return will babble about Trump's tax returns to try to create a false moral equivalence. Speaker Pelosi, who at age 80 has had brain freezes of her own in recent years, ridiculed Trump for being "morbidly obese"[540] (someone should ask Stacey Abrams and Jerry Nadler their opinion on the subject). Trump did release his health records, and Biden needs to do likewise. With older people, the decline does not happen gradually. It is a rapid descent, and voters need to know that Biden is declining. Reagan was lucid at the 1992 GOP Convention. By 1994, he was announcing that he had Alzheimer's disease. Whatever is affecting Biden, he needs to let voters know now.

Biden stands for nothing. Bush Senior struggled with what he called "the vision thing." Dole once joked about going into a Pearl Vision Center so that he could get one.[541] Massachusetts Senator Ted Kennedy, Hillary Clinton, and Dole were three candidates in recent decades who were never able to articulate why they wanted to be president. Senator Kennedy was pressured by his father. Hillary worships power. She wanted the job because she wanted the job.

Presidential candidates with core beliefs can clearly articulate what those beliefs are. Voters know what their priorities are, whether they are ideological or not. Obama's campaign focused on the three issues of healthcare, education, and the environment and energy. He was as ideological on the left as Reagan was on the right. Trump focused on trade and immigration, the same two issues he has been speaking about for the last 35 years. Trump is nonideological, but he still had his core beliefs.

Trying to decipher the overarching theme of Biden's campaign is as tough as trying to decipher his sentences. Like Hillary, Biden seems to be running an "Orange Man Bad" campaign designed to make him the default option. "I'm uninspiring, but my opponent is far worse and scary" is not a winning campaign strategy.

Biden had 40 years to articulate his political philosophy. Because he stood for nothing, this left him open to be all things to all people. This brings us to his next problem.

Biden is a flip-flopper. For all his wacky behavior, Biden has never been a leftist radical or a revolutionary. He was a mainstream center-left traditional Democrat. The Democratic Party moved sharply leftward in the twenty-first century. In 2008 and 2012, labeling Obama a socialist was considered an insult. In 2016 and 2020, Sanders ran as a proud socialist and nearly captured the Democratic nomination. Biden wanted to run a centrist campaign, but the radicals who devoured his party threatened to send him down to a third humiliating presidential primary defeat (Dole never won the White House, but he did on his third try win his party's nomination). It is one thing to have a genuine conversion on an issue. It is quite another to change on every issue, especially in an election year.

- **Abortion.** Biden used to be a somewhat pro-life Catholic Democrat. Pennsylvania is one of the few states where those people still exist. In 1974, he stated that the landmark *Roe v. Wade* decision of 1973 "went too far." He staunchly supported the middle-ground position that kept the two sides from killing each other. The (Henry) Hyde Amendment denied federal funding for women having abortions. If a woman wanted an abortion, she would have to pay for it herself rather than use taxpayer dollars. After decades of holding this position, Biden in 2019 reversed himself and supported repealing the Hyde Amendment.[542]

- **Guns.** Biden cast "a vote in favor of a 1986 bill that the NRA has called 'the law that saved gun rights' in America." A few years later he reversed course and supported the 1994 assault weapons ban. As vice president from 2009 to 2017, Biden spoke in favor of gun control but took virtually no action. It was the one issue that Obama did not try to forcefully push because of political expediency. In 2020, Biden vowed to appoint Beto O'Rourke as his gun czar. O'Rourke goes beyond gun control. He publicly announced his support for gun confiscation, which he would do through government force.[543]
- **Immigration.** In 2007, Biden supported a crackdown on illegal immigration, including a border wall. He held the exact same position as Trump. In 2020, Biden fell in line and declared border walls and other immigration enforcement mechanisms racist.[544]
- **Crime and race.** Biden enthusiastically supported the 1994 crime bill that cracked down on inner-city crime. When Trump in December 2018 passed the Second Chance Act, Democrats were terrified of his making serious inroads with black voters. Biden all of a sudden became a supporter of criminal justice reform.[545]
- **Gay rights.** In the 1990s, Biden supported "Don't Ask, Don't Tell" (DADT) and the Defense of Marriage Act (DOMA). The former banned gays from serving in the military, and the latter banned gay marriage. In 2012, with the Obama-Biden team in reelection trouble, Biden came out in favor of gay marriage. This actually forced Obama's hand, and Obama quickly rolled the dice and adopted the same position.[546]

There are plenty of other examples, but this should be a sufficient start. Because Biden lacks core beliefs, he does what the party wants. He is a follower, not a leader.

Biden corrupted the judicial confirmation process and polarized America. Biden is running as a uniter to bring people together from the divisive Trump presidency. Very few people did more to divide Americans than Biden. His time as the Senate Judiciary Committee chairman forever poisoned a once-collegial process. Confirming judges used to be a routine, boring affair. Absent clear malfeasance, Republicans and Democrats banged the gavel, asked a few questions that only the nominee knew the answer to, pretended to stay awake during the answers, banged the gavel again, voted yes, and went to lunch. Ideology was not a factor in confirming judges. It was well understood that elected American presidents could nominate whichever judges they chose. Then came the 1987 Robert Bork Supreme Court nomination hearings.

Bork was one of the finest legal minds ever nominated to the high court. However, after years of liberals dominating the Supreme Court, it was now in danger of becoming conservative. It was easy to be collegial when Democrats controlled everything. Now Republicans were on the verge of winning a Supreme Court majority. This meant a possible overturning of *Roe v. Wade.* When it comes to Democrats and abortion, the ends justify the means. Collegiality had to be tossed out the window. Bork had to be destroyed. Senators Kennedy and Biden led the charge.[547]

Bork's video rental history was leaked to the press. His choice of movies was unremarkable, but it led to the enactment of the 1988 Video Privacy Act. Biden's history of obtaining private records started long before he targeted Flynn. In 1986, Biden stated in an interview that a hypothetical Bork nomination would meet his approval. By 1987, Biden was in full presidential campaign mode. Democrats wanted Bork's head on a platter by any means necessary, and Biden followed his marching orders. Bork's only sin was being a strict constructionist originalist who would have repealed *Roe.*

In 1991, Clarence Thomas found himself in Biden's crosshairs for the exact same reason. Thomas was a textualist to the core in the mold of the conservative icon Scalia. Thomas did not sugarcoat his conservatism or his originalism. When it appeared that Thomas had the votes to be confirmed, Democrats through Anita Hill launched a desperate eleventh-hour sexual harassment accusation against him.

Because Thomas is a black conservative, Democrats were even more hell-bent on ripping him to pieces. Luckily for Thomas, Republicans still seething from the Bork hearings were finally ready to fight back. They did not defend Bork. Thomas was unwilling to be a sitting duck. He offered a passionate defense of his character. Thomas rejected Democratic charges at the hearings in a moment for the ages:

> This is not an opportunity to talk about difficult matters privately or in a closed environment. This is a circus. It's a national disgrace. And from my standpoint, as a black American, as far as I'm concerned it is a high-tech lynching for uppity blacks who in any way deign to think for themselves, to do for themselves, to have different ideas, and it is a message that unless you kowtow to an old order, this is what will happen to you. You will be lynched, destroyed, caricatured by a committee of the U.S. Senate rather than hung from a tree.[548]

Thomas was confirmed, but Biden and his fellow Democrats learned the wrong lesson. Rather than return to civility, Democrats lost that battle because they had not been brutal enough. Republicans tried the civility approach in the Clinton administration. Although Ruth Bader Ginsburg was a leftist ideologue, she was confirmed 97–3. The civility ended when Republicans won back the White House. Democrats launched destructive attacks against Sam Alito[549] and Brett Kavanaugh.[550] The same tactic of alleging unproven sexual harassment charges against Thomas was later amplified against Kavanaugh. Alito and Kavanaugh were both confirmed, but the reputational damage was done. The stakes changed significantly in 2007 when former Senate Majority Leader

Harry Reid began stalling George W. Bush judicial nominees from even getting a vote.[551] Bloody death matches became the norm for judicial confirmation hearings. Joe Biden's embrace of political poison has forever divided us and politicized the one branch that must be seen by both sides as apolitical. Biden wrecked an entire branch of government.

Biden has a history of sexually inappropriate behavior. Biden's Delaware neighbors have alleged for years that Biden used to get drunk and swim in his backyard naked for all to see.[552] What is not an allegation is Biden's hypocrisy regarding his conduct toward women. The man who fought to bring down Thomas and Kavanaugh over sexual misconduct has a lifetime of accusations regarding his own inappropriate behavior toward the fairer sex. The charges range from inappropriate touching up to and including far more serious acts such as sexual assault.

Business Insider compiled a comprehensive list of the eight women who alleged varying degrees of inappropriate behavior by Biden. These accusations spanned the entire range from crude comments to sexual assault.

- **Tara Reade** alleged in April 2019 that Biden touched her in ways that made her feel uncomfortable while she worked in his Senate office in 1993. In March 2020, Reade alleged that Biden sexually assaulted her in 1993.
- **Ally Coll**, a former Democratic staffer, told the *Washington Post* in April 2019 that when she met Biden in 2008, he complimented her smile, squeezed her shoulders, and held her "for a beat too long."
- **Amy Stokes Lappos** alleges Biden pulled her face close to him during a 2009 political fund-raiser.
- **D. J. Hill** alleges Biden rested his hand on her shoulder and moved it down her back at a 2012 fund-raising event in Minneapolis. Hill said the encounter made her "very uncomfortable."

- **Vail Kohnert-Yount**, a former White House intern, said that when she met Biden in 2013, he "put his hand on the back of my head and pressed his forehead to my forehead." Kohnert-Yount also said that Biden called her a "pretty girl."
- **Lucy Flores** alleged in March 2019 that Biden grasped her shoulders from behind and kissed the back of her head without her consent during a campaign event in 2014.
- **Sofie Karasek**, a progressive organizer, was photographed holding hands and touching foreheads with Biden at the 2016 Academy Awards. Karasek said that she felt that Biden violated her personal space in that interaction.
- **Caitlyn Caruso** said that after she shared her story of sexual assault at a University of Nevada event in 2016, Biden hugged her "just a little bit too long" and put his hand on her thigh.[553]

Some of the charges involve salacious details left out of this book for the sake of politeness. Biden deserves the presumption of innocence, but he was never willing to give the benefit of the doubt to accused Republicans from Thomas to Kavanaugh.

All of these women are Democrats. There is no right-wing conspiracy here.

Sadly, Democrats have proven that they will always put the politics of abortion above truly protecting the rights of women. In 1998, Clinton had a sexual relationship with White House intern Monica Lewinsky. Enough liberal women believed that the ends justified the means. Writer Nina Burleigh summed it up in vulgar liberal fashion: "I would be happy to give him a blowjob just to thank him for keeping abortion legal. I think American women should be lining up with their Presidential kneepads on to show their gratitude for keeping the theocracy off our backs."[554]

A new decade brought the same Democrats and the same morally bankrupt whitewashing. In May 2020, Kathy Pollitt of *The Nation* wrote a column subtitled, "I Would Vote for Joe Biden Even if I Believed Tara Reade's Account." The first line of her monstrous column stated, "I would vote for Joe Biden if he boiled babies and ate them."[555]

The White House beat reporters took a different approach. They absolutely refused to cover any of this. Lengthy interviews with Biden would end without a single question on this topic. Follow-ups were out of the question. The truth is known.

Beyond Biden's bad behavior is his hypocrisy. He favored the very changes to Title IX that led to many young men on campuses being treated as guilty and having to prove their innocence. Betsy DeVos reversed those draconian rules. Before the reversal, Biden would have been convicted without due process of the very charges he currently faces.[556]

Biden is a liar. Forget the standard broken promises of your average politician. This is about character. In Biden's case, it is about a lack of character that transcends politics.

During the 2020 campaign, Biden tried to clean up one of his many racially insensitive flubs by claiming an NAACP endorsement. The NAACP quickly refuted his claim, insisting that it was a non-partisan organization that has never endorsed anyone in a presidential race.[557] Biden also claimed that he had a full college scholarship and finished in the top half of his class. He had a partial scholarship and finished near the bottom 10 percent of his class.[558] Biden has a history of whoppers, including an odd story about a gangster named Corn Pop.[559] These are dismissed as harmless, but his worst lie was as harmful as it gets.

By now, the whole world knows about the tragic 1972 car crash that took the life of Biden's first wife and their young daughter. His two sons were injured but recovered. Biden himself was not in the car. It was a horror no man should experience. As awful as the loss of his wife is, having a child predecease a parent is every parent's nightmare. Biden almost quit his political career before it began but decided to serve. He found love again and seems to be very happy with his second wife, Dr. Jill Biden. He gets choked up talking about his first wife, as any decent husband and father would. All of this is true.

For whatever reason, perhaps to ease the pain, Biden chose to lie about the circumstances surrounding the crash. To this day, Biden claims that his wife and daughter were the victims of a drunk guy on a tractor trailer. The trailer driver did collide with Mrs. Biden's car. However, the accident was her fault. She blew through a stop sign. The trailer driver immediately rushed over to Neilia Biden and tried to save her. He clutched her to him and got her blood all over his clothing. He called the police immediately. The police investigated fully and determined that Mrs. Biden was indeed at fault. The truck driver had zero alcohol or drugs in his system. This was a tragic accident, and the living victim truck driver tried to be the Good Samaritan. Until the day he died, it bothered him that a rich, powerful senator and then vice president accused him of being a drunk and a killer.

Biden must give a small measure of comfort to the truck driver's daughter. Her father's name was Curtis C. Dunn. For the last 27 years of his life, he was slandered by Biden in the worst way.[560] Mr. Dunn deserves to have his good name restored. Biden has spent 27 years squandering away anything remotely resembling a good name.

Biden has been wrong on foreign policy for 40 years. Pick any bad actor, and Biden has been on the wrong side.

- **China.** Biden ridiculed Trump for claiming that China was a strategic competitor and a threat. The COVID-19 pandemic threw Biden for a loop. He began arguing two completely contradictory foreign policy approaches. On the one hand, Trump blames China to cover up his own failures. On the other hand, Trump is too soft on China, and Biden would be much tougher. Biden cannot make up his mind. Biden never said what he would do, but Trump has been tougher on China than any of his predecessors. China is a nuclear power, which means that any retaliation must be economic. When

China saber-rattled against Taiwan and slowly dismantled freedoms in Hong Kong, Obama and Biden said nothing and did nothing. When China engaged in massive cyberhacking and theft of intellectual property of American consumers and products, Obama and Biden said nothing and did nothing.[561]

- **Iraq.** Biden opposed the first Gulf War in 1990. That war was the epitome of the very multilateralism that Democrats cherish. The war was quick, decisive, and successful. Saddam Hussein was driven out of Kuwait, and those who opposed the war looked foolish for their doomsday predictions. Biden did support the second Gulf War in 2003 before turning against it just in time for his 2008 presidential run (the liberal base was rabidly anti-war). He also recommended a completely unworkable plan to partition Iraq into three separate countries. The Obama-Biden administration's dreadful decision to withdraw from Iraq led to the creation of a new terror group called ISIS.[562]

- **Iran.** Biden supported the disastrous Iran deal[563] that had Iran on a glide path to a nuclear bomb. Trump withdrew from the deal, increased sanctions, and put Iran in a financial straitjacket. Trump's targeted drone strike of Soleimani was a complete success.[564] Biden condemned the strike and predicted an imminent Iran war. Trump correctly predicted Iran's subsequent meekness.

- **Israel.** Biden claims to be pro-Israel, but left-wing pressure had him adopting the Palestinian platform. Trump is revered in Israel and has streets named after him. Secretary Pompeo reversed 40 years of anti-Israel State Department policy by declaring Jewish homes in Judea and Samaria fully legal and compliant with international law.[565] The Obama-Biden team declared them illegal and repeatedly pressured Israel to make suicidal concessions. Trump closed PLO offices on American soil. Biden vowed to reopen them.[566]

- **Russia.** When 2012 GOP nominee Mitt Romney warned about Russia, Obama mocked him in a debate. Obama and Biden totally dismissed the idea of Russia as a threat.[567] When Vladimir Putin's Russia gobbled up Crimea, Obama and Biden impotently watched, said nothing, and did nothing.[568] When Putin took steps to become president for life, Obama and Biden said nothing and did nothing.

- **Ukraine.** When Ukraine begged for self-defense weapons, Obama and Biden left them high and dry. Trump got them the needed weapons.[569] Trump encouraged the Ukrainian leader to crack down on corruption. Biden is part of that very corruption.

- **ISIS.** This organization did not exist until Obama and Biden fled Iraq on an arbitrary timetable. This was solely to keep a campaign promise, ignoring reality on the ground. ISIS came in and captured mass amounts of territory in their goal of a regional caliphate. Biden ridiculed Trump's plan to "bomb the hell out of ISIS" as bluster. Trump meant it. General Mattis did exactly that, eradicating ISIS in a total and complete victory.[570] The successful raid that killed of ISIS leader Abu Bakr al-Baghdadi was an exclamation point.

- **Al-Qaeda.** Biden spent the 2012 campaign bragging that the Obama administration got Osama bin Laden and put al-Qaeda on the run. Biden was against the strike on bin Laden and was lucky that Obama overruled him (after chickening out the first three times because Valerie Jarrett worried about political fallout).[571] Killing bin Laden was a symbolic victory, but the organization was still thriving until Trump came in and took the shackles off the U.S. military. The killing of bin Laden by Rob O'Neill[572] of Seal Team Six happened with help from Bush-Cheney coercive interrogation methods that Obama and Biden wanted to make illegal.[573]

There are not enough trees to produce the pages needed to cover all of Biden's wrong actions, wrong inactions, and overall bungled actions. As bad as he has been, the current state of his party will make him worse.

Biden is a puppet of the radical left. Because of his advanced age, cognitive decline, and lack of core beliefs and a governing philosophy, Biden, if elected, would be a very weak leader. He wanted to run a centrist campaign, but his party would not let him. He was not strong enough to push back against the left like Bill Clinton did. Biden won the nomination by default because the Democratic National Committee was desperate in 2016 and 2020 to stop Sanders at all costs. Biden was dead in the water until House Majority Whip James Clyburn rescued him in South Carolina. Biden owes his political life to black voters. He knows it, and they know it. Biden also backed himself into a corner by promising during one of the primary debates that his vice presidential choice would be a woman.

Because of his giving in to identity politics, Biden had to placate various leftist constituencies that will hurt him among moderate voters. The increasing influence of the squad led by AOC and Omar are an albatross around his neck. His failure to stand up to them was a major factor in his undoing.

While Biden was an inconsequential vice president, his own choice for the vice presidency will be very consequential. The five main contenders are all awful for a variety of reasons. They all come with drawbacks.

- **Stacey Abrams** of Georgia never won a statewide race. She never held an actual job. She has financial scandals swirling around her student loans and her various community organizing groups that seem to be nothing more than political rabble rouser training grounds. She is a black woman who openly campaigned for the vice presidency and threatened Biden that he would lose unless he picked a black woman.[574]
- **Gretchen Whitmer** of Michigan is a first-term governor who is growing more hated by the day. While her state is

strategically important, her draconian lockdown measures during the COVID-19 crisis backfired and energized Republicans in her state.[575] Biden needs a very capable teammate. Whitmer seemed to blow a shot at that label.

- **Liz Warren** of Massachusetts is the darling of the angry left. She has a fairly safe senate seat but zero appeal in the other 49 states. She engenders more hostility among Republicans than Hillary Clinton, an impressive accomplishment. Warren never expanded her appeal beyond upper-class older white liberals. The younger leftists preferred Sanders. Warren is also incapable of giving a speech without screaming her lungs out. Trump all but begged to run against her. Her history of lying about everything from her ethnicity to job history to her family was the last strike.[576]

- **Kamala Harris** of California is vapid, and everyone in Democratic circles knows it. On paper, she looks perfect. When she speaks, she is underwhelming. She had to explain why she would campaign with a man that she labeled a racist when she was running against him.[577] The black community had high hopes for her, but her record on putting plenty of black people in jail on minor drug offenses worked against her. Her own fellow Senator Dianne Feinstein endorsed Biden over her. She has the looks and the charm but not the substance. She has a history of fibs about her background. How she even got to where she is politically is too scandalous to print. Ask Willie Brown.[578]

- **Amy Klobuchar** of Minnesota is the closest thing Democrats have to a normal person. She was the only Democrat who questioned Judge Kavanaugh in a manner that was remotely dignified.[579] Minnesota is an important state, and Klobuchar is well regarded in her home state. She would be the favorite if not for her being white. Black voters absolutely did not want her. She is the most sane and the least objectionable of the bunch, but the bar is low. Like Biden, she is cagey about what she actually stands for.

Whoever Biden picks, one constant remains. Biden is a complete disaster personally, politically, and on policy. He is not remotely qualified to be president. Trump is more successful than Biden on every level and every honest metric.

Trump successfully governed as a conservative. Conservatism works. Biden surrendered to the hard left. Leftism is failure.

The decision is easy. Donald J. Trump deserves to be reelected as the president of the United States.

Part V

A BONUS
CHAPTER

Babies Are Beautiful
and So Are Women's Rights

Abortion

A lot has changed radically and recently in this most sensitive of American political policy arenas. On the pro-choice side, the Reproductive Health Act of New York was passed on January 22, 2019. Prior to the passage of the Reproductive Health Act (RHA), New York law banned third-trimester abortions except when necessary to save the life of a pregnant woman. Unborn children can now be aborted at the time of dilation on the day of birth. Before the RHA was passed, New York law required that only licensed physicians perform abortions. Now licensed healthcare practitioners can perform them. The RHA also removed abortion from the criminal code, with potential consequences for crimes against pregnant women. It passed in a room full of cheers and applause led by Democrat Governor Cuomo as a landmark passage and a pinnacle of victory for women's rights.

Democrat Governor Ralph Northam signed Virginia House Bill 2491. The new law rolled back a number of prior abortion requirements, including a 24-hour waiting period and a mandate that second-trimester abortions take place in a hospital. House Bill 2491 also changed the prior laws requiring women during their third trimester of pregnancy to be evaluated by three doctors to confirm that the pregnancy is life-threatening before an abortion is permitted. Now only one doctor is required to do the evaluation, and terminating the pregnancy is permissible if the mother's "mental or physical health is threatened." Abortion opponents argued that, like the New York law, this new law would technically allow abortion until the point of birth if the sole doctor deemed it was necessary.

In Virginia, more so than New York, several more restrictive elements still exist. A woman can generally still only receive an abortion up until 25 weeks of gestation. Other minor stipulations also remain in place. In order to receive an abortion, a woman must have an ultrasound performed at least 24 hours beforehand. She must be given the option to view the ultrasound image. She must also have state-directed counseling with information designed to discourage an abortion 24 hours before an abortion is performed. A minor seeking an abortion must receive the consent of a parent or legal guardian.[580]

On the pro-life side, the Alabama legislature passed House Bill 314, also known as the Human Life Protection Act (HLPA). HLPA fully banned abortion, aside from very limited exceptions. House Bill 314 is the nation's most restrictive abortion law. Performing abortion at any stage of pregnancy is a felony with a possible penalty of life in prison for the mother or doctor performing the procedure.

Georgia passed the hotly contested House Bill 481 that would have outlawed abortions as early as six weeks into a pregnancy at the start of 2020. District Judge Steve C. Jones stopped the bill from taking effect on January 1. The Georgia Chapter of the American Civil Liberties Union (ACLU) sued the state. The Georgia ACLU claimed that House Bill 481, which bans most abortions once a doctor can detect fetal cardiac activity, violates a woman's constitutional right to abortion established by the Supreme Court ruling in *Roe v. Wade*.[581]

Abortion has always been a difficult topic for Americans.
The CDC found that virtually all U.S. abortions occur within 13
weeks of gestation. Two-thirds of abortions occur within 8 weeks.
About only 1 percent of abortions take place after 21 weeks. As for
this 1 percent of over 638,169 (or as many as 832,000 total abortions
including illegal abortions) that take place per year in America, our
citizenry has become even more divided on the fate of these approximately 6,300 to 8,000 unborn children.[582]

These recent American policy changes have even more greatly
fueled the fire of conflict regarding abortion nationwide. The questions of the primacy of life, women's rights, and even the barbarism
of possible infanticide have been aggressively raised. The issue is so
personal and so primal. It has moved beyond politics in its most
essential nature.

For just this reason, I approach this bonus chapter much more
personally than globally. There is also a reason that this chapter was
labeled "Chapter 13½," even though abortion is far from just an
afterthought or merits less than a full chapter.

When it comes to abortion, there should be a struggle in any
compassionate evolved country. This is a sign of both the moral and
mental health of our country.

It may be unpopular to say, but before I am a Republican or a
conservative, I am first an American. I trust that when we struggle,
we are thinking. Then we fight passionately on issues. Democracies
thrive on this debate and require it.

The abortion issue is powerful and unique. It is so essential to our
personhood that it falls outside of our social, foreign, and domestic
policies, our national identity, and even ideological lines themselves.
As for the reasons "not to be a liberal," it's not that simple.

The abortion issue, agree or disagree, does not an ideology make.
Regardless of what liberals try to tell you, you can be a pro-choice
conservative and still benefit from the rest of the timeless truths the
Framers intended for you. Individual rights, free markets, and natural rights make up a strong conservative ideology.

The vote composition of the pro-life versus pro-choice split itself reflects the complexity of this struggle clearly. People *should* struggle on who has primacy when it comes to abortion, the rights of American women and the rights of unborn American children.

Nate Silver in a *FiveThirtyEight* column called, "The Abortion Debate Isn't as Partisan as Politicians Make It Seem," points out:

> The issue is not a 50/50 Democrat/Republican split, as the plurality of Americans consistently take the "pro-choice" position over the "pro-life" one. Yet the public, unlike political elites, is not completely divided along party lines on this issue. There is a large bloc of Republicans who support abortion rights. There is a smaller, but still sizable group called "Democrats for Life" that has 45 House members who oppose abortion rights.
>
> On top of that, a recent national poll showed 22 percent of voting Democrats are pro-life. 34 percent of Republicans are pro-choice and say that abortion should be legal or agree with the *Roe v. Wade* decision. That's not a small number of citizens to be counter to their party position.[583]

Furthermore, who knows where Americans as a whole really stand on this highly politicized yet deeply personal issue? Abortion undeniably highly influences American female voters, and many politicians put power before convictions in the modern day. These numbers may be far from accurate.

On the Democratic side, there was once a larger bloc of anti-abortion Democrats in Congress, but many of those members were from the South. Republicans now largely control those seats and the region.

On the Republican side, Susan Bevan and Susan Cullman led a group called "Republican Majority for Choice." They announced that they would leave the GOP and that their group would cease operations, arguing that there was no room for their cause in the current

Republican Party. They claimed that there is "hostility to women within the Republican culture."[584] They simply chose to dodge the bullet and focus on other policies because of votes regardless of their convictions.

As Silver continues:

Also, just as the Christian right made it a key GOP policy goal to reverse *Roe v. Wade* and limit abortions, pro-abortion-rights groups pushed the Democrat Party into making abortion rights more central to the party's identity—so much so that the party inserted a provision into its 2016 platform that called for the government to overturn a ban on using federal funding to pay for abortions. The ban, called the Hyde Amendment, has been in place since the 1970s.[585]

The sanctity of life versus the sanctity of women's right to their own bodies is an emotionally messy picture. Democrats admittedly lean more pro-choice and Republicans pro-life. Because this issue is about the paramount matter of human life beyond a typical policy battle (and the abortion issue has huge political and emotional clout), it's important to be not only aware of but also compassionate toward this issue of real demographic complexity.

On this issue, it's easy to just default to the woman's right to choose. There is a reason for this. It is undeniably her body. "Hell hath no fury like a woman scorned" is particularly relevant when it comes to abortion, as shown by the millions of women willing to march in the pouring rain on this very issue.

I, adhering to the ideal of both colorblind and gender-blind conservatism, politically view people, including myself, as citizens first and everything else second. I'm still primarily concerned with the message our policies stand for and mean to the world. We are not alone. Our standard of living is both viewed by and monitored by the world.

Life is sacred. Let's temporarily move away from the lens of the rights of American women (and all women) for one moment. I believe, given all that I have said throughout this book, that no one portends that any decent American citizen disagrees with this fact.

There's a reason our Constitution's "Life, Liberty and the pursuit of Happiness," places this sacred word *life* first. America is a moral leader of the world not by choice as much as by chance of the fates of history. We are not Europe. We are not China. We are not the Middle East. We are America. How we treat our citizens from the cradle to the grave or even farther back from the womb to the tomb matters. It is once again not about us alone. This is the cost of leadership and our great blessings.

JFK's inaugural address was a call to action for the greater good. If you indeed love America and the planet and seek world peace, our ethics must be global.

At inception or at birth, our citizens' value is an example to the world of how we as citizens value the sanctity of life. This is especially true in our American role in the defense against global evil. We always take it.

The numbers are staggering: More than 638,169 legally induced abortions were reported to the CDC as of its last fully reported year of record. This is down from approximately 1.4 million in 1980, but note that the abortion pill's use is harder to track.

When China took a position of death due to its one-child policy, abortions became excessive. The state was causing abortions. Estimates counted 336 million abortions total, or around 13 million abortions a year during this policy. Since 2016, all Chinese couples have been allowed two children. This eased abortions, yet China is now ordering families to have abortions or pay huge fines. Because of state control, there are now also 61 million children left behind, many being raised by their grandparents as parents work in distant factories. Many loyal Communist Party women are simply told when they must abort. They must remember and believe that the state knows best. Society's needs are greater than those of individuals. We are not China, and this is hard to even imagine for a free American woman. Yet some context matters because we are discussing a very sensitive issue.

Notably, American women are radically free already, according to the Guttmacher Institute:

Out of 195 global countries, 26 countries fully ban abortion: Andorra; Malta; San Marino; Angola; Congo-Brazzaville; Congo-Kinshasa; Egypt; Gabon; Guinea-Bissau; Madagascar; Mauritania; São Tomé & Príncipe; Senegal; Iraq; Laos; Marshall Islands; Micronesia; Palau; Philippines; Tonga; Dominican Republic; El Salvador; Haiti; Honduras; Nicaragua; and Suriname.

Another 37 countries ban abortion unless it is necessary to save the life of the woman. These include major economies such as Mexico, Brazil, Nigeria, Indonesia, and the UAE. Another 36 countries restrict access unless an abortion is necessary to protect the woman's physical health. These include three European countries—Poland, Lichtenstein and Monaco—as well as South Korea, Jordan, Argentina and Costa Rica.

Another 24 countries include protecting the woman's mental health as grounds for access. These include New Zealand, Israel, Malaysia, Colombia and Thailand. In El Salvador, where abortion is totally banned, authorities can prosecute women whose pregnancies end before 40 weeks even if by miscarriage or stillbirth if they are suspected of harming their fetus. Prison sentences range from two to eight years. Some women have been convicted on charges of aggravated homicide and sentenced for up to 30 years.

Overall, only 37 percent of the world's 1.64 billion women of reproductive age live in countries where unrestricted abortion is permitted. Additionally, according to a UN report, in the last five years only nine countries in the world have a higher reported abortion rate than the United States. They are Bulgaria, Cuba, Estonia, Georgia, Kazakhstan, Romania, Russia, Sweden, and the Ukraine.

Many liberals glamourize Europe as a good progressive secular model that America should follow. With regard to abortion, that is decisively untrue. Europe is less pro-choice than America. In Germany all abortion is illegal after 12 weeks. There is a three-day waiting period and mandated counseling even during the first 12 weeks. This is more restrictive than Texas. America's states vary from 20 to 25 weeks with seven states allowing abortion at any time. France, Belgium, Denmark and Finland only allow abortion during the first 12 weeks, and only after a six-day waiting period to reconsider the decision. Sweden allows abortion only up to 18 weeks. After that, approval by a medical board is required.[586]

The United States, in turn, remains incredibly free when it comes to aborting the unborn.

Again, the overarching point is how America handles the rights of its citizenry. America is always on trial on the global stage.

After years of in-depth research and personal conflict, I stand solidly to the right of center on this issue, but with some cautious moderation. I believe that as Americans, not just men or women, we should allow our government to hold the position of protecting the sanctity of life for these many global and ethical reasons. Yet I also believe that we should allow the states to do as they choose without penalty, as the Federalist system was created. It remains an undeniably increasingly complex issue.

Although it may be inconvenient and idealistic, today's women can vote with their feet about where they want to live or choose to cross state lines. We can still honor both considerations of the national sanctity of life and states' rights. This is not because I want to restrict women's rights. I am a Federalist when it comes to our Bill of Rights.

The 1973 *Roe v. Wade* decision legalized abortion nationwide, but it is imperative to understand that overturning Roe would not mean a nationwide abortion ban. It would give jurisdiction back to the states, each of which would be able to decide whether or not to allow abortion within its borders.[587] This could possibly restrict 21 states, but political advocates would quickly create the infrastructures to get women to nearby states with citizen-based funding. Others could move if the restrictions so dictated.

Some women might choose to have children in their home states rather than travel. Many adopting couples wait in states with strict abortion restrictions. Some sources estimate that there are about 2 million couples currently waiting to adopt in the United States. This translates to as many as 36 couples waiting for every one child who is placed for adoption. There are estimated to be between 600,000 and 800,000 abortions a year in the United States. As sterile and clinical as this sounds, there is more demand than supply for children to be born rather than aborted. If demand didn't meet supply, this could be addressed by easing the highly bureaucratic U.S. adoption laws. It remains a noble choice to take a baby to term for the many families seeking to adopt. Although some adopted children do have difficulties adjusting, adoption far outweighs the chance to never experience consciousness, life, love, school, work, marriage, parenthood, and old age. Cumbersome U.S. adoption regulations force many families to spend tens of thousands of dollars adopting babies from Russia, China, and elsewhere.

Abortion can also lead to long-term psychological pain that should never be minimized from this discussion. There are many side effects of abortion, the greatest being emotional. Dr. David C. Reardon studied the link between abortion and domestic violence:

There is an important connection between violence in the womb and violence in the home. Certainly not every abortion leads to domestic violence, nor is every case of domestic violence rooted in the trauma of a prior abortion. Still,

abortion and domestic violence rates have risen together
during the last twenty-five years. That is not coincidental. Correlation is so compelling that it is beyond dispute. The two key elements related to post-abortion violence
are: 1) increased levels of irritability, anger, and rage, and 2)
increased tendencies toward risk-taking, self-destructive,
and suicidal behaviors.

In an Elliot Institute study of 260 women, 53 percent stated
that after their abortion, they started losing their temper more easily.
Forty-eight percent became more violent when angered. Self-hatred,
hatred of the male, and hatred of men in general were all significantly
correlated with each other. In this same sample, 56 percent reported
experiencing suicidal feelings, with 28 percent actually attempting
suicide one or more times. Approximately 37 percent described
themselves as self-destructive. Another 13 percent were unwilling to
rule out the possibility that they had become self-destructive.

Suicidal tendencies and self-destructive behavior were statistically associated with shorter tempers and increased anger and violence levels. Short-temperedness and self-destructive behavior were
significantly associated with feeling less in touch with one's emotions, feeling unable to grieve, fake displays of happiness, and feeling
less control over one's life.[588]

This is a far cry from a morally relativistic net-zero equation.
It's hard to lose a potential child on the body of a mother. There are
long-term, path-altering life consequences for those who go through
abortion.

I'd like to get personal as I conclude this book.

I'm an ex-liberal turned conservative and pro-life today only after a whole decade of struggling with every facet of this complex issue. I also admit hypocrisy on this matter.

Fortunately, for many years I've had the great benefit of my faith to deal with my imperfections and hypocrisies as I have grown. I have also had a large circle of compassionate, loving friends and family to grant me emotional support in regard to the more challenging events of my life. They and God have given me enough compassion over the years to openly discuss these personal truths here now. I think it is important for the purpose of this chapter to speak more personally. Looking directly at the reality of life and yourself is, as I have stated repeatedly, the essence of being a conservative.

As a young liberal man, I had my own experiences with abortion.

The first experience happened while I was in college. My deeply embedded liberal values from my hard-left college did not empower me to advocate for what I wanted: the opportunity to have the child, even if we were to put it up for adoption. It was a horrible experience.

As a parent today, I know that this unborn being may have been the greatest blessing of our lives regardless of the personal, societal, career, or financial costs that may have followed. Now, later in life, I also know that God, just as he always has, would have provided for us all, regardless of whether we stayed together. Sadly, we didn't yet have the right ideology in place to know and trust these greater truths at that youthful time.

A decade later in Los Angeles and still a liberal, the woman I was involved with decided to terminate a pregnancy without consulting me—there were extenuating medical circumstances—but the fact remains I was not fully informed beforehand.

Given my political party of the time, I cannot say if I would still have had a voice to stand for the life of our unborn child. Obviously, our potentially unborn child never had his or hers. As a liberal, I was overwhelmingly educated that a woman's right to choose was unequivocally dominant to the right for a child to be born or my own rights as a father. We never spoke of it again.

My own actions were irresponsible, but once again, I found myself silenced by my liberal programming. Of course, it was her choice ultimately, but my party's ideological positions had engineered me to become morally relative about life. The noble struggle to always do what is highest and best, regardless of inconvenience, risk, or consequence, where one boldly takes full responsibility for oneself in the light of both God and natural law, was not yet ensconced.

Another significant event also greatly evolved my position on the abortion issue. Years later, my prior business partner, an intense but kind man, came into my life. He was the result of an unwanted pregnancy and was put up for adoption at birth. He went on from this very precarious beginning to enlist and fight in the Marines in Operation Desert Storm. In the Gulf War, he served as a point man destroying tanks with hand-held weaponry. He went on to college on the G.I. Bill and later became very successful in real estate.

When we first met, I was newly married with two stepdaughters and had just entered commercial real estate. We had no savings and nothing to fall back on. I was scrambling, and it was not yet going as well as it is today. After meeting in random circumstances, my future partner decided that he liked my work ethic. Despite my much lower than average abilities, he took a great risk on scouting me for one of the nation's top five financial institutions. Through many bureaucratic denials, he fought for and succeeded in bringing me in. This event radically changed me, my wife, and the lives of our children.

A relentless bulldog, every two weeks for three years straight, he would fly into Los Angeles from Texas and push me from 6:00 a.m. to 2:00 a.m. into exhausted dizziness training me. As the ex-Marine he was, he drilled into me how to achieve excellence in our field via solely intense hard work, high ethics, and intelligent hustle. Within a few years, I had fought from the very bottom to the top by working hard, passionate American 18 to 20 hour days under his intense and believing hand.

A proud, respected American with six wonderful children of his own, he partially retired. He remains passionately active in his church, coaching, and raising his kids. He later found his birth parents, who cried when they reunited, telling him he was a miracle.

They told him how poor and broke they were at the time they gave him up. It was only at the very last minute that they walked out of the abortion clinic just as his mother was getting on the procedural table.

He has since returned to be a beloved son of both his birth and adoptive families and goes to a large biannual reunion of over 100 newfound relatives. Given the chance to live, he has been blessed by both his faith and the free markets to have the ability to now emotionally and financially care for his birth parents, his adoptive parents, his own family of six, and his community.

I often wonder, had I not abdicated my more enduring beliefs because of my deep liberal indoctrination (via my leftist college, my years in the Hollywood entertainment sector, and later as a Democrat Party activist), what paths my children and I may have taken. Not a season passes that I don't think about where they might be and what deeds, like my friend, they may have accomplished.

All that being said, rather than have those first two children in both my early twenties and thirties, I later raised two lovely stepdaughters. I was blessed with the joyous, painful, grand, and selfless journey of parenthood anyway. God works in mysterious ways indeed.

That's the abortion issue. It is not just a right or left issue to our individual citizenry. It is not a reason to accept or reject an entire political ideology based on this sole issue.

This chapter ultimately transcends ideology. As for the further arguments on this very sensitive personal topic, I leave the deeper questions and answers up to you.

It is not a comfortable conversation to have, yet it is a noble one to never cease having. Just like this ongoing conversation, we must never cease debating about our great country and its sacred future as well.

Conclusion

First Principles, Final Thoughts

Certain themes become truer over time. History, by definition, takes time. The Revolutionary War in 1775 did not come full circle until 1788 when New Hampshire became the ninth and final state required to fully adopt the Constitution. Change also takes time. My own journey to conservatism took a decade and a half.

Regardless of emotions, opinions, or any given news cycle, it remains true that natural law and the divine continue to be the bedrock philosophical anchors holding our great American ship in its unique and sacred harbor. They are my principles as well. They are also ideals that are timeless and true. These ideals are beyond relativity or subjectivity. Aligning with these principles doesn't mean being regressive or stuck in the past. It means that we simply don't deconstruct those things good, true, and enduring that work regarding the highest freedom and natural rights of the American individual. We conserve these principles —thus, the essence of conservatism.

This is the true north behind all the previous chapters on the issues. Sadly, these ideals and principles have more than ever become the opposite of current liberal ideology. To be a part of the liberal movement is no longer simply to be a Democrat. Liberalism and progressivism have lives of their own. The push for liberal progressivism has become exceedingly anti-foundational in nature.

Liberalism today offers open-bordered globalism over nationalism, shame about our heritage over patriotism, overreliance on the state versus fierce individual freedom, and hypersensitivity and political correctness over the rough-and-tumble American durability of spirit. Extreme liberalism, which is growing in strength, sacrifices tangible, measured returns in favor of the failed socialist and communist experiments of the past.

Limited government works. Truly free markets work. Over-regulation of the human entrepreneurial spirit does not work. Expanding protected classes of victims over using more eternal standards of justice and equality for all citizens does not work. The evidence is clear, and the examples are legion.

There are many problems and challenges ahead for our country if the trend toward perfecting human beings through greater government increases any further. Modern liberalism's universal approach underwrites a postnational globalism that could ultimately destroy American politics and usher in an elitist, destructive new technocratic empire.

Progressivism's intentions remain full of nonexecutable lofty ideals at odds with the true nature of humanity and reality itself. The very idea that government itself can protect people from all the pains and inequalities of life remains folly.[589] This book clearly reveals this repeatedly and in careful detail. In opposition to what is sold to the masses, there is no fullest and final achievement of civilization. Nothing gives rise to a final triumph that the new brand of liberalism seems to promise.

It's just not the nature of things. By contrast, the inequalities that life inherently has in store for all of us can best be endured and overcome by self-determination and a deep inner journey supported by faith, friends, and family. If government ever takes on those three roles, all is lost. Our founding tries to guarantee that the state is simply here to serve us in limited form to allow us to go on these journeys as individuals. With its recent near-religious zeal and anti-conservative heresy hunting, contemporary liberalism claims to be the last and only hope for humanity. Nothing could be further from the truth. Less government and trusting American citizens' own individual liberty are the solution.

That is the greater fight. To fight in matters social and political, we must stay open-minded and listen humbly with an intention to learn and understand.

This may not sound political, but this contrarian position derives directly from the biblical rule of loving your neighbor as yourself. If you love America, you must love her citizens even when fiercely fighting for your own contra beliefs. Their dissent is their God-given American birthright. We true conservatives must take only one road, the high road.

It has been said that 70 percent of Americans in theory pretty much agree on 70 percent of the issues. This gives us a lot of operating room in any discussion. We also must stay vigilantly informed from multiple sources. We must avoid groupthink and stay "conscious." With our modern media and ever-intrusive technology and big business and big politics increasing their capacity to influence our thoughts and minds, we must remain vigilantly aware. Presenting facts and history to get past labels has never been so important. Whether it is a social media post or a one-on-one encounter, let us never forget that we all help shape public policy on a collective level via every discussion we have had.

We are all negotiating. We are all just trying to make a deal.

In essence, that is how America works.

Epilogue

The George Floyd Riots

A s this book went to press, a decade of rioting by disparate leftist organizations reached a crescendo after the murder of George Floyd. Although the officers were charged within four days of the murder, that was not enough to satiate the mob. Floyd was the excuse, but these were preplanned riots that were carefully funded and organized. Bricks were carefully deposited and strategically placed in cities throughout America. The rioters knew exactly where to pick up the bricks. Social media allowed rioters to coordinate attacks on vulnerable areas and avoid areas with a stronger police presence. Leftist mayors ordered police to stand down and allow the chaos to spread. Looters robbed stores blind and arsonists set businesses ablaze. Even the tiny fraction of people who were arrested were released on their own recognizance under cashless bail laws. These mayors threw their police departments under the bus.

Antifa, Black Lives Matter, and other leftist agitators began by setting Minneapolis on fire. Mayor Jacob Frey ordered police officers to abandon the Third Police Precinct. The mob then burned that police station to the ground. Upon seeing the complete surrender of police officers, emboldened leftist mobs wreaked havoc in other cities as well.

Seattle became the first city in America to develop a no-go zone modeled after Islamic mini-caliphates in France. The Capitol Hill Autonomous Zone (CHAZ) covered six blocks of downtown Seattle. Despite a police precinct being within the CHAZ zone, self-appointed armed guards banned police from the area. CHAZ then changed its name to CHOP, the Capitol Hill Organized Protest. Residents and business owners within the CHOP zone begged police for help, but assistance never came. Seattle Mayor Jenny Durkan smugly declared that CHOP was a peaceful protest that would turn into a "Summer of Love." As was expected, the mob then turned on Durkan and protested outside her home. Only then did she declare the riots problematic. She ordered the CHOP zone closed down once her own safety became an issue.

An Antifa splinter group calling itself the Pacific Northwest Youth Liberation Front (PNYLF) wreaked havoc in Portland. Mayor Ted Wheeler prohibited the police from using force to disperse the PNYLF. As expected, the PNYLF rioted daily for two straight months without interruption.

New York City Mayor Bill de Blasio allowed Black Lives Matter protesters to ignore curfews and loot stores at will. He pleaded for patience and offered platitudes about not harming police officers. The officers themselves saw his words as insincere, and the criminals took full advantage. Assaults on officers drastically increased.

Frey, Durkan, Wheeler, and de Blasio are all white leftists. Their states of Minnesota, Washington, Oregon, and New York all have white leftist governors who permitted the mayors to undermine the police officers.

Black Lives Matter provided the fig leaf for the violence, but many of the businesses that burned down in the Minneapolis riots were owned by black people. A large majority of the most violent of the protesters were young upper-class white people. White-collar professionals with six-figure jobs were tossing Molotov cocktails at police cars.

The looting and burning of businesses was just the start. Two more dangerous developments began in the aftermath. The leftist mobs demanded that their cities defund the police. This led to a split between Democrats. The hardcore left wanted police departments abolished. Other Democrats soon realized that this idea was politically toxic in an election year. These Democrats decided that defunding the police did not really mean what its proponents explicitly said it meant. New buzzword phrases included "reimagining the police," "reallocating resources," and "reforming the police." Linguistic gymnastics aside, the result was the same. Leftist city councils drastically reduced law-enforcement budgets. De Blasio slashed one billion dollars from the New York Police Department, a 17 percent cut. Seattle and Minneapolis led efforts to completely abolish their police departments altogether. Even those not willing to completely abolish the police worked to end qualified immunity, which shields police officers from lawsuits.

The consequences were dire. Many officers retired or quit. The reduced police presence led to a rapid increase in violent crime. Murders skyrocketed, and minorities were the ones hurt the most. New York went from being a safe big city to the lawless crime haven it was in the 1970s. Even the murder of a one-year-old girl in Brooklyn did not stop the violence.

Chicago has been a violent city for decades, but now things were spiraling beyond all control. Several children, including a 20-month-old toddler, were killed in the second half of June 2020 alone. A beloved 76-year-old black police officer named David Dorn was murdered by a 24-year-old black man with a history of violent crime. Chicago Mayor Lori Lightfoot took the typical leftist position. She pled for calm, got ignored, refused outside help, and blamed the federal government offering that help.

In addition to coddling the mobs, leftist mayors cracked down hard on police officers and private citizens trying to defend themselves.

Atlanta Mayor Keisha Lance Bottoms demanded that police officer Garrett Rolfe be charged with first-degree murder for the death of Rashard Brooks. Mr. Brooks resisted arrest, grabbed Officer Rolfe's taser, and pointed it at Rolfe. The video of the incident showed a clear case of self-defense. The mayor and an overzealous prosecutor facing his own ethical clouds piled the charges on high and deep.

St. Louis saw the mob forcefully breach a security gate and enter a very wealthy area of the city. The mob finally faced resistance when it reached the home of Mark and Patricia McCloskey. The McCloskeys were told that no police were coming to their aid, so they exercised their Second Amendment rights. They pointed their guns at the mob, and the mob retreated without shots being fired. Leftist St. Louis Mayor Lyda Krewson responded over one week later by finally sending police officers. The mob was long gone. The officers were there to seize the McClosekys' guns. The McCloskeys were under a threat of indictment for legally defending themselves. The mere possession of guns allowed the McCloskeys to keep their home from being torched.

Unlike other cities, Atlanta and St. Louis are blue cities with red state Georgia and Missouri governors. These Republican governors are in contact with the federal government regarding Officer Brooks and the McCloskeys. Jail time for any of these innocent individuals is unlikely. Innocent victims in cities controlled by blue state governors still face the danger of being railroaded by unequal justice based on ideology.

The worst component of the riots came in the form of erasing history. Leftist mobs went beyond demanding the removal of offensive symbols. The mobs physically removed statues in direct violation of existing laws. Statues of Confederate soldiers were vandalized, taken down, broken and burned. Then statues of the Founding

Fathers were targeted for removal. Presidents George Washington and Abraham Lincoln were derided as racist slave-owning bigots. Even noted black abolitionists were vandalized and removed.

Cancel culture spread everywhere. Democrats demanded the removal of everyone and everything they had praised only several years earlier. Mount Rushmore was deemed a racist symbol. The National Anthem was targeted for replacement. These combined actions constituted nothing less than the attempted eradication of American history. Businesses unwilling to placate the social justice left were threatened with boycotts. A harmless food company named Goya spent decades feeding and providing jobs for thousands of Hispanics. The Hispanic Goya CEO was targeted with a boycott for praising the president in July 2020.

Looting stores, burning down buildings, defunding the police, and tearing down statues are all acts of lawlessness. Rather than bolster the police presence, leftist mayors did the precise opposite. Throw in the seizing of guns and additional quarantine lockdowns. The results are a dangerous suppression of human liberty and freedom.

The president repeatedly offered to send in federal help to restore order and calm. The few mayors who initially accepted his help saw the violence decrease. The National Guard successfully restored order. The most hardened of the leftist mayors who continually refused his help saw their cities engulfed in crime and violence. Those mayors have all but dared the president to send in military troops in an election year. Meanwhile, innocent people, including children, kept getting shot to death. Cities are on the verge of complete societal breakdown and collapse. Leftist mayors responded by demanding federal bailouts to repair the damage that their own supporters committed and they condoned. Their demands were rejected outright.

The federal government by executive order reiterated and expanded 1964 legislation that declared any vandalism of a statue a federal crime punishable by a decade in prison. Antifa members have complained about getting arrested. If the left wins the White

House and controls the election, the lawlessness in the cities will explode exponentially. The previous decade provides the evidence.

Notes

1. Prager, Dennis, "The Bigger the Government, the Smaller the Citizen," Prager.com, September 1, 2009.
2. Friedman, Milton, "Interview with Richard Heffner," *Open Mind*, December 7, 1975.
3. Lemon, Don, CNN, July 29, 2013.
4. "A Rebirth of Self-Reliance? Food Stamp, Welfare, Medicaid, Disability Rolls All Dropping under Trump," *Investor's Business Daily*, April 27, 2018.
5. Jacoby, Jeff, "Frank's Fingerprints Are All over the Financial Fiasco," *Boston Globe*, September 28, 2008.
6. Obama, Barack, Remarks to his Jobs and Competitive Council, June 13, 2011.
7. Obama, Barack, Campaign rallies from June 2009 through June 2010.
8. Drobnic Holan, Angie, "Lie of the Year," Politico, December 12, 2013.
9. "Solyndra," Wikipedia.
10. Obama, Barack, Campaign rally in Columbia, Missouri, October 30, 2008.
11. Emanuel, Rahm, "CEO Council 2008: Shaping the New Agenda," *Wall Street Journal*, November 17, 2008.
12. "My Pillow Founder Opens Up about Addiction," Salvationarmynorth.org, December 29, 2015.
13. Marshall, John, "The Power to Tax Is the Power to Destroy," *McCulloch v. Maryland*, 1789.
14. Del Beccaro, Thomas, *The New Conservative Paradigm*, TMK Books, January 2008.
15. "The Return of 3 Percent Growth," *Wall Street Journal*, July 28, 2018.
16. Epstein, Gene, "Un-Spinning the Obama, Trump GDP Numbers," *Barrons*, March 28, 2019.
17. Hershey, Jr., Robert D., "Last Quarter's Growth Revised to Robust 4.8 Percent," *New York Times*, February 27, 1993.
18. Trugman, Jonathan, "Obama Was Terrible for Economic Growth," *New York Post*, April 1, 2017.

19. Lambro, Donald, "Clinton, Bush Prove Cutting Capital Gains Rate Works," Townhall.com, October 26, 2010.
20. Wells, Nick, "Companies Are Holding a $2.6 Trillion Pile of Cash That's Still Growing," CNBC.com, April 28, 2017.
21. Giuliani, Rudy, campaign event in Beverly Hills, 2008.
22. Jefferson, Thomas, Declaration of Independence, 1776.
23. Ibid.
24. "Growth of French Economy Slows in Blow for Macron," Thelocal.fr, July 30, 2019.
25. "Brexit," Wikipedia.com.
26. "Nixon Shock," Wikipedia.com.
27. United States Constitution Sixteenth Amendment, ratified February 3, 1913.
28. Heriot, Gail, "The Sad Irony of Affirmative Action," *National Affairs*, Winter 2013.
29. Houseman, John, Smith Barney commercial, 1979.
30. "Obamacare and the '29ers," *Wall Street Journal*, February 26, 2013.
31. Bush, George H. W., Republican National Convention presidential nomination speech in New Orleans, Louisiana, 1988.
32. "Boat Builders Scuttled by Yacht Tax," *South Florida Sun Sentinel*, August 16, 1993.
33. Biren, Curt, "'Economic Justice' Isn't Just," *The American Mind*, October 11, 2019.
34. National Football League Players Association (NFLPA), 2018.
35. Johnson, Roy S., "The Jordan Effect," *Fortune Magazine*, June 22, 1998.
36. Friedman, Milton, *Free to Choose*, Harcourt Brace and Company, 1979.
37. Finley, Mordecai, Ohr Hatorah Synagogue, Los Angeles, Sermon, December 2012.
38. Dorfman, Jeffrey, "Ten Free Market Economic Reasons to Be Thankful," *Forbes*, November 23, 2016.
39. "Wet markets," Wikipedia.com.
40. Baier, Bret, *Special Report*, Fox News, April 15, 2020.
41. Brooks, Brad, and Holland, Steve, "'Howdy, Modi!': Thousands, plus Trump, Rally in Texas for India's Leader," Reuters, September 22, 2020.
42. Stein, Jeff, "U.S. Official Crafting Retaliatory Actions against China over Coronavirus as President Trump Fumes," *Washington Post*, April 30, 2020.
43. Goldberg, Michelle, "Bernie Sanders' Radical Past," *Slate*, February 24, 2016.
44. Haltiwanger, John, "Here's the Difference Between a Socialist and a Democratic Socialist," *Business Insider*, November 7, 2018.
45. Fernandez-Villaverde, Jesus, and Ohanian, Lee E., "How Sweden Overcame Socialism," *Wall Street Journal*, January 9, 2019.
46. "2018 Index of Economic Freedom," Heritage.org, 2018.
47. Soros, George, et al., "An Open Letter to the 2020 Presidential Candidates: It's Time to Tax Us More," Medium.com, June 24, 2019.

48. Biren, Curt, "'Economic Justice' Isn't Just," *The American Mind*, October 11, 2019.
49. Madison, James, *Federalist Papers*, No. 51 (February 8, 1788).
50. Madison, James, *Federalist Papers*, No. 10 (November 22, 1787).
51. Biren, Curt, "'Economic Justice'" Isn't Just," *The American Mind*, October 11, 2019.
52. Small Business Administration, 2017.
53. Yager, Sarah, "Doritos Locos Tacos: How Taco Bell and Frito Lay Put Together One of the Most Successful Products in Fast-Food History," *The Atlantic*, July 2014.
54. Cuban, Mark, "Owning a Sports Team Is Unlike Any Other Business," Blog Maverick, February 12, 2013.
55. *Shark Tank*, ABC, premiered August 9, 2009.
56. Thunberg, Greta, Speech to United Nations, September 23, 2019.
57. "When the End of Human Civilization Is Your Day Job," *Esquire*, July 20, 2015.
58. Treiger, Dr. Marvin, Millennial Policy Center, 2019.
59. Broecker, Wallace Smith, Wikipedia.com.
60. Dove, Michael R., *The Anthropology of Climate Change: An Historical Reader* (2014).
61. Intergovernmental Panel on Climate Change, *IPCC Fifth Assessment Report* (2014).
62. Rensburg, Willem Van, "Climate Change Skepticism: A Conceptual Re-Evaluation," *SAGE Journals*, May 27, 2015.
63. Happer, Dr. William, "The Great Climate Change Swindle," CO_2 Coalition, December 3, 2015.
64. Pew Research Center, "The Politics off Climate," *Science & Society*, October 4, 2016.
65. Peterson, Dr. Jordan B., address to Cambridge University, 2018.
66. Perry, Mark J., "There Is No Climate Emergency, say 500 Experts in Letter to the United Nations," Aei.org, October 1, 2019.
67. "31,000 Scientists Say 'No Convincing Evidence,'" Ossfoundation.us, October 2007.
68. Epstein, Alex, "'97 Percent of Climate Scientists Agree' Is 100 Percent Wrong," *Forbes*, January 6, 2015.
69. "Falsifiability," Wikipedia.com.
70. "Environmental Protection Agency," Wikipedia.com.
71. "Clean Air Act," Wikipedia.com.
72. Maraniss, David, and Weisskopf, Michael, "In Arkansas, the Game Is Chicken," *Washington Post*, March 22, 1992.
73. Greenfield, Larry, Executive Director, Reagan Legacy Foundation, various 2008 mock presidential debates.
74. "Marvin the Martian," Wikipedia.com.
75. Brown, Aaron, "Did You Know the Greatest Two-Year Global Cooling Event Just Took Place?," Realclearmarkets.com, April 24, 2018.
76. "Climate Change: How Do We Know?," Climate.nasa.gov, 2019.

77. "Cold Water Currently Slowing Fastest Greenland Glacier," Climate.nasa. gov, March 25, 2019.
78. "Study: Mass Gains of Antarctic Ice Sheet Greater than Losses," Climate .nasa.gov, November 5, 2015.
79. Taylor, James, "New NASA Data Blow Gaping Hole in Global Warming Alarmism," *Forbes*, July 27, 2011.
80. Pomeroy, Ross, "Trump's NASA Chief Changed His Mind on Climate Change. He Is a Scientific Hero," Space.com, June 12, 2018.
81. "NASA Says That CO_2 Is a Coolant Not a Warming Gas," Coldclimatechange.com, March 12, 2018.
82. "Climate Scientists Agree on Warming, Disagree on Dangers, and Don't Trust the Media's Coverage of Climate Change" desmogblog.com126. April 24, 2008
83. "*Exxon Valdez*," Wikipedia.com.
84. "Swedish Police Stop Bill Murray in Golf Cart," Reuters, August 22, 2007.
85. Gibbs, Robert, daily press briefing, May 3, 2010.
86. Holland, Steve, "Obama Wants to Plug the Damn Hole," Reuters, May 25, 2010.
87. "Yogi Bear," Wikipedia.com (created in 1958 by Hanna-Barbera).
88. "The Ten Big US Government Failures of the 21st Century," 247wallst.com, April 26, 2011.
89. Pruitt, Scott, White House press conference, June 3, 2017.
90. Watts, Anthony, "EPA Leaves out the Most Vital Number in Their Fact Sheet," Wattsupwiththat.com, June 12, 2014.
91. "Jones, Van," Wikipedia.com.
92. "Tracking Deregulation in the Trump Era," Brookings Institution, November 12, 2019.
93. "U.S. Petroleum Exports Exceed Imports in September," Eia.gov, December 5, 2019.
94. De Lea, Brittany, "Trump Says US Is a Net Energy Exporter: Fact Check," Fox Business, February 6, 2019.
95. McAleer, Phelim, and McElhinney, Ann, "Fracknation," January 7, 2013.
96. Deutsch, Breanna, "Wind Investments Blow Pickens off the Forbes 400 List," Daily Caller, September 26, 2013.
97. Steyn, Mark, *The Rush Limbaugh Show*.
98. Luft, Gal, speech to Republican Jewish Coalition, March 4, 2009.
99. "Obama's Green Jobs Fraud Exposed," *Investor's Business Daily*, June 21, 2012.
100. Hoium, Travis, "Solar City: Tesla's Solar Boondoggle," *The Motley Fool*, October 18, 2017.
101. "Chicago Climate Exchange," Wikipedia.com.
102. Kuhner, Jeffrey, "The Hypocrisy of Michael Moore," *Washington Times*, February 10, 2011.
103. "Despite What You've Heard, Global Warming Isn't Making Weather More Extreme," *Investor's Business Daily*, January 4, 2018.

104. Hope, Jessica, "The Dark Side of the Hybrid: Lead Acid Batteries," Hazardouswasteexperts.com, October 2, 2014.
105. Trenberth, Kevin, National Center for Atmospheric Research, email dated October 12, 2009.
106. Lott, Maxim, "Arbitrary Adjustments Exaggerate Sea Level Rise, Study Finds," Foxnews.com, December 13, 2017.
107. Rose, David, "World's Top Climate Scientists Confess: Global Warming Is Just a QUARTER What We Thought—and Computers Got the Effects of Greenhouse Gases Wrong," *Daily Mail*, September 14, 2013.
108. "Lisa P. Jackson," Wikipedia.com.
109. Sayet, Evan, "Right to Laugh" comedy tour, debuted in 2008.
110. "The Education of Al Gore," *Washington Times*, March 25, 2000.
111. "The True Meaning of That Green New Deal," Heritage Foundation, February 13, 2019.
112. Kaufman, Alexander C., "Alexandria Ocasio-Cortez Will Be the Leading Democrat on Climate Change," Huffpost.com, June 27, 2018.
113. Ocasio-Cortez, Congresswoman Alexandra, Interview with Ta-Nehisi Coates, January 22, 2019.
114. Berwyn, Bob, "What Does '12 Years to Act on Climate Change' (Now 11 Years) Really Mean?," Insideclimatenews.org, August 27, 2019.
115. Borter, Gabriella, "U.S. Rep. Ocasio-Cortez 'Encouraged' Despite Senate Rejecting 'Green New Deal,'" Reuters, March 29, 2019.
116. Elder, Larry, *What's Race Got to Do with It?* (2009).
117. Tolstoy, Leo, *War and Peace* (1867).
118. "Republican Party," Wikipedia.com.
119. Lincoln, Abraham, Emancipation Proclamation, January 1, 1863.
120. Foner, Eric, *A Short History of Reconstruction* (1990).
121. Tourgee, Albio, Attorney for Plessy in *Plessy v. Ferguson*, 1896.
122. The 1975 Civil Rights Act, Senate.gov.
123. United States Constitution, Nineteenth Amendment, ratified on August 18, 1920.
124. Gop.com-our-party/our-history.
125. Ibid.
126. Ibid.
127. Ibid.
128. Ibid.
129. Ibid.
130. Ibid.
131. Ibid.
132. Ibid.
133. Hagelin, Rebecca, "Planned Parenthood Founded on Racism, Belief in Protecting Society from the Unfit," *Washington Times*, April 23, 2017.
134. "Snipes, Brenda," Wikipedia.com.
135. "Stained Sheets, Pills but No Clarity on Gillum Hotel Run-In," *Associated Press*, April 23, 2020.

136. Trump, Jr., Donald J., "What's Authentic about an Irish Guy Pretending to Be Hispanic?," Twitter tweet, October 15, 2018.
137. Cillizza, Chris, "Elizabeth Warren's Native-American Heritage Reveal Was Just as Bad as You Thought It Was," CNN.com, December 7, 2018.
138. "Harris, Kamala," Wikipedia.com.
139. United States Constitution, Preamble, written in September of 1787.
140. United States Constitution, Article III, 1787.
141. "List of Amendments to the United States Constitution," Wikipedia.com.
142. "*Obergefell v. Hodges*," Wikipedia.com.
143. "Neoplatonism," Wikipedia.com.
144. "Magna Carta," Wikipedia.com.
145. United States Constitution, Tenth Amendment, ratified on December 15, 1791.
146. Jefferson, Thomas, "Jefferson on the Supreme Court," *New York Times*, June 23, 1861.
147. Scalia, Antonin, Speech to Iona College, January 23, 2012.
148. Scalia, Antonin, Interview with Piers Morgan, CNN, 2012.
149. Roy, Avik, "The Inside Story of how Roberts Changed His Supreme Court Vote on Obamacare," *Forbes*, July 1, 2012.
150. "Dirksen, Everett," Inspiringquotes.us.
151. Roberts, John, Supreme Court confirmation hearings, September 12, 2005.
152. "Woke," Wikipedia.com.
153. "*Social Justice* (Periodical)," Wikipedia.com.
154. Hayek, Friedrich, *Law, Legislation and Liberty, Vol. 2: The Mirage of Social Justice* (1976).
155. "Taparelli, Luigi," Wikipedia.com.
156. Goldberg, Jonah, "What Is Social Justice?," Remarks to Prager University, March 24, 2014.
157. Ekins, Emily, "71 Percent of Americans Say Political Correctness Has Silenced Discussions Society Needs to Have. 58 Percent Have Political Views They're Afraid to Share," Cato Institute poll, October 31, 2017.
158. Yiannopoulos, Milo, Speech at University of Houston, September 19, 2016.
159. United States Constitution, First Amendment, ratified on December 15, 1791.
160. "Pan-sexuality," Wikipedia.com.
161. Starnes, Todd, "'His Majesty': Student Single-Handedly Defeats an Army of Gender-Neutral Activists," Foxnews.com, September 30, 2016.
162. Goldberg, Jonah, *Liberal Fascism* (2008).
163. Rolling Stones, "You Can't Always Get What You Want," *Let It Bleed*, 1969.
164. "#MeToo," Wikipedia.com.
165. "Brainwashing," Wikipedia.com.
166. Long, Alex, "The Mind Hacks Behind Brainwashing," Null Byte Blog, February 18, 2012.
167. Ibid.

168. Kurtus, Ron, "Four Noble Truths of Buddhism," Schoolforchampions.com, October 6, 2018.
169. Silverman, Sarah, *The Bedwetter* (2010).
170. Silverman, Sarah, *Jesus Is Magic* (2005).
171. "Churchill, Winston," BrainyQuote.com.
172. Hill, Benny, *The Benny Hill Show*, premiered 1955.
173. Kinglake, Alexander William, *Eothen* (1830).
174. "*New York v. Feiner*," Wikipedia.com (decided on January 15, 1951).
175. "Hall, Evelyn Beatrice," BrainyQuote.com.
176. Limbaugh, Rush. *The Way Things Ought to Be*, published in 1992
177. New Testament, Matthew 5:14.
178. "Massachusetts Bay: The City Upon on a Hill," Ushistory.org.
179. Podhoretz, Norman, "Is America Exceptional?," *Imprimus*, October 2012.
180. "Stalin, Joseph (1929), The History of American Exceptionalism," Wikipedia.com.
181. "Marx, Karl," Wikipedia.com.
182. Kennedy, John F., Address to Massachusetts State House in Boston on January 9, 1961, p. 61.
183. Reagan, Ronald, Farewell Address to the Nation, January 11, 1989.
184. Obama, Barack, remarks to a reporter in France, April 2009.
185. Krauthammer, Dr. Charles, "Decline Is a Choice," *Weekly Standard*, October 19, 2009.
186. Reagan, Ronald, presidential campaign ad, 1980.
187. Obama, Barack, campaign speech in Roanoke, Virginia, July 13, 2012.
188. Gingrich, Newt, *A Nation Like No Other: Why American Exceptionalism Matters* (2011).
189. Little, Becky, "A Few Things You (Probably) Don't Know about Thanksgiving," *National Geographic*, November 20, 2018.
190. Sayet, Evan, "Right to Laugh" comedy tour, debuted in 2008.
191. Montgomery, Marion, "That's Life," released 1963.
192. "*Caddyshack*: The Snobs Against the Slobs," Hollywoodsuite.ca, June 24, 2016.
193. "How the U.S. Helped Fight the Global AIDS Epidemic," *All Things Considered*, NPR, December 17, 2013.
194. "Killing of George Floyd," Wikipedia.com.
195. United States Constitution, Fifth Amendment, ratified December 15, 1791.
196. Ryan, Paul, Speaker.gov, March 24, 2016.
197. "Jerusalem Embassy Act," Wikipedia.com.
198. "When the End of Human Civilization Is Your Day Job," *Esquire*, July 20, 2015.
199. Dershowitz, Alan, *The Case for Israel*, Wiley, 2003.
200. Aust, Jerold, "The Religious Roots of America's Founding Fathers," Ucg.org, July 3, 2011.
201. Paine, Thomas, *Age of Reason*, Part First, Section 1 (1794).
202. Hall, Mark David, "Did America Have a Christian Founding?," Heritage Foundation, June 7, 2011.

203. United States Constitution, First Amendment, ratified December 15, 1791.
204. United States Constitution, Fourteenth Amendment, ratified July 9, 1868.
205. "Williams, Roger," Wikipedia.com.
206. State.gov, updated in 2018.
207. Newport, Frank, "In U.S., 77 Percent Identify as Christian," News.gallup. com, December 24, 2012.
208. *Engel v. Vitale*, decided by the U.S. Supreme Court on June 25, 1962.
209. Lattin, Don, "Standoff over the National Anthem/NBA Suspension of Muslim Stirs Free Speech Debate," Sfgate.com, March 14, 1996.
210. Elk Grove Unified School District v. Newdow, decided by U.S. Supreme Court in 2004.
211. "Bet Din," Wikipedia.com.
212. Chalmers, Robert, "Pamela Geller: American Patriot or Extremist Firebrand?," Independent.co.uk, May 15, 2011.
213. "Radical Islam in America: Is Islam Truly a Religion of Peace?," *Hannity*, October 13, 2014.
214. Buckley, William F., *In Search of Anti-Semitism* (1992).
215. Sommer, Allison Kaplan, "Women's March Faces Crisis as Jewish Activists Lose Faith Amid Farrakhan Firestorm," *Haaretz*, March 11, 2018.
216. "The Jewish Divide over the Iran Nuclear Deal," *New York Times*, September 3, 2015.
217. Democratic National Convention floor fight, September 5, 2012.
218. "Arab Citizens in Israel," Wikipedia.com.
219. "Little Satan," Wikipedia.com.
220. "Sherman, William Tecumseh," BrainyQuote.com.
221. "Military-Industrial Complex," Wikipedia.com.
222. United States Declaration of Independence, July 4, 1776.
223. Roosevelt, Theodore, personal letter written on January 26, 1900.
224. Ballou, Adin, Christian *Non-Resistance: In All It's Important Bearings, Illustrated and Defended* (1846).
225. "Costs of War," Watson.brown.edu/costsofwar, updated 2018.
226. Kagan, Frederick W., Criticalthreats.org.
227. Bush, George W., State of the Union Address, January 29, 2002.
228. Paris Peace Accords, signed January 27, 1973.
229. Ford, Gerald, Address to the Nation, April 10, 1975.
230. "United Nations Security Council Resolution 1441," Wikipedia.com.
231. Esterbrook, John, "Salaries for Suicide Bombers," CBSNews.com, April 3, 2002.
232. Quigley, Samantha L., "Munitions Found in Iraq Meet WMD Criteria, Official Says," American Forces Press Service, June 29, 2006.
233. Prager, Dennis, Dennisprager.com, November 27, 2007.
234. Gillespie, Nick, and Welch, Matt, "How 'Dallas' Won the Cold War," *Washington Post*, April 27, 2008.
235. "Schmidt, Harald," Wikipedia.com.
236. Roberts, Joel, "Bush, Japan's PM Do Graceland," CBSNews.com, June 30, 2006.

237. Geller, Andy, "Saddam's Ex-Lover; She Tells of Viagra-Popping Butcher,"
      New York Post, September 8, 2002.
238. "The Purple Finger Remains a Hopeful Symbol in Iraq, as Iraqis Go to the
      Polls," Pri.org, April 30, 2014.
239. "Brexit," Wikipedia.com.
240. French, David, "It's Time for an Iran Deal Reckoning," *National Review*,
      June 6, 2018.
241. McVeigh, Tracy, "Michelle Obama Raises Pressure Over Kidnapped
      Schoolgirls," Theguardian.com, May 10, 2014.
242. "Conclusion: U.S. Military Power," Heritage.org, October 4, 2018.
243. Kennedy, John F., Inaugural Address, January 20, 1961.
244. "Loathing Joe Lieberman," *The Economist*, November 26, 2009.
245. "Bush Takes on Critics," CNN.com, February 24, 2004.
246. Murdock, Deroy, "Give Thanks That ISIS Is Going, Going . . . ," *National
      Review*, November 22, 2018.
247. "Boston Marathon Bombing," Wikipedia.com (happened April 15, 2013).
248. "Fort Hood Shooting," Wikipedia.com (happened November 5, 2009).
249. "2015 San Bernardino Attack," Wikipedia.com (happened December 2,
      2015).
250. "Orlando Nightclub Shooting," Wikipedia.com (happened June 12, 2016).
251. Altman, Howard, and Ziezulewicz, Geoff, "FBI Identifies Suspect
      Identified in NAS Corpus Christi Shooting It Believes Is 'Terrorism
      Related,'" NavyTimes.com, May 22, 2020.
252. Siders, David, "Democrat Struggle to Make Voters Care about Climate
      Change," Politico, September 14, 2018.
253. Sakuma, Amanda, "Mexico's Other Border," MSNBC.com.
254. Ingraham, Christopher, "There Are Now More Guns Than People in the
      United States," *Washington Post*, October 5, 2015.
255. "America's Complex Relationship with Guns," Pew Research Center Social
      and Demographic Trends, June 22, 2017.
256. French, David, "Why the Left Won't Win the Gun Control Debate,"
      National Review, March 5, 2018.
257. United States Constitution, Second Amendment, Ratified December 15,
      1791.
258. "Case Studies, Gun Control," BBC.co.uk, October 16, 2014.
259. Pavlich, Katie, "Gun Rights Are Women's Rights," Prager University,
      October 16, 2017.
260. Ibid.
261. "Brexit," Wikipedia.com.
262. Justfacts.com/guncontrol.
263. Lott, John R., *More Guns, Less Crime* (1998).
264. Madison, James, *The Federalist Papers* (1788).
265. Antonio Wright, Mark, "Australia's 1996 Gun Confiscation Didn't Work:
      And It Wouldn't Work in America," *National Review*, October 2, 2015.
266. "ATF Gun-Walking Scandal," Wikipedia.com.

267. "Ban on Assault Weapons Didn't Reduce Violence," *Washington Times*, August 16, 2004.

268. Malcolm, John, "Here Are 8 Stubborn Facts on Gun Violence in America," Heritage Foundation, March 14, 2018.

269. Boyer, Edward J., and Ford, Andrea, "Black-Owned Businesses Pay a Heavy Price," *Los Angeles Times*, May 8, 1992.

270. Hanna, Jason, Karimi, Faith, and Grinberg, Emanuella, "Gunman Confessed to High School Shooting, Police Say," CNN.com, February 15, 2018.

271. Johnson, Kevin, and Vanden Brook, Tom, "Feds: Airport Shooting Suspect Complained of Mind Control," *USA Today*, January 6, 2017.

272. "Orlando Nightclub Shooting," Wikipedia.com, (happened June 12, 2016).

273. "Unclassified Summary of Information Handling and Sharing Prior to the April 15, 2013 Boston Marathon Bombings," prepared by the Inspector General of the Intelligence Community, April 10, 2014.

274. "Obama Bans Terms Islam and Jihad from U.S. Security Document," *Haaretz*, July 4, 2010.

275. "75 Shot, 5 Arrested: The Many Ways Chicago Police Can Solve More Violent Crimes," *Chicago Tribune*, October 31, 2019.

276. "*McDonald v. City of Chicago*," Wikipedia.com.

277. Halbrook, Stephen P., "How the Nazis Used Gun Control," *National Review*, December 2, 2013.

278. "Warsaw Ghetto Uprising," Wikipedia.com.

279. Kopel, David B., "The Racist Roots of Gun Control," Encounterbooks.com, February 23, 2018.

280. "Mass Public Shootings Keep Occurring in Gun-Free Zones," Crime Research Prevention Center, June 15, 2018.

281. Sayet, Evan, "Right to Laugh" comedy tour, debuted in 2008.

282. Shackford, Scott, "No, Trump Did Not Make It Easier for Mentally Ill People to Buy Guns," Reason.com, February 15, 2018.

283. Greenwald, Glenn, "Obama DOJ Formally Accuses Journalist in Leak Case of Committing Crimes," Theguardian.com, May 20, 2013.

284. "George Washington Conversation with Thomas Jefferson," Senate.gov.

285. "Immigration to the United States," Wikipedia.com.

286. Vaughan, Jessica M., "Trends in Chain Migration," Cis.org, September 27, 2017.

287. "Race and Ethnicity in the United States," Wikipedia.com.

288. Fazel-Zarandi, Mohammad, "The Number of Undocumented Immigrants in the United States: Estimates Based on Demographic Modeling with Data from 1990 to 2016," Journals.plos.org, September 21, 2018.

289. "Population of New York City," in *Essential New York City Guide* (updated 2012).

290. Rampton, Roberta, and Cornwell, Susan, "Trump Seeks $25 Billion for Border Wall, Offers 'Dreamer' Citizenship," Reuters, January 24, 2018.

291. Borjas, George J., "The Wage Impact of the Marielitos: A Reappraisal," Harvard University, October 2015.

292. D'Hippolito, Joseph, "When Jerry Brown Tried to Keep Immigrants out of California," *Wall Street Journal*, March 9, 2018.
293. Dinan, Stephen. "Lawmakers Strike Deal to Double Number of Guest Visas," *Washington Times*, November 26, 2018.
294. "Hispanics in the US Fast Facts," CNN.com, March 22, 2018.
295. "Democrats' Immigration Platform Focuses on Amnesty, Calls for 'Limits' to Legal Immigration," Numbersusa.com, July 26, 2016.
296. Dudley, Mary Jo, "These U.S. Industries Can't Work Without Illegal Immigrants," CBSNews.com, June 25, 2018.
297. Lempert, Phil, "3 Big Reasons the Food Industry Needs Immigrants," *Forbes*, February 28, 2017.
298. Melnick, Jordan, "Who's Working in Your Kitchen?," Qsrmagazine.com, April 21, 2011.
299. Dudley, Mary Jo, "These U.S. Industries Can't Work Without Illegal Immigrants," CBSNews.com, June 25, 2018.
300. "Immigration Labor Statistics," Pew Research Center, updated 2018.
301. "History of 'Si, Se Puede,'" Ufw.org.
302. Planas, Roque, "Cesar Chavez Used Terms 'Wetbacks,' 'Illegals' to Describe Immigrants," *Huffington Post Latino Voices*, April 3, 2013.
303. Loudon, Trevor, *The Enemies Within* (2013).
304. "Gender Bias and Immigration Policy," Legalmomentum.org, 2019.
305. Kennedy, John F., Inaugural Address, January 20, 1961.
306. "Here's How a $54 Billion Deficit Will Hurt Californians," CalMatters.org, May 7, 2020.
307. Holcombe, Madeline, and Shoichet, Catherine, "Why California Is Giving Its Own Stimulus Checks to Undocumented Immigrants," CNN.com, April 16, 2020.
308. Meotti, Giulio, "Only Israel's Fences Save Lives," Israelnationalnews.com, June 10, 2017.
309. "Love It or Leave It," Wikipedia.com.
310. "Omar, Ilhan," Wikipedia.com.
311. "Curriculum Guide: Japanese American Internment," FDRlibrary.org.
312. Sink, Justin, "President Obama's Ebola Problem," TheHill.com, October 16, 2014.
313. Rudan, Igor, "A Cascade of Causes That Led to the COVID-19 Tragedy in Italy and in Other Countries," Ncbi.nlm.nih.gov, April 4, 2020.
314. Romero, Dennis, and Blankenstein, Andrew, "Typhus Zone: Rats and Trash Infest Los Angeles' Skid Row, Fueling Disease," NBCNews.com, October 14, 2018.
315. "Steinle, Kate," Wikipedia.com.
316. "Immigration Act of 1924," Wikipedia.com
317. Gertsein, Josh, and Hesson, Ted, "Supreme Court Upholds Trump Travel Ban," Politico, June 26, 2018.
318. X, Malcolm, "The Ballot or the Bullet," Speech, April 3, 1964.
319. "Ayers, Bill," Wikipedia.com.
320. "McVeigh, Timothy," Wikipedia.com.

321. "Kaczynski, Theodore," Wikipedia.com.
322. "Sierra Club at a Glance," Biggreenradicals.com.
323. "Earth Liberation Front," Wikipedia.com.
324. *ALF*, NBC, debuted September 22, 1986.
325. "Animal Liberation Front," Wikipedia.com.
326. "Crown Heights Riot," Wikipedia.com (took place August 19–21, 1991).
327. Jones, Sam, and Pignal, Stanley, "Soros Fails to Quash Insider Trading Conviction," *Financial Times*, October 6, 2011.
328. Samuels, David, "The Aspiring Novelist Who Became Obama's Foreign Policy Guru," *New York Times Magazine*, May 6, 2016.
329. "New Black Panther Voter Intimidation Case," Wikipedia.com.
330. "Knockout Game," Wikipedia.com.
331. "Occupy Wall Street," Wikipedia.com (formed in New York on September 17, 2011).
332. "Code Pink," Wikipedia.com (founded on November 17, 2002).
333. "The Spiritual Plan for Aztlan," Liberation Conference in Denver, Colorado, March 1969.
334. Connor, Joseph F., "In Agreement with America's Enemies," *Washington Times*, April 23, 2015.
335. Shapiro, Ben, "CNN Labels Zimmerman White Hispanic," Breitbart.com, July 11, 2013.
336. Obama, Barack, press conference, July 24, 2009.
337. "Garner, Eric," Wikipedia.com.
338. "Brown, Mike," Wikipedia.com.
339. "Black Lives Matter," Wikipedia.com (founded on July 13, 2013).
340. "Antifa," Wikipedia.com (formed in 2017).
341. Riley, Jason, *Please Stop Helping Us* (2014).
342. Centers for Disease Control and Prevention, data published August 2012.
343. Treacher, Jim, "Did Emanuel Cleaver Really Get Spit On?," *Daily Caller*, March 24, 2010.
344. Stein, Jeff, "Tea Party Groups Targeted by the IRS Are Now Eligible for Government Payouts," *Washington Post*, April 20, 2018.
345. Johnson, Kevin, Locker, Ray, Heath, Brad, and Madhani, Aamer, "'It's Time to Destroy Trump & Co.': Scalise Shooter Raged on Facebook," *USA Today*, June 15, 2017.
346. White, Chris, "Neighbors Say Rand Paul's Attacker Was an Avowed Socialist," *Daily Caller*, November 5, 2017.
347. Carelle, Katelyn, "Man Attempts to Stab Republican Running Against Eric Swalwell," *Washington Examiner*, September 11, 2018.
348. Bradner, Eric, and Shih, Adrienne, "Local GOP Office in North Carolina Firebombed," CNN.com, October 17, 2016.
349. "'We Are Outraged!' Florida Republicans Express Anger over Jacksonville Attack on Trump Supporters Registering Voters," FirstCoastNews.com, February 10, 2020.
350. Simon, Carolina, "Sarah Huckabee Sanders Visits the Red Hen, and Lexington, Virginia, Reels in the Aftermath," *USA Today*, June 26, 2018.

351. Wilson, Kirby, and Contorno, Steve, "Pam Bondi Confronted by Protesters Outside Mr. Rogers Movie," *Tampa Bay Times*, June 23, 2016.
352. Ehrlich, Jamie, "Maxine Waters Encourages Supporters to Harass Trump Administration Officials," CNN.com, June 25, 2018.
353. Lemon, Don, CNN, October 23, 2017.
354. President Trump Campaign Rally in Tampa, Florida, on July 31, 2018.
355. Wead, Doug, "Media Unbelievably Blames Trump for Murder of Khashoggi," Newsmax.com, October 23, 2018.
356. Trump, Donald, Twitter tweet on February 17, 2017.
357. Houck, Curtis, "Liberal April Ryan Hilariously Claims She Doesn't 'Have an Agenda' after Tense Exchange with Spicer," Newsbusters.org, March 28, 2017.
358. Wulfsohn, Joseph, "CNN's Jim Acosta Continues to Prove He Is a Political Activist, Not a Journalist," *The Federalist*, August 3, 2018.
359. "Can Trump's White House Legally Ban Reporters?," Theconversation.com, August 9, 2018.
360. Adams, Jerome, White House Corona Task Force briefing, April 10, 2020.
361. Trump, Donald, White House Corona Task Force briefing, May 12, 2020.
362. Jiang, Weijia, Twitter tweet on March 17, 2020.
363. Nordyke, Kimberly, "CNN Reporter Kaitlan Collins Apologizes for Gay Slurs in Resurfaced Tweets," HollywoodReporter.com, October 7, 2018.
364. Pavlich, Katie, "Eric Holder Regrets Not Using Better Language to Target Fox News' James Rosen," Townhall.com, October 30, 2014.
365. Caton, Alex, "Why Democrats Are Dropping More F-Bombs than Ever," Politico, April 25, 2017.
366. Rosiak, Luke, "Sources: Wasserman Schultz Screamed at House Officials to Kill Hacking Probe, Intervened in Pakistani Criminal Matter," *Daily Caller*, June 4, 2018.
367. Haberman, Maggie, "Dean's Howling for Shot to Lead DNC into Future Battle to Head Democrats," *New York Daily News*, January 30, 2005.
368. Green, Miranda, "Sen. Kirsten Gillibrand Drops F-Bomb during Speech," CNN.com, June 9, 2017.
369. Trump, Donald, Press Conference at Trump Tower, August 15, 2017.
370. Drobnic Holan, Angie, "In Context: Donald Trump's 'Very Fine People on Both Sides' Remarks (Transcript)," PolitiFact.com, April 26, 2019.
371. Vadum, Matthew, "Is Antifa Changing Its Strategy?," Capitalresearchcenter .org, May 1, 2018.
372. Chang, Ailsa, "Some Left-Wing Protesters Were Ready to Trade Blows in Charlottesville," NPR, August 17, 2017.
373. Trump, Donald, Presidential Campaign Announcement, June 16, 2015.
374. Martinez, Alberto A., "Did Trump Not Rent to Black People?," Newstandardpress.com, December 19, 2016.
375. "Schwarzenegger, Gustav," Wikipedia.com.
376. Stead Sellers, Frances, "Donald Trump, a Champion of Women? His Female Employees Think So," *Washington Post*, November 24, 2015.

377. Ralph, Pat, "Where Are They Now? Every Winner of 'The Apprentice' and 'Celebrity Apprentice,'" *Business Insider*, July 7, 2018.
378. "List of Honors and Awards Received by Donald Trump," Wikipedia.com.
379. "Dolezal, Rachel," Wikipedia.com.
380. Carrey, Jim, Ace Ventura, Pet Detective, released February 4, 1994.
381. "Porn Star Stormy Daniels Is Taking a Victory Lap after Michael Cohen's Guilty Plea. Here's a Timeline of Trump's Many Marriages and Rumored Affairs," *Business Insider*, August 25, 2018.
382. Little, Becky, "Historic Presidential Affairs That Never Made It to the Tabloids," History.com, May 7, 2018.
383. Miller, Arthur, *The Crucible* (first performed January 22, 1953).
384. "Access Hollywood," Billy Bush interview with Donald Trump, 2005.
385. David Letterman interview with Howard Stern, Netflix, May 31, 2018.
386. Howard Stern radio interview with Donald Trump, 1997.
387. Anderson Cooper interview with Stormy Daniels, *60 Minutes*, March 25, 2018.
388. Mangan, Dan, "Michael Avenatti Announces He Will Not Run for President in 2020," CNBC.com, December 4, 2018.
389. Pirani, Fiza, "Harvey Weinstein to Matt Lauer: 2017 Sexual Harassment Scandals List," *Atlanta Journal-Constitution*, May 25, 2018.
390. "Hill, Katie," Wikipedia.com.
391. John, Arit, "Republican Mike Garcia Sworn in to Serve the Remainder of Former Rep. Katie Hill's Term," LATimes.com, May 19, 2020.
392. Boothe, Lisa, "Judge Kavanaugh and the Weaponization of #MeToo," *The Hill*, September 25, 2018.
393. George Stephanopoulos interview with presidential candidate Donald Trump, *ABC's This Week*, July, 2016.
394. Tucker Carlson interview with Alan Dershowitz. Fox News, December 7, 2018.
395. Schwartz, Ian, "Sara Carter: We Will See Concerted Effort That Dossier Was Used to Get Warrant, Hillary Paid for It," RealClearPolitics.com, February 2, 2018.
396. Solomon, John, "Hillary Clinton's Russia IOU: The Answers She Owes America," TheHill.com, June 3, 2019.
397. "Stone, Roger," Wikipedia.com.
398. McCarthy, Andrew, "The FBI's Trump-Russia Investigation Was Opened under False Pretenses," *National Review*, May 26, 2019.
399. Cohen, Zachary, "Acting Intelligence Chief Has Declassified Names of Obama Officials Who 'Unmasked' Flynn," CNN.com, May 15, 2020.
400. Polantz, Katelyn, "Judge in Michael Flynn Case Hires Prominent DC Law Firm to Help with Appeal," CNN.com, May 24, 2020.
401. "The Vindication of Michael Flynn," *Wall Street Journal*, May 7, 2020.
402. Singman, Brooke, and Spunt, David, "List of Officials Who Sought to Unmask Flynn Released: Biden, Comey, Obama Chief of Staff Among Them," FoxNews.com, May 13, 2020.

403. Polantz, Katelyn, "FISA Court Slams FBI conduct in Carter Page Surveillance Warrant Applications," CNN.com, December 17, 2019.
404. Singman, Brooke, and Spunt, David, "List of Officials Who Sought to Unmask Flynn Released: Biden, Comey, Obama Chief of Staff Among Them," FoxNews.com, May 13, 2020.
405. Memmott, Mark, "Report: Obama White House OK'd Spying on Other Leaders," NPR.org, October 29, 2013.
406. Ibid.
407. Wemple, Erik, "Seizing Journalists' Records: An Outrage That Obama 'Normalized,'" *Washington Post*, June 8, 2018.
408. "Durham, John," Wikipedia.com.
409. Mordock, Jeff, and Dinan, Stephen, "Justice Department Clears Trump of Wrongdoing on Ukraine Call," *Washington Times*, September 25, 2019.
410. Schwartz, Ian, "One America News: John Brennan Hand-Picked Whistleblower for White House," Realclearpolitics.com, November 14, 2019.
411. "BREAKING: Intel Community Secretly Changed the Whistle-Blower Rules to Allow the Trump-Ukraine Complaint Just Days Before It Was Filed," Redstate.com, September 27, 2019.
412. Roberts, Katabella, "Ukrainian Prosecutor Says Yovanovitch Lied to Congress," TheEpochTimes.com, December 10, 2019.
413. Fink, Jenni, "Tulsi Gabbard Defends Donald Trump Firing Alexander Vindman. 'Whether People Like It or Not, There Are Consequences to Elections,'" Newsweek.com, February 10, 2020.
414. Smith, Lee, "Adam Schiff Lied about the Trump Investigation—and the Media Let Him," NYPost.com, May 8, 2020.
415. Klein, Betsy, "Trump's Beef with Nadler Is Decades Old and Fairly Nasty," CNN.com, April 9, 2019.
416. Bauder, David, "CBS' Early Exit Shows Decisions Networks Face on Impeachment," ABCNews.go.com, January 21, 2020.
417. Melugin, Bill, "Republican Challenger Accuses Adam Schiff of Neglecting District's Homeless Problem," FoxLA.com, February 27, 2020.
418. Cox, Jeff, "Trump Has Set Economic Growth on Fire. Here Is How He Did It," CNBC.com, September 7, 2018.
419. Ibid.
420. Cox, Jeff, "Trump Has Set Economic Growth on Fire. Here Is How He Did It," CNBC.com, September 7, 2018.
421. Ibid.
422. Fitzgerald, Maggie, "Black and Hispanic Unemployment Is at a Record Low," CNBC.com, October 4, 2019.
423. "U.S. Purchase Mortgage Activity Hits Seven-Year High: MBA," Reuters, June 7, 2017.
424. Dudley, Susan E., "Documenting Deregulation," *Forbes*, August 14, 2018.
425. Pramuk, Jacob, "Trump Signs Bank Bill Rolling Back Some Dodd-Frank Regulations," CNBC.com, May 24, 2018.

426. Chen, Celia, "Foxconn Gives Trump's Jobs Vow a Shot in the Arm with Multi-Billion Dollar Investment in Michigan," *South China Morning Post*, August 6, 2017.

427. Hodge, Scott A., "Testimony: The Positive Economic Growth Effects of the Tax Cuts and Jobs Act," Testimony before the United States Joint Economic Committee, September 6, 2018.

428. Amadeo, Kimberly, "Dow Jones Closing History: Top Highs, Lows since 1929," Thebalance.com, October 13, 2018.

429. Executive Order 13783: Energy Development. Environment, signed by President Donald Trump on March 28, 2017, Law.harvard.edu.

430. DiChristopher, Tom, "Trump Signs Executive Actions to Advance Keystone XL Dakota Access Pipelines," CNBC.com, January 25, 2017.

431. Tubb, Katie, "In Big Win for Utah, Trump Scales Back Federal Land Grab from Obama Administration," Heritage Foundation, December 5, 2017.

432. Frey, William H., "US Population Disperses to Suburbs, Exurbs, Rural Areas, and 'Middle of the Country' Metros," Brookings Institution, March 26, 2018.

433. Barnes, Robert, "The Kavanaugh Court Is Decades in the Making: How Fast Will It Shift Right?," *Washington Post*, October 6, 2018.

434. "Promoting Women in Entrepreneurship Act, Signed by President Donald Trump on February 28, 2017," Wikipedia.com.

435. Docket Number DEA-476, Deadiversion.usdoj.gov, December 29, 2017.

436. "Media Mostly Silent on Second Amendment Repeal Poll Results," *Accuracy in Media*, April 3, 2018.

437. Trump, Donald, Whitehouse.gov, May 3, 2018.

438. Trump, Donald, G-20 Summit Press Conference in Buenos Aires, Argentina, with Enrique Pena Nieto and Justin Trudeau, November 30, 2018.

439. Trump, Donald, White House Oval Office signing ceremony, January 23, 2017.

440. Trump, Donald, White House Rose Garden ceremony, June 1, 2017.

441. Trump, Donald, Speech in Miami, Florida, on June 16, 2017.

442. Mosher, Steven W., "Trump Represents the US Far Better in Asia Trip Than Obama Ever Did," Fox News, October 15, 2017.

443. Trump, Donald, Oval Office signing ceremony, February 9, 2017.

444. "Joint Statement from President Donald J. Trump and President Jair Bolsonaro," Whitehouse.gov, March 19, 2019.

445. Ibid.

446. Trump, Donald, Whitehouse.gov, May 3, 2018.

447. Donald Trump Executive Order signed January 25, 2017, ICE.gov.

448. Greene, Emily, "What Is the First Step Act?," Prisonfellowship.org, 2019.

449. Zazueta-Castro, Lorenzo, "Border Apprehensions in May Exceed 140,000," Themonitor.com, June 5, 2019.

450. Barnes, Robert, "Supreme Court Upholds Trump Travel Ban," *Washington Post*, June 26, 2018.

451. Office of National Drug Policy, Donald Trump Executive Order signed March 29, 2017, Whitehouse.gov.

452. U.S. Department of Agriculture, updated 2017.

453. Trump, Donald, Oval Office signing ceremony, February 9, 2017.

454. Samuels, Brett, "Trump Donates Quarterly Salary to Small Business Administration," *The Hill*, October 3, 2018.

455. Chang, Ellen, "This Is Why You Will Pay the Lowest Price for Gas since 2005 on Fourth of July Weekend," Thestreet.com, July 2, 2017.

456. Trump, Donald, Whitehouse.gov, April 18, 2017.

457. Trump, Donald, White House Executive Memorandum, signed January 28, 2017.

458. "U.S. Department of Labor Announces Award of $48.1 Million in Grants for Workforce Reintegration of Homeless Veterans," DOL.gov, 2019.

459. Garamone, Jim, "Trump Signs Fiscal Year 2018 Defense Authorization," Defense.gov, December 12, 2017.

460. Kheel, Rebecca, "Price of Air Force's F-35 Drops below $90 Million for First Time," *The Hill*, September 28, 2018.

461. Shane III, Leo, "Remains of Fallen American Troops Headed Back from North Korea," Militarytimes.com, July 26, 2018.

462. Trump, Donald, White House Speech on September 19, 2017.

463. Kube, Courtney, and Lee, Carol E., "Trump Administration Has New Plan to Drive Iran out of Syria," NBCNews.com, October 16, 2018.

464. Popalzai, Ehsan, and Smith-Spark, Laura, "'Mother of All Bombs' Killed 94 ISIS Fighters, Afghan Official Says," CNN, April 15, 2017.

465. DiMicco, Dan, "Trump Should Stay Tough on China at the G-20," *The Hill*, November 30, 2018.

466. Kerns, Jen, "President Trump Is Tougher on Russia in 18 Months Than Obama in Eight Years," *The Hill*, July 16, 2018.

467. Tibon, Amir, "Israelis Love Trump More Than Any Other Nation, Poll Shows," *Haaretz*, October 2, 2018.

468. Pompeo, Mike, White House State Department press conference, November 18, 2019.

469. Taylor, Adam, "Why Trump's Flight from Saudi Arabia to Israel Is a Big Deal," *Washington Post*, May 22, 2017.

470. Trump, Donald, Remarks at NATO Summit in Brussels, Belgium, July 12, 2018.

471. Wilner, Michael, and Gamez Torres, Nora, "Trump's Next Move against Venezuela's Maduro Relies on Action from Allies," Mcclatchydc.com, October 1, 2019.

472. Fritze, Jon, and Shesgreen, Dierdre, "Trump Says U.S. Citizen Danny Burch Held in Yemen Has Returned to Family." USAToday.com, February 25, 2019.

473. Trump, Donald, Rose Garden Signing Ceremony on June 6, 2018.

474. Ujifusa, Andrew, "Donald Trump Signs First Major Education Bill of His Presidency," Edweek.org, July 31, 2018.

475. Mangan, Dan, "Trump Touts Repeal of Obamacare Individual Mandate," CNBC.com, January 30, 2018.

476. Collins, Terry, "Donald Trump's Itchy Twitter Thumbs Have Redefined Politics," CNET.com, January 20, 2018.

477. Zwirz, Elizabeth, "Stumping in Missouri, Trump Says He'll Clear out 'Lingering Stench' at FBI, DOJ," Fox News, September 21, 2018.

478. Thiessen, Marc A., "Trump Isn't Attacking NATO. He's Strengthening It," *Washington Post*, July 12, 2018.

479. Superville, Darlene, "Trump Signs Major Public Lands, Conservation Bill into Law," AP, March 12, 2019.

480. "HHS Finalizes Rule Requiring Manufacturers Disclose Drug Prices in TV Ads to Increase Drug Pricing Transparency," HHS.gov, May 8, 2019.

481. "U.S. Departments of Health and Human Services, Labor, and the Treasury Expand Access to Quality, Affordable Health Coverage Through Health Reimbursement Arrangements," HHS.gov, June 13, 2019.

482. "Drug Overdoses Drop in U.S. for First Time since 1990," CDC, July 18, 2019.

483. Schnirring, Lisa, "Trump Signs Executive Order to Improve Flu Vaccines," Center for Infectious Disease Research and Policy, September 20, 2019.

484. Penney, Joe, "Racism, Rather than Facts, Drove U.S. Coronavirus Travel Bans," TheIntercept.com, May 16, 2020.

485. Cathey, Libby, and Flaherty, Anne, "Government Response to Coronavirus: Fauci Backs Trump Travel Ban, Says Testing System 'a Failing,'" ABCNews.go.com, April 12, 2020.

486. Medaris Miller, Anna, "Nursing Home Residents and Workers Make Up a Third of Coronavirus Deaths. In Some States They Account for Half," BusinessInsider.com, May 9, 2020.

487. Murdock, Deroy, appearance on *Fox and Friends*, May 16, 2020.

488. Wulfsohn, Joseph A., "CNN's Chris Cuomo Reemergence Claim from Coronavirus Quarantine Gets Panned on Social Media," FoxNews.com, April 21, 2020.

489. "White House Coronavirus Task Force," Wikipedia.com.

490. Soave, Robby, "A Progressive Media Group Demanded Censorship of Trump's Coronavirus Press Conferences. The FCC Said No," Reason.com, April 6, 2020.

491. Neumann, Sean, "Dr. Fauci Says Trump Has Listened to His Recommendations and He's Not Being Forced to Say So," People.com, April 13, 2020.

492. "Donald Trump's Fiercest Critics Are Praising His Handling of Coronavirus," Newsweek.com, March 19, 2020.

493. LeBlanc, Beth, "Attorney: Shiawassee Judge Denies Shutdown of Owosso Barbershop," DetroitNews.com, May 11, 2020.

494. Trump, Donald, Coronavirus Task Force press conference, May 22, 2020.

495. Johnson, Kevin, "DOJ Warns California that Reopening Could 'Discriminate' against Religious Groups," USAToday.com, May 19, 2020.

496. Wilkie, Christina, "Trump Says Coronavirus 'Bailouts' for Blue States Are Unfair to Republicans," CNBC.com, May 5, 2020.

497. Ward, Myah, "White House Officials Push Back on Calls to Activate DPA for Critical Medical Supplies," Politico.com, March 26, 2020.

498. "'Celebrity Apprentice,'" Wikipedia.com.

499. Saldivia, Gabriela, "Trump Urges Car Companies to Make Ventilators without Imposing Defense Production Act," NPR.org, March 22, 2020.

500. Herb, Jeremy, "Nancy Pelosi–Steve Mnuchin Relationship Key to Federal Government's Coronavirus Response," CNN.com, March 19, 2020.

501. Trump, Donald J. Independence Day celebration of America from Mt. Rushmore, South Dakota, July 3, 2020.

502. Ibid.

503. Santucci, Jeanine, "Republicans Call for DOJ Investigation into Planned Parenthood over Coronavirus Relief Loans," USAToday.com, May 22, 2020.

504. "Unemployment Insurance Relief during COVID-19 Outbreak," DOL.gov, March 27, 2020.

505. Trump, Donald, Remarks in a Roundtable with Restaurant Executives and Industry Leaders, WhiteHouse.gov, May 18, 2020.

506. Trump, Donald, White House Coronavirus Task Force press conference, April 16, 2020.

507. "Roarty, Michael," Wikipedia.com.

508. "East Bound and Down," Wikipedia.com.

509. Toosi, Nahal, "Trump, the 'King of Ventilators' May Donate Some Machines to African Countries," Politico.com, April 21, 2020.

510. "2020 Stock Market Crash," Wikipedia.com.

511. Whitsett, Karen, Appearance on *The Ingraham Angle*, April 6, 2020.

512. LeBlanc, Beth, "Democrats Plan to Censure Lawmaker Who Credited Trump for COVID-19 Recovery," DetroitNews.com, April 23, 2020.

513. Hoonhout, Tobias, "Woman Who Blamed Trump after Giving Her Husband Fish-Tank Cleaner Now under Investigation for Murder," *National Review*, April 29, 2020.

514. Cooke, Charles W., "No, President Trump Did Not Make Anyone Ingest Fish Tank Cleaner," *National Review*, March 24, 2020.

515. "Teenagers Are Eating Tide Pods. Yes, Really," Advisory.com, January 26, 2018.

516. Curley, Grace, "Democrats Not About to Let a Good Pandemic Go to Waste," *Boston Herald*, May 24, 2020.

517. Pelosi, Nancy, Appearance on *Late, Late Show with James Corden*, April 14, 2020.

518. Fite, Elizabeth, "Georgia Gov. Kemp Balances Health Effects of Unemployment, COVID-19 in State's Reopening Plan," TimesFreePress .com, May 4, 2020.

519. Noem, Kristi, appearance on *Fox News at Night with Shannon Bream*, May 12, 2020.

520. Sibilla, Nick, "Michigan Bans Many Stores from Selling Seeds, Home Gardening Supplies, Calls Them 'Not Necessary,'" Forbes.com, April 16, 2020.

521. "Coronavirus Response Highlights Deepening Partisan Divide," CNBC.com, March 30, 2020.

522. Durkin, Erin, and Goldenberg, Sally, "'Scapegoating Jews': Outrage after de Blasio faults 'Jewish Community' for Crowded Brooklyn Funeral," Politico.com, April 29, 2020.

523. Shelton, Caitlyn, "Feeling the Pressures of the Pandemic: Suicide Hotlines See 800 Percent Spike in Calls," Fox17.com, April 14, 2020.

524. Maass, Brian, "New Covid-19 Death Dispute: Colorado Coroner Says State Mischaracterized Deaths," Denver.CBSLocal.com, May 14, 2020.

525. Herbert, Geoff, "Hunter Biden Fathered Child with Woman While Dating Brother's Widow, DNA Test Reveals," Syracuse.com, November 21, 2019.

526. Stimson, Brie, "Hunter Biden Got $83G per Month for Ukraine 'Ceremonial' Gig: Report Says," FoxNews.com, October 19, 2019.

527. Biden, Joe, Speech to Council on Foreign Relations, January 23, 2018.

528. Mordock, Jeff, and Dinan, Stephen, "Justice Department Clears Trump of Wrongdoing on Ukraine Call," *Washington Times*, September 25, 2019.

529. "Joe Biden 1988 Presidential Campaign," Wikipedia.com.

530. Korecki, Natasha, "Biden Has Fought a Pandemic Before. It Did Not Go Smoothly," Politico.com, May 4, 2020.

531. Biden, Joe, "Road to the White House," C-Span, July 7, 2006.

532. "Biden's Description of Obama Draws Scrutiny," CNN.com, February 9, 2007.

533. Biden, Joe, "Remarks by the President and the Vice President at a Memorial for Senator Robert C. Byrd," Obamawhitehouse.archives.gov, July 2, 2010.

534. Biden, Joe, speech to the Asian and Latino Coalition in Des Moines, Iowa, August 8, 2019.

535. Biden, Joe, interview with Charlamagne tha God on *The Breakfast Club*, May 22, 2020.

536. Tapper, Jake, and Kulman, Betsy, "The Macaca Heard Round the World," ABCNews.go.com, August 17, 2006.

537. Golshan, Tara, "How Hillary Clinton's Health Passed from an Online Conspiracy to a Mainstream Debate," Vox.com, September 13, 2016.

538. Bates, Josiah, "Joe Biden Challenges Iowa Man to a Push-Up Contest during Heated Exchange," Time.com, December 5, 2019.

539. "Joe Biden 1988 Presidential Campaign," Wikipedia.com.

540. Pelosi, Nancy, interview on *360 with Anderson Cooper*, May 18, 2020.

541. Margolis, Jon, and Dole, Robert J., *The Quotable Bob Dole* (1996).

542. Bradner, Eric, "Biden Reverses Long-Held Position on Abortion Funding Amid Criticism," CNN.com, June 7, 2019.

543. Seitz-Wald, Alex, "Biden Voted with the NRA When the Senate, and the Nation, Were Very Different," NBCNews.com, April 24, 2019.

544. Nguyen, Tina, "Here's a Video of Joe Biden Sounding a Lot Like Trump," VanityFair.com, May 10, 2019.
545. Tapper, Jake, "Fact Check: Biden's Misleading Claims on 1994 Crime Bill," CNN.com, July 18, 2019.
546. Yellin, Jessica, "Biden Apologizes to Obama for Marriage Controversy," CNN.com, May 10, 2012.
547. "A Bad Biden Benchmark," Heritage.org, October 24, 2008.
548. Thomas, Clarence, testimony before the Senate Judiciary Committee, October 11, 1991.
549. Marlantes, Liz, "Alito Grilling Gets Too Intense for Some," ABCNews.go .com, January 12, 2006.
550. "Brett Kavanaugh Supreme Court Nomination," Wikipedia.com.
551. Cooper, Matthew, "Who Boke Washington? Blame Harry Reid," TheAtlantic.com, October 2, 2013.
552. Nelson, Steven, "Biden Swims Naked, Upsetting Female Secret Service Agents, Book Claims," USNews.com, August 1, 2014.
553. Relman, Eliza, and Sheth, Sonam, "Here Are All the Times Joe Biden Has Been Accused of Acting Inappropriately Toward Women and Girls," BusinessInsider.com, May 4, 2020.
554. "Burleigh, Nina," Wikipedia.com.
555. Pollitt, Kathy, "We Should Take Women's Accusations Seriously. But Tara Reade's Fall Short," TheNation.com, May 20, 2020.
556. Lowry, Rich, "Everyone Deserves to Live under the Biden Standard," Politico.com, May 6, 2020.
557. Johnson, Derrick, "NAACP Statement on Endorsement Comment by Former Vice President Joe Biden," NAACP.com, May 22, 2020.
558. Dreyfuss, Ben, "That Time Joe Biden Lied about His Academic Credentials," Motherjones.com, May 3, 2019.
559. Fearnow, Benjamin, "Twitter Mocks Joe Biden o 'Corn Pop' Black Gang Leader Story as 'Only White Lifeguard,'" Newsweek.com, September 15, 2019.
560. Hamilton, Carl, "Daughter of Man in '72 Biden Crash Seeks Apology from Widowed Senator," NewarkPostOnline.com, October 30, 2008.
561. Frye, Nels, "Why China Is Rooting for Joe Biden to Win 2020 Presidential Race," NYPost.com, March 12, 2020.
562. Torrance, Kelly Jane, "'Ignoring Reality': Biden Got It Wrong in Iraq, Mattis Says," WashingtonExaminer.com, August 30, 2019.
563. Ghosh, Bobby, "Biden's Call to Ease Iran Sanctions Fits a Bad Pattern," Bloomberg, April 8, 2020.
564. Trump Gives Dramatic Account of Soleimani's Last Minutes before Death: CNN," Reuters, January 18, 2020.
565. Hansler, Jennifer, "Pompeo Announces Reversal of Longstanding US Policy on Israeli settlements," CNN.com, November 18, 2019.
566. "Biden Pledges to Reopen PLO Mission and Resume US Assistance to Palestinians," JNS.org, May 6, 2020.
567. *2016 Presidential Debate*, CNN, July 21, 2016.

568. Haddad, Benjamin, and Polyakova, Alina, "Don't Rehabilitate Obama on Russia," Brookings.edu, March 5, 2018.

569. Thiessen, Marc A., "Joe Biden Is a Hypocrite on Ukraine," WashingtonPost.com, October 8, 2019.

570. Murdock, Deroy, "The Defeat of ISIS Is Another Trump Promise Made, Promise Kept . . . and Nearly Ignored by the Liberal Media," FoxNews.com, April 9, 2019.

571. Bennett, John T., "Biden Was Against bin Laden Raid before He Was for It," RollCall.com, October 20, 2015.

572. "O'Neill, Rob," Wikipedia.com.

573. Blair, Dennis, "CIA Torture Report Helped Us Catch Osama bin Laden," Telegraph.com.uk, December 10, 2014.

574. Oprysko, Caitlin, "Stacey Abrams Signals 'Concern' if Biden's VP Pick Isn't a Woman of Color," Politico.com, April 22, 2020.

575. "GOP Lawmakers Reject Michigan's Virus Order; Whitmer Unfazed," Politico.com, April 23, 2020.

576. Curl, Joseph, "Pathological Liar Elizabeth Warren Thinks Presidential Candidates Should Tell Truth," WashingtonTimes.com, January 21, 2020.

577. Harris, Kamala, *Democrat Presidential Primary Debate*, NBC, June 27, 2019.

578. Cummings, William, "Former S.F. Mayor Willie Brown Writes about Dating Kamala Harris, Appointing Her to Posts," USAToday.com, January 27, 2019.

579. Cillizza, Chris, "Amy Klobuchar's Moment in the Brett Kavanaugh Confirmation Hearings," CNN.com, October 1, 2018.

580. Black, Shelby, "What Are the New Abortion Laws in New York and Virginia? They're Controversial," Elitedaily.com, February 6, 2019.

581. Jorgenson, Dawn, "Here Are Virginia's Rules on Abortion: How Do They Compare to Other States?," *10 News Virginia Today*, May 24, 2019.

582. "CDCs Abortion Surveillance System FAQs," CDC.gov, 2019.

583. "The Abortion Debate Isn't as Partisan as Politicians Make It Seem," Nate Silver, FiveThirtyEight.com, July 10, 2018 (p. 134).

584. Bevan, Susan, and Cullman, Susan, "Why We Are Leaving the GOP," *New York Times*, June 24, 2018.

585. Bradner, Eric, "Biden Reverses Long-Held Position on Abortion Funding Amid Criticism," CNN.com, June 7, 2019.

586. Singh, Susheela, Remez, Lisa, Sedgh, Gilda, Kwok, Lorraine, and Onda, Tsuyoshi, "Abortion Worldwide 2017: Uneven Progress and Unequal Access," The Guttmacher Institute, March 2018.

587. Horn, Dan, "Ending *Roe v. Wade* Wouldn't End Abortion in America. This Is What Happens Next," *Cincinnati Enquirer*, May 15, 2019.

588. Reardon, Dr. David C., "Abortion and Domestic Violence," *Post-Abortion Review*, 1996.

589. Bryson, D., "Technocratic Liberalism and Social Science," *Radical History Review*, 1996.

Acknowledgments

To Buddhist teacher Dr. Marvin Treiger, thank you for awakening me to conservatism after 9/11. To my late father, Jack Dunning, thank you for your patriotism and constant teachings of the importance of keeping government (whenever rationally possible) out of our private lives. To my Conservative Conversation Book Group for challenging all my beliefs, pushing my mind, and our decade-long journey that always ends up back at "First Things" and "The Divine." To Eric Golub, Lowell Cauffiel, Evan Sayet, and Michael Loftus for their instrumental role in helping and pushing me to write, finish, and bring this book to fruition. To my esteemed literary agent and great American Karen Gantz for her love of all literature across the political spectrum and her tireless passion and enthusiasm. To Mary E. Glenn and Keith Pfeffer of Humanix Books for championing this work and making it happen. To my beloved wife, Angela, thank you for your love, support, and our daughters: the ever-ebullient Ava for being so open-minded while also challenging my every position along the journey, and the real writer in our family, Grace.

Further Acknowledgments

S pecial thanks to my dear friend, speaker, author, and conservative comedian Eric Golub for his long trek to a log cabin in rural North Carolina to argue with me for a month. Also thanks to Buddhist teacher Marvin Treiger for my conversion to conservatism after 9/11. Furthermore, this book could never have been written without the ongoing support of my Politicon panelist friends: comedian and Emmy Award–winning TV writer Adam Yenser; author, TV writer, and conservative comedian Evan Sayet; TV writer Sonya Schmidt; TV comedy writer, comedian, and creator and host of *The Loftus Party* and *The Flipside* and our new show together *Bulletpoints!*, Michael Loftus; and my prior *Conservatively Unplugged!* cohosts, the wonderful Canadian-American comedian Adam Richmond and the amazing improv actor Carrie Long. I also thank all those involved in our TV show *Conservatively Unplugged!*, Carrie Long, Michael DeVorzon, Quinton Flynn, Lowell Cauffiel, Teo Karolkev, Chris Garcia, Rob Nelson, and all my friends in West Los Angeles and Hollywood (whose names I can't use because of the fact that they live in West Los Angeles and Hollywood); my wife and daughters for frequently challenging me; my late father, Jack Dunning; my uncle and second father, Lon Whitner; Jesus Christ for being simply amazing; Pastor Brad Bailey of the West Los Angeles Vineyard Church; Lowell C., Clay T., and Mike B.

for the greater life guidance; liberal-centrist Rabbi Mordecai
Finley of the Ohr Hatorah Synagogue, my business coach Marjorie
Dudley; all my liberal friends for their listening and intelligence; our
Founding Fathers for their sacrifice; the West Los Angeles Veterans
Administration Volunteer Program; American veterans everywhere;
and Europe for failing my expectations.

Of course, I want to take a final moment to thank all my other
racist, homophobic, transphobic, xenophobic, greedy, middle-class-
abandoning, religiously repressive, gun crazy, war hungry, grabby,
misogynistic, stupid, mean, privileged, and corrupt conservative,
deplorable, irredeemable, smelly Walmart-shopping friends. So
what if the mainstream media often state that they hate you? I love
you, regardless.

Index

About the Author

Judd Dunning is an author, host, producer, and president of CU Media Group.

CU Media Group brings together some of the biggest names in politics and entertainment, offering its own unique, unconventional, and highly-entertaining brand of political discourse. Inspired by a three-decade-long political journey from liberal to conservative activist, Judd cohosts the weekly show *BulletPoints!* with Fox News' Michael Loftus, and their new *BulletPoints 1 on 1* interview show.

Previously, Judd hosted and produced several versions of his show *Conservatively Unplugged! with Judd Dunning* and *Judd Dunning Unplugged!*, often cohosted with comedians Adam Richmond and Carrie Long. A frequent Politicon talent, Judd hosted and produced the popular celebrity panels *Right-Wing Comedy in These Trumptastic Times*, *13½ Reasons Why Not to Be a Liberal, Judd Dunning Unplugged!* with guest Michael Knowles, and also premiered his 30-minute television pilot *CU! News Goes to Politicon*, which aired to packed theaters.

While he graduated pre-law from Colorado State University, with minors in political science and economics, Judd first pursued his passion for the arts. He attended the American Conservatory Theater and worked as an actor, filmmaker, writer, and comedian for 17 years. He directed more than ten projects while also performing in numerous film, television, and stage projects, and touring North America as a comedian. As a conservative political correspondent, he recently appeared on Andy Cohen's "Then and Now," OANN, and many others. Also, an activist, Judd, just organized the peaceful #openlanowandsafely shutdown protest, just covered by the *Los Angeles Times*, KABC, and numerous other outlets.

Later, Judd excelled in commercial real estate, becoming a leading Institutional Capital Markets advisor and real estate investment syndicator. He has successfully sold millions of square feet of institutional real estate and raised over $300 million in private equity. Personally, he co-owns two "practical environmental" clean water and clean gas businesses.

Judd is a fifteen year ongoing member of private Los Angeles think tank "Conservative Conversations" and is an avid surfer. He lives in West Los Angeles, where he attends the Westside Vineyard Christian Church and Ohr Hatorah Synagogue, with his wife and two Jewish stepdaughters who are his life, making any other hobbies unnecessary and impossible. He wouldn't have it any other way.

Follow Judd's show and book on YouTube, Facebook, Parler, and Instagram @BulletPointNation, at Twitter @BPNinsider, and on the web at www.bulletpointnation.com.

More Titles From Humanix Books You May Be Interested In:

Mike Huckabee says:
"One of the most intellectually compelling and rational defenses of Christianity's role in America."

In *Dark Agenda: The War to Destroy Christian America*, David Horowitz examines how our elites — increasingly secular and atheist — are pushing a radical agenda. A *New York Times* bestselling author and leading conservative thinker, Horowitz warns that the rising attacks on Christians and their beliefs threaten all Americans — including Jews like himself.

Warren Buffett says:
"My friend, Ben Stein, has written a short book that tells you everything you need to know about investing (and in words you can understand). Follow Ben's advice and you will do far better than almost all investors (and I include pension funds, universities and the super-rich) who pay high fees to advisors."

In his entertaining and informative style that has captivated generations, beloved *New York Times* bestselling author, actor, and financial expert Ben Stein sets the record straight about capitalism in the United States — it is not the "rigged system" young people are led to believe.

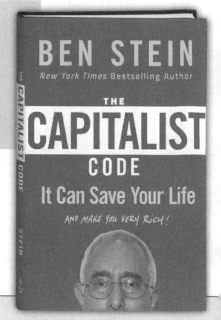

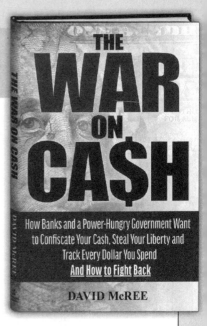